April 16 '07

To great friends from Eric – Rita would have been delighted to send this to you.

EVy–

Think Kind Thoughts

by

Harriet (Rita) Prince Parrish Youngquist
Eric V. Youngquist

Part 1 - Rita

Part 2 – Our Life Together:
From Academia into the Foreign Service

Voyageur Publishing Co., Inc.
Nashville, Tennessee

Think Kind Thoughts

Part I – Rita

Part 2 – Our Life Together:
From Academia into the Foreign Service

Copyright 2007 Voyageur Publishing Co., Inc.

All rights reserved.
Printed in the United States of America

ISBN: 0-929146-06-9
ISBN 13: 978-0-929146-06-5

Editor: Eric V. Youngquist
Cover design by John R. Robinson
This book may not be reproduced in whole or in part, by mimeograph or any other means, without advance permission. For information, address: Voyageur Publishing Co, Inc., 1012 Greenwich Park, Nashville, TN 37215.

Special Numbered Edition – Limited to 150 copies

Copy Number −56− *EVy*

Contents

Prologue   1

Genealogy   Prince   2

Dodge   5

Alden   7

Mitchell   8

Part 1 – Rita

Photographs for Part 1   11

Rita's Grandfather – Earl Henry Prince (E.H.)   25

Rita's Grandmother - Minnie Harriet Jones Prince (Mama)   41

Rita's Mother - Sarah Harriet Prince Parrish (Honey)   45

Rita's Father - William Mallow Parrish (Bo)   55

Rita

Childhood and Early Years   75

Trip back to Louisiana and the Plantation   85

Avery Coonley School   87

High School and Music   91

Rita and Kay in Japan 1947 – 1948   93

Sumo, Silk, Earthquakes, and Leading Families   96

Climbing Fuji   99

Sendai   107

Mary Suwada's Grandfather's Farm   108

Back at Michigan 1948 – 1950   111

We find one Another   111

Marriage   133

Photographs for Part 2   136

**Part 2 – Our Life Together:
From Academia into the Foreign Service**   143

Note on reading Rita   145

University of Wisconsin

Maple Bluffs and Summer-time   149

237 Langdon   152

Rita and Teaching   156

Getting Ready for Norway   161

On Stage   165

Norway (1951 - 1952)

Trip over on SS *Stavangerfjord*   167

Visit to Rjukan   175

Trip to Paris, London, and Glasgow   177

Apartment in the Suburbs   181

Honey Arrives   185

A Nation on Skis   187

Practicing my Norwegian   189

Winter Olympics   192

More Skiing   195

New Arrival   197

Spring in Oslo   203

Back to America   207

On to Cornell (1952 - 1954)

Bricks and Books   211

Moving to Ithaca   213

Settling in   217

Jobs, Jobs   218

Teaching Fellow   221

Daily Living   222

Ithaca Rifle and Pistol Club   229

Home Life 231

The Big Payoff 241

Catching the Foreign Service Bug 245

Final Semester at Cornell 249

Getting Ready for the Oral Examination 255

Waiting for the Service 259

Into the Foreign Service (January – February, 1955) 263

Prologue

Genealogies are just names and dates, and yet the people mentioned in them are our ancestors. They were living people, carrying our genes, living in very different times, coping with life and passing life on to us.

My grandmother, Minnie Prince (Mama) wrote a little book of memories, so that later generations would know her parents and their times. Now Eric and I will do the same. The present seems so permanent, and yet I know that the world will change, and some day our experiences will seem strange to our descendants. These pages are for those children of our children, to help them know a bit more about their forebears.

Rita Prince Parrish Youngquist

Prince Genealogy

The following genealogy was taken from Rita's application for DAR membership while she was in high school. She could also have qualified for DAR membership on the basis of her father's ancestors (the Mitchell line). The starting point is Rita's maternal grandfather, Earl Henry Prince.

EARL H. PRINCE Born 10/10/1861 at Roxbury, VT.
                Died Dixon, IL 2/8/1940.
                Married 5/3/1887 to
MINNIE JONES PRINCE Born 11/7/1866 at Northfield, VT.
        Died 10/6/1946 at Downers Grove, IL. See **Dodge Genealogy**

EARL H. PRINCE was son of

    JOSEPH FREEMAN PRINCE Born 10/28/1820.
                      Died 1/12/1899 at S. Randolph, VT
  and
SARAH CLARK (2nd wife) Born 7/1/1837 Married 8/28/1853.

The said JOSEPH FREEMAN PRINCE was son of

    JOHN PRINCE Born 1/17/1795 at Amherst, NH.
           Died 6/6/1866 at Randolph, VT.
    Married 3/25/1817 to
MARY MCINTOSH PRINCE Born 1795.
                    Died 1864 at Randolph, VT.

The said JOHN PRINCE was son of
    JOSEPH PRINCE, JR. Born 1752 at Amherst, NH.
              Died 1800 at Amherst, NH.
      Married 12/6/1775 to
    SARAH WYATT Born 8/12/1751 at Danvers, MA.
      Died   at Amherst, NH.

The said JOSEPH PRINCE JR. was son of

    JOSEPH PRINCE, SR. Born 1704 at Salem Village, NH.
              Died 1789 at Amherst, NH.
      Married 1746 to
    ELIZABETH ROLLINS Born 1725.
              Died 1823 at Amherst, NH.

JOSEPH PRINCE, JR. AND JOSEPH PRINCE, SR. were signers of Test Articles:

    In consequence of the resolution of the Hon. Continental Congress, and to show our determination in joining our American Brethren in defending the Lives, Liberties and Properties of the Inhabitants of the United Colonies -- We the subscribers do hereby engage and promise that we will to the utmost of our power at the risque of our Lives and Fortunes with arms, to oppose the Hostile proceedings of the British fleets and armies against the colonies.
                                                          April 1776

Source: *History of Amherst*, page 374.

JOSEPH PRINCE appears on the rolls of officers and men on board the grannicide commissioned by Capt. John Fish in 1776 in Boston Harbor.

Here are extracts about the Prince family from *History of Amherst*:

> JOSEPH and ABEL PRINCE were in the legislature. p. 106.
> ABEL PRINCE was in Col. Baldwin's regiment. p. 378.
>> This regiment was raised in September, 1776, and marched to assist the army in New York. It was in the Battle of White Plains, October 28, 1776, and was dismissed at North Castle, NY about the first of December of that year.

EARL H. PRINCE had two brothers and three sisters:

> EDMUND born 5/17/58 died 9/15/1942 Married to
>> ABBIE born 6/1/1856 died 9/15/1924.
>
> HATTIE born 1863
> NELLIE born 1866
> LEO born 11/24/1873
> BERTHA born 1877

The Dodge Family Genealogy

The following is taken from Mama Prince's book *Memories:*

1. JOHN DODGE came from Somerset Shire, England. His wife was Margery Deacon.

2. DEACON WILLIAM DODGE came to Salem in 1629. He was a Selectman, grand juryman, and member of many committees.

3. WILLIAM DODGE was born in 1640 and died in 1720. He was a Captain, maltster, deputy, overseer in 1679. Representative in 1690. He fought the Narragansetts in 1675. He married Mary Conant Balch. She died and he married Joanna Larkin, widow, daughter of Deacon Robert Hale of Charlestown, Mass.

4. ROBERT DODGE was born 1686 and died in 1764. A Surveyor. He married Lydia Woodbury, daughter of Isaac, and Elizabeth (Herrick) of Chebacco Parish.

5. WILLIAM DODGE of Beverly was born in 1741 and died in 1810. He was a Joiner, Cabinet Maker and deacon of the Second Church.

6. SIMEON DODGE was born in 1755 in Beverly and died in Francestown, N.H. in 1827. He served in the Revolution from February 13, 1777 to February 13, 1780, under Captain Billy Porter and Colonel Tupper. He was at the Battle of Concord and Lexington. Following the British back to Boston he had to hide in a cellar to save his live. He was married December 31, 1780 to Mary Balch of Salem.

7. SAMUEL DAVIS DODGE was born January 20, 1799 in Francestown, N.H. He died in Northfield, Vt., August 30, 1887. He married Harriet Gardner at Temple, N.H. February 27, 1825. Harriet Gardner was born July 22, 1801 and died at

Northfield December 17, 1877. He was a Clothier and wool carder. Harriet Garner was the daughter of Abel and Susanna (Bryant) Gardner.

8. HARRIET ELIZABETH DODGE was born December 19, 1830 in Plainfield, Vt. She married E.K. Jones of Northfield December 31, 1852. They had four children:
    FRED ANSON, born September 23, 1854;
    SUSIE ELSIE, born March 23, 1865;
    MINNIE HARRIET, born November 7, 1866 [**MAMA PRINCE**]
    JESSIE AURORA, born April 24, 1869.

Alden Genealogy

I don't claim complete accuracy for the following genealogical record, but this is what I prepared based on research:

John Alden (Mayflower passenger) born Hartfordshire 1599 and died 1687

John's son: Joseph Alden born 1624

Joseph's son: Isaac Alden born 1665 Bridgewater, Massachusetts

Isaac's daughter Thankful born 1737 Needham, Mass. of Isaac's second wife

Thankful Alden married 1763 to John Pratt born 1733

Their son John Jr. was born in 1773

John Pratt Jr. married Margaret Houghton

Their **daughter Rhoda** was born 3/17/1798 (died 7/16/1830}

Rhoda Pratt married Daniel Jones Aug. 1, 1819

Their son **Edwin Kent Jones married Harriet Elizabeth Dodge**

Edwin Kent Jones born June 4, 1828 Randolph, Vt. and died Feb. 2, 1909 at Northfield, Vt.

Harriet Elizabeth Dodge born Dec. 19, 1830 at Plainfield Vt. and died December 17, 1894 at Northfield, Vt.

Their **daughter, Sarah Harriet Jones, married Earl Henry Prince**

They had two children: **Sarah Harriet** and Earl Samuel.

Sarah Harriet Prince (Honey) married William M. Parrish (Bo)

Mitchell (Bo's) Genealogy

This genealogy is taken from a typewritten account by William S. Mitchell, entitled *Mitchell Ancestry*. We begin with Mitchell's own account; the rest is a summary.

The first trace I have been able to find of our Family, was through Uncle Elijah Mitchell, the oldest child of my Grandfather, William Mitchell. Uncle Elijah said he had from good authority that one **Anthony Mitchell**, a single man, emigrated to Dumfries County or Province, Scotland, from Germany.

That said Anthony Mitchell was married to **Mary Dalrymple**, and among the children born to that marriage was one son, **Robert Mitchell**, and who, in good season was married to a woman whose maiden name I have been unable to learn; and born to that latter marriage was one daughter, Elizabeth, and one son, **Robert Mitchell,** (my Great Grandfather) who grew to manhood in Scotland.

He served two enlistments in the British Army; in the first enlistment, he learned the art of a baker, and in the second, the art of music—all soldiers in that age of the world being required to learn some art or profession during the term of their service.

Bo's lineage goes back to that **Robert Mitchell**, who came to America from Dumfries County, Scotland. He brought his family to the Colony of Virginia and located at Lunenburg. Church records show that he served as Senior Warden of the Episcopal Church there.

According to U.S. War Department records, **Robert Mitchell** enlisted in the Army **November 27, 1776** and was on the Army rolls as late as **May, 1779.** He served as a drum-major under Virginia regiments (11th, 15th and 7th) commanded by Colonel

Daniel Morgan. (Letter dated January 15, 1901, from F.C. Ainsworth, Chief of the Record and Pension Office)

Robert Mitchell's name also appears in the list of soldiers of the Revolutionary War for purposes of eligibility for membership in the Daughters of the Revolutionary War and Sons of the Revolutionary War.

Robert had four sons:
- **William,** born June 18, 1779; died April 4, 1839
- Andrew
- Peter
- James

William was married to **Sarah Myers** of New Jersey on March 22, 1810 in Adams County, Ohio. They had the following children:

- Aaron
- Elijah
- **Joseph**, born March 4, 1817; died March ___, 1880
- John
- Sarah

Joseph was married to **Louisa Melinda Kendall** January 30, 1889. They had the following children:

- **Mary Catherine**, born January 1, 1846; died October 11, 1896
- Sarah E
- Martha J.
- Rebecca E
- William C
- Alice
- John Hull
- Oliver Morton
- Carry Bell
- Julia Etta

Mary Catherine married **Jesse M. Parrish**. They had the following children:

>Lew Wallace
>Rebecca
>Quincy T.
>Frank W.
>Chester C
>Jessie Pearl
>Joseph A
>**William Mallow** (Bo)

Part 1 – Rita
Photographs

E. H. Prince
Graduation from Norwich
Successful Businessman
E. H. and his family (Leo at bottom left)

Mama Prince
Before marriage
When E.H. was at Michigan
As Rita remembered her
On porch of Princeholm

Honey
As a young woman
Wedding party
With Bo at wedding
Riding
As Eric remembered her
With Bo and children
As Rita remembered her

Bo
As a child
As a young man
With International Harvester
At trade fair for International Harvester

Rita
Rita playing by Princeholm
Playing on porch of Princeholm
At Avery Coonley with Mickey Carpenter opposite
Rita as a young girl
With Peter and Kay

Growing up
High School Graduate

Rita back at U. of Michigan
Rita's sketch of Eric
Rita's graduation picture
Rita and Eric at prom
Marriage
Rita descending staircase with Bo
Bride and groom
After the ceremony
Parents, minister and bridal couple
Wedding party
Honeymoon - untying cans from car
Honeymoon – on the way
Honeymoon - White Pines State Park
Honeymoon - on beach at Mackinaw Island

E.H. Prince

Graduation from Norwich

Successful Businessman

E. H. and his family (Leo at Bottom left)

Mama Prince

Before Marriage

When E.H was at Michigan

As Rita remembered her

On porch of Princeholm

Honey

As a young woman

With Bo at wedding

Wedding Party

Riding

As Eric remembered her

With Bo and children

As Rita remembered her

Bo

As a child

As a young man

With International Harvester

At trade fair for International Harvester

Rita playing by Princeholm

Playing on porch of Princeholm

At Avery Coonley with Mickey Carpenter opposite

Rita as a young girl

With Peter and Kay

Growing up

High School Graduate

Rita back at U. of Michigan

Rita's sketch of Eric

Rita's graduation picture

Rita and Eric at prom

Marriage

Rita descending staircase with Bo

Bride and groom

After the ceremony

Parents, minister and bridal couple

Wedding party

Honeymoon-untying cans from car

Honeymoon-on the way

Honeymoon-White Pines State Park

Honeymoon-on beach at Mackinaw Island

Rita's Grandfather
Earl Henry Prince (E.H.)
(1861-1940)

Until Rita went off to the University of Michigan in 1944, her life was pretty well limited to Downers Grove, Illinois, a small western suburb of Chicago on the Burlington Railroad. It was because of the railroad connection with Chicago that her grandfather E.H. Prince decided to buy land there and become a developer.

The following is from an article about E.H. that appeared in the *Downers Grove Reporter* after he passed away February 8, 1940:

> [Mr. Prince] formed a company of which Emerson Young Foote was a member, and later, Charles Linscott. The company acquired 225 acres of land in Downers Grove for subdivision purposes which included practically all between the Burlington tracks and the old Plank road (now Ogden Avenue), extending east and west from Highland Avenue to Montgomery Street. This was in 1890. The firm prospered until the depression that followed the World's Fair of 1893. At this time the gold rush to Alaska was fermenting and Mr. Prince and his brother, Leo, after elaborate preparation, joined the others who went on this hazardous undertaking. They were gone a year and never regretted the experience although it was not materially profitable. Following his return he spent several years in mining operations in Cobalt, Ontario. For the last twenty years he has been identified with the ice industry, establishing himself in Dixon. . . .
>
> Christian Science services were held at his home in Dixon Saturday afternoon following which the body was placed in a

mausoleum. It will be sent East in the spring and interred in the family plot at South Randolph, Vt.

The following article about E.H. appeared in the Dixon, Illinois, newspaper:

Earl H. Prince, one of Dixon's most outstanding citizens, passed away last evening at about 6:30 o'clock at his home, 618 East Second street, his passing terminating an illness with which he has been suffering for the past three years. Mr. Prince came to Dixon in 1923 when he purchased the Dixon Distilled Water Ice Company, which he has operated since. Under his careful guidance, the business increased materially and many improvements were added to the plant.

Since coming to Dixon from Chicago he has been one of the city's leading residents. Always maintaining a keen interest in civic affairs, Mr. Prince was one of Dixon's most successful citizens. He was a most interesting personality and his experiences had been many and varied...

He was affiliated with the Sigma Chi fraternity and held membership in the University club in Chicago and the Chicago Stock Exchange.

Mr. Prince spent some years in prospecting in the western states and in Alaska. He was one of the subjects in the book "Sourdough Gold," which was written concerning the hardships and dangers of miners' lives in the early mining days of Alaska, where he spent many months. He was also active in prospecting silver, cobalt and coal in the western states during his young manhood.

Mr. Prince was a member of the Dixon Chamber of Commerce, the Dixon Country Club and Dixon lodge of Elks as well as having been a member of other civic organizations. He is survived by . . . .

Rita's grandfather was born in Roxbury, Vermont, into a large family that soon moved to Bethel, where he completed his early education.

He entered Norwich Military Academy (now Norwich University) in 1881, after attending State Normal School at Randolph. He graduated from Norwich in 1886, with a B.S. in Civil Engineering, He and Minnie Harriet Jones (Mama Prince) were married in May, 1887, and they went to Ann Arbor, Michigan, where E.H. entered the University of Michigan law school that fall.

After receiving his law degree in 1889 he took his young bride and moved further west, to Chicago, where he planned to set himself up in business. Interested in real estate, he looked at different areas and narrowed his search down to two possibilities.

One was Evanston to the north, but he decided that the climate would discourage people from living there. He looked to the west along the Burlington Railroad, and finally settled on Downers Grove, just 24 miles from the Loop.

E.H., as he was called, was a colorful, dynamic person, and he made an indelible impression on Downers Grove. The home he built there—Princeholm—was his three-story success statement to the world. This is how Rita described it.:

Daddy Prince built Princeholm thinking that all his children and grandchildren would stay with him as in olden days. It was finished in 1893, just in time for the World's Fair, and his relatives were coming from Vermont for the occasion. There were 26 rooms, with three fireplaces. Daddy Prince loved wood, so each room was in a different paneling and molding. The entrance had oak paneling. The parlor and living room were mahogany. The library was cherry, the dining room oak. There may have been walnut, too, but I don't remember.

The front stairs were wide and oak paneled, with beveled glass windows halfway down the stairs. In the entryway was a beautiful stained glass window, a vase with flowers, which was lovely. The kitchen was big, with a marble sink and a table in the center to work on. There was a food pantry, with bins for fifty pounds of flour and sugar, and two other bins. Then there was a dish pantry as you walked into the kitchen. The back stairs went to the second floor, and the back bedroom there was for the maid.

The house had tall windows and high ceilings, and it creaked and groaned with weather changes. It was a scary place to be alone in if you had a vivid imagination. My room during college days was in the maid's room at the top of the back stairs, and many times I was SURE that someone was coming up those stairs.

The house was surrounded by tall old oaks, which would sway with the wind in a storm. Our fear was that either there would be a fire in Princeholm or one of the oaks would fall on it. Lightning hit one of the trees every year, so electric storms were a worry.

E.H. Prince lived a full and eventful life. He was truly a many-sided person, and larger than life to those who knew him. He seemed almost driven by an inner force, or battling against his own private demons. In any event he was much more than the embittered old man that Rita remembered.

This becomes quite clear from the direct and often passionate letters he wrote to his wife during his Klondike adventure. Rita did her best to decipher and transcribe the many scrawled notes that E.H. wrote to his wife Minnie (all of which she saved) during the year he spent during his 1898 venture into the north. E.H.'s year in Alaska had a lasting impact on him. While he didn't find gold or riches there, he learned a lot about himself. He confronted many severe physical and emotional challenges, and he not only survived them but also came away much strengthened in body and spirit.

He and his younger brother Leo decided to join the thousands of men and women who were attracted to the Yukon Territory by gold that was found there in 1897. In March, 1898, the two traveled by train to Seattle, and spent the next eight days making certain that they had the food supplies and equipment that they would need.

They found Seattle inundated by a flood of hopeful prospectors, almost all of whom were woefully ignorant of the obstacles they would be facing. There were plenty of people taking advantage of the travelers:

> This city is filled with sharks and frauds like a big fair: everything to catch the Klondiker. I am glad I brought what I did from Chicago . . . .

Earl Prince was no wide-eyed innocent. Raised on a farm in Vermont, he was used to hard physical work, and knew what living in the cold was like. He made sure that they would have what they needed up there, and nothing more. But how could he have foreseen the immense difficulties that he and his brother would face – beginning with landing their gear?

The two left Seattle March 21, 1898, and stopped briefly at Victoria, Vancouver, Juneau, and Skagway before arriving at Dyea March 26. The captain anchored a mile from shore at high tide, not wanting to get stuck on the beach when the tide ran out. Earl evidently heard what was going to happen, and he took action. Before the ship arrived, he went into the hold and got all their things together, so that they would be ready for the first teams that were available to land goods on the beach at low tide. As a consequence Earl and Leo landed with their equipment two days before many of the other passengers. That earned Earl the reputation of being a "hustler."

They started the long and difficult transport of their things from Dyea up to Sheep Camp, and then to the Scales, where the Canadian Mounted Police weighed their effects. Fearful that prospectors might starve going to the Yukon Territory, they would not let anyone go over Chilkoot Pass unless he had at least 1,150 pounds of food. Many did what Earl and Leo did, which was hire Native Americans to carry their things up the steep and rocky incline, which consisted of steps cut out of the snow and a rope to hang onto for balance.

But Chilkoot was just the beginning of a prospector's difficulties. They then had to transport their things overland to Lake Bennett, where they could either hire a boat to take their things down the turbulent headwaters of the Yukon and through dangerous, narrow channels on the way to Dawson or build one themselves..

Along with their new partner Dr. James Foster Scott, they decided to build their own boat. They felled and trimmed trees, dragged the trunks to their camp, sawed them into boards using a pit saw, and constructed their own vessel. Earl did most of the construction work, being an excellent carpenter, and their vessel, called *The Harriet*, received many compliments. A good sailor/navigator was essential, though, and they were fortunate that their party of three included Dr. Scott, whose adventures were later chronicled in *Sourdough Gold*. The good doctor had been a member of the Yale rowing crew, so he handled the steering of their craft while Earl and Leo manned the oars.

Maybe Earl's being so far away from home stimulated introspection as well as remorse for having destroyed his marital relationship, for this is what he wrote while their ship was docked at Juneau:

> . . . I trust that you and my little ones are well and happy. You must try to be happy without me as I do not believe you will ever be happy with me there. I am not so bad a man, and yet I have been very cruel to you, Minnie. If it was in my power to undo all the wrongs I have done you I would cheerfully bury myself in the bosom of this great ocean, as it seems at times she is calling me to take my troubled and weary soul.
>
> As I came into this world so shall I depart when it shall please my maker, then and not till then. In the meantime I will fight as hot a battle as it is in my power. All the powers that are given me I will use and then when it shall please my God to call me I am ready. Let it come when it may – I am content. As for getting happiness, I am satisfied that it is not for me. . . .

Many of his letters included similar remarks, expressing self-doubts, concern about what he considered mankind's weaknesses for sin and corruption, and uncertainty over how long he might stay. At the same time, he found that he had developed great strength and endurance during his months on the trail, and that gave him great satisfaction.

> It seems like many years since I left home. I doubt if you would at first know me in my present dress with a full beard. Those who knew me in Seattle and saw a good deal of me do not know me and say that they cannot see a trace of the man they saw there. I am quite thin yet strong and powerful. I doubt if there are

any here that can follow me on the trail. My power and endurance were never better. I am ready to push on when those with me have given out. . . .

Earl's letters also reveal a passionate and emotional side, as one can see in his many loving references to his beloved daughter Harriet (Honey to Rita) and his baby son Earl Samuel. He ended almost every letter in similar fashion:

> How is Harriet? The same sweet child, no doubt. Tell her Papa would like to see her and get a kiss, and Earl the same baby, chubby sweet boy as ever. I would like to get hold of him and give him a little hug and a kiss.

Earl also felt stimulated by the many challenges that Alaska presented, and seemed to thrive on them. Well-organized, handy with tools, and full of energy, he became an indispensable member of his Klondike team. He organized their outfit well, he helped to extricate victims buried by the horrendous April 1898 snow avalanches at the Chilkoot Pass, he hunted quail, ptarmigan and other game for food for his party of three, and also helped build a small hospital where Dr. Scott practiced.

In his last letter, dated January 31, Earl told Minnie that he would soon be leaving Alaska.

> . . . .My plans now are to take Leo and go out over the ice as soon as I can get ready, which will take at least ten days or two weeks. I hope I will find father in his right mind and out of danger although I fear the worst. Since my return Saturday last I have been on the jump looking to my trip out. 600 miles over the ice is quite a trip at this season, although I neither dread nor fear it, but shall be glad of the day when I can make the start. My plan is to get two or three dogs to draw our food and blankets. I hasten to write this letter as I have just learned that a mail leaves tomorrow and closes today at 4:00 p.m.

While up the creek I shot another moose, so we have plenty of good meat. . . .

I have had many hard experiences since my last letter, battling with the elements in this country which I hope to detail in person to you. However, I came out of them with all my limbs and am in perfect condition for my trip over the ice. Nearly a year of battling life in this unfriendly country has given me new life and courage for the future battles which I hope to win before this life is ended.

Kiss and hug the babies for me. The many questions you ask in the three letters and the many questions I have to ask I hope to answer and have answered when we can be face to face in the sweet future. We have many ugly and hard questions to settle which I hope may be settled for the good and happiness of all.

Earl and Leo arrived in Seattle March 11, 1989, almost exactly a year after they first arrived there from Chicago to begin their Alaskan adventure.

The book *Sourdough Gold* mentioned in E.H.'s Dixon obituary was written by Mary Lee Davis. She based her story on Dr. Scott's log book about his stay in Alaska. Scott was a physician, and wanted to explore a great river. His aim, he said, was not to find gold, but to find a spiritual truth about himself—to "escape the care-free verdict of the world, drift down it, and seek there for something hidden." He chose the Yukon, and met E.H. and Leo soon after he landed in Alaska at Dyea.

A well-educated and cultured man who had spent his early years in India, Scott was drawn to Earl and brother Leo. This is how the book described their meeting and friendship:

Until I reached Dyea, I was a lone traveler. I had formed no alliance back in the States, in the belief that better partners would be found, if partners should seem needful, when on the trail. And then at Dyea I had met two brothers—manly, efficient, and congenial men—to whom I drew at once, and they to me. These were my company, in close and pleasant fellowship, from that time on until the next winter.

We were not strictly partners for we drew no legal covenant, and surely wind-swept Dyea boasted no lairdly coven-tree beneath which we could sign our articles. Our compact was concluded, sealed, solely through the look of the eye, the clasp of the hand; yet it was one which bound, which steadily grew firmer with our better acquaintance. . . .

My good companions were Earl and Leo Prince, whose early home had been a farmstead in Vermont. Earl was thirty-six years old, a graduate of Ann Arbor who had been in real estate business in Chicago. He was an excellent carpenter, practical and skilled, a hustler and competent in many ways. Leo, aged twenty-five, had many a fine quirk of character, too. . . .

The brothers were not tall men, were both of dark complexion. I'm sure I could have found no better-fitted partners, if I had combed the country. Both of them, being farm-bred, were 'facultized,' as New Englanders would say, and had the native Yankee mechanical genius for contriving. Earl could rig up anything. . . .

So, in my John Bunyan's *"pilgrim's progress"* with a pack upon my back, I was most fortunate to have for my companions two honest men of admirable and wholesome qualities. . . .

Later in the book, a February 1899 entry from Scott's log told of E.H. and Leo leaving Alaska:

My partners of the Trail left Dawson for the Outside, with Ginnold of the Arctic Express and his dogs. They are to walk and run for the six hundred miles we previously navigated together in our boat. So long, Mates!

The story that Mary Lee Davis published was a lot more than Scott's own log; she had discussed his story with him at length, and embellished it and added much of her own flair. Whenever she used the word *we* in describing Dr. Scott's first year in Alaska, it can be assumed that she meant Scott, E.H. and Leo.

Many years later, Scott and E.H. made contact with one another by letter. E.H. wrote to Dr. Scott October 26, 1933, and the following exchange took place.:

Dr. James Foster Scott
McLean, Virginia

Dear old friend of the trail:

My daughter, Mrs. Parrish, who lives in our old home in Downers Grove found in Marshall Field in Chicago your diary "Sourdough Gold" edited by Mary Lee Davis. She was all excited, getting it on Saturday and rushing out here Sunday to Dixon to see me with a copy of the book and we had a jolly and thrilling time going over it together. Her husband, Mr. Parrish, seemed to enjoy it as we did.

It brought to mind so many dear old memories. I certainly would like to see you and talk it over. When I came to your description of our Lake Bennett camp I was in perfect accord. I have thought of that camp so very very often and idealized it as a camp that could not be repeated. I spent two or three years in Northern Ontario mining and prospecting and often had my son and daughter up there on those lakes for their vacations in the summer and we had many wonderful camps, but none so perfect as the Lake Bennett.

When I see Leo, who is a druggist in Webb City, Missouri, we go over those days counting them as among the richest of our lives and Leo is always saying, "I wish I could see Dr." and repeats the many jokes we had. I see you failed to get them into your diary...the girl tripping out of the canvas toilet at the back of the boat. That never fails to throw Leo into convulsions of laughter.

I wrote to your friend, the compiler of your diary, and sent it to the editors to be forwarded to her. In response to it I got your address and a long interesting letter from her. She must be an exciting interesting woman. Should I have a chance to go up that way I will not fail to call on her, and I surely will "dog" you down in your retreat and go over the old days.

My son, Earl, is interested with me in business and also for himself in Sterling, the next town west and I am in business here. My daughter and her husband, W. Parrish live at Downers Grove. He is with the International Harvester Co. We are all getting much out of life and prospering fairly well in spite of what they say about the times.

Write me, Dr., and tell me about yourself. While our association was not so long, it was so close and intimate and pleasant with no jars that I cherish it as one of the most fruitful of all my life.

Your old friend of the Klondike, Earl H. Prince

Dr. Scott wrote back to E.H. almost immediately. The following is from his letter dated October 31, 1933:

My very dear old Earl:

It had been a long time since any letter gave me as much joy as yours. About thirty years ago I wrote up my diary and it has been lying idle ever since. Mrs. Davis was to write another book and she talked much with me and I also lent her what I had written. I had no idea that she was going to make me the villain of her book, and I rebelled strongly. Now please don't think that I have become a doddering idiot and forgotten the things that were burned indelibly into our memories. . . .

Do not think that she and I wrote the book; it is entirely hers. . . .

You and Leo were just grand companions, and if I were going off again I should hold both of you up at the point of a gun, if necessary, to make you come along, but I hope you would come without coercion. Try as we would I doubt if we could develop such a camp as we had at Bennett. I have described it several times to Boy Scouts and made their mouths water. Leo and I were mighty hunters; with our two guns one of us managed to hit a fool-hen [ptarmigan] about three feet away. He thinks that he hit it, and I am sure that I did, and we can never come to an agreement on that. Do you remember when I was sitting on a rock on Thirty-mile communing with Nature in a serious mood that was not altogether beyond the reproach of society, and a scow with several ladies and gentlemen whisked close by to my annoyance? I think you do. The innumerable jokes of the Klondikers were not meant for drawing rooms. Do you recollect the time when you wore out Brimstone on your marathon hike? Of course you have forgotten about the two moose which fell to your gun. I still possess the mighty hammer which gave you a thrill, and it should be put in a glass case. . . .

When you come this way prepare to stay with me for several days. I can make you comfortable in a real bed, and keep you alive with food. It would be a treat to have a long talk and many walks with you. I still keep the Shakespeare you left with me, and I treasure it. . . .

E.H. wrote back to Dr. Scott November 23, 1933. His letter shows very clearly how much he cherished his time in Alaska and his friendship with Scott.

My dear old friend, Dr. Scott:

Was I pleased when your letter came. I do not know when I have had such pleasant thrills and I went directly back to the Dyea Beach, Sheep Camp, snow slides, over the Summit, Lake LaBarge, and down to our never-to-be-forgotten-camp on Lake Bennett and later on to Dawson.

I treasure all that adventure as among the richest of my life. Leo would certainly be excited to see you. He is always asking about you and I assure you he has not forgotten the many quaint things that happened and the jokes. He often speaks and laughs at the consternation of us all when you were caught so unfortunately that morning just after breakfast when we were preparing to hit the Thirty-Mile River. I can even now hear the yell that went up from that bunch in the boat.

I enjoyed every word of your trip from Dawson to St. Michael. I think the experience we got in the North was well worth while. Everything in your account seemed so like you and I think I appreciate just how you felt about your river. Perhaps we both found ourselves while in that lonely, wild country where we had lots of time to think and meditate. I could not possibly sufficiently impress you with the depths of feeling which it strikes in me even yet, and makes me long for the North woods. I enjoyed the winters and enjoyed the summers. They were so delightful and I enjoyed the return trip from Dawson to Skagway and can see you as we pulled up the river from Dawson on that 8th day of February. I was awfully sorry to leave you behind, as I felt at the time that you should come out with us.

Kosnick we never heard of but once, and that was at St. Michael. Washburn, President of the Alaska Commercial Co., told us that he applied to him for a passage to Seattle and he asked him to go to work and help him to load the vessels as he needed men badly, and he never saw him after that. Poor old Kosnick. That country was too much for him.

You remember the currants I brought down from Flat Creek in a pail for you and the next day the gray backs that disturbed the peace of your mind when I charged you with harboring some of those fellows on your person. Oh! what days.

I carefully read every word of Mary Lee Davis and your book. I think I knew when it was you speaking and when it was Mrs. Davis speaking. It is all good and entertaining, but the second part I have read slowly and with care and can see and enjoy your philosophy of life, your river, your experience, the finding of yourself, as you put it. It is fine, Dr., well done, and I hope and believe many will read it and enjoy it as I have. It did me good and will do others good if they will read it and I am sure many will. I received a shipment of six books today which I am going to pass around among some of my friends that I want to have them. I shall get more. One is going to Leo with a copy of your letter. It will be such a pleasant surprise to him.

Leo was a pretty good cook and I think we both enjoyed his meals. I am sure I did. You and I weren't so good. You probably got to be a good one before you left. Your experience in St. Michael was interesting together with your experience when you left Seattle. I certainly did think you took undue chances in coming in your little boat through the latter part of the trip to St. Michael and would not recommend it to be tried again. I always love to think of our experience in shooting Miles Canyon and White Horse. You certainly took us through fine. It was all great.

    I shall see you, Dr., my first opportunity and we will have a nice long visit. I cannot say when that may be.

    With great esteem and admiration, and sincerest love,

        Your old friend,   Earl H. Prince.

In Rita's papers I also found an October, 1933, letter to E.H. from Mary Lee Davis. She wrote, in part:

    I think that 100 times while I was writing "Sourdough Gold" I wondered "Will the Prince boys ever read this? Are they alive? and where? What fun it would be to hear from them. I wonder if I ever will!" So when your letter came yesterday it gave me genuine joy and I sincerely thank you for it. . . .

    He [Scott] isn't very good at describing people, and so I may have missed up sometimes (not willfully) in telling of "the Prince boys." But I came to be very <u>fond</u> of you both.

Alaska was not E.H.'s only adventure, of course. He also prospected in Canada, bought a plantation in Louisiana, and ran a ranch in North Dakota [he had the foresight to retain mineral rights to alternating sections on the land]. As you know from the articles about him, he established an ice cream and ice plant in Dixon. That ice cream plant led to creation of Prince Castles, a forerunner of fast-food enterprises like McDonalds. Each one of his adventures would be worth a separate book, but that is outside the scope of this one.

Speaking of McDonalds, we probably never would have had McDonald fast-food shops at all if it hadn't been for E.H.'s son Earl S. Prince. It was Earl who invented what he called the Multimixer, a device that made it possible to make four milkshakes simultaneously. His national sales representative for the Multimixer received several orders for it from a little company in California. Curious to learn about this apparently very successful business, he went out to visit them and saw a golden opportunity. That national sales representative was Ray Krok, and he had the foresight to purchase the right to use that little store's name—McDonald's—and the rest is history.

When Rita came on the scene in 1926, E.H. was no longer living at Princeholm . For reasons that are outside the purpose of this book, Rita's grandmother had divorced him. Rita's relationship with E.H. was not positive. She wrote:

I think that Honey more than anything would have wanted me to remember her father. I never saw him through her eyes, however. She saw love; I saw criticism, but never love. I thought that at any moment he would spank me, and Honey wouldn't stop him. His death, so grievous to Honey, meant nothing to me.

Rita's Grandmother

Minnie Harriet Jones Prince (Mama)
(1866 – 1946)

The relationship between Rita and her grandmother ("Mama" to Rita) was special. Mama was truly like a mother to her: loving, compassionate, gentle, kind, patient, considerate, and full of useful advice about proper living. Her Mama believed in living her Christian faith, not just talking about it, and she stressed to Rita the importance of staying clear of liquor, premarital sex, profanity, and unkind thoughts or behavior. Rita would often repeat what Mama said about not judging people: "Think kind thoughts." That became a lifelong guide for her. In all the years we shared, Rita only deviated once, and that was when she commented on General Douglas MacArthur, whom she could not stand.

Mama Prince was an old-line Vermonter whose ancestors had come to America very early. One genealogist thought that her line went back to John Alden of Mayflower fame, but in any case her ancestors were clearly in New England very shortly after. One of the famous Salem witches (Sarah Osborne) was definitely related to Rita; her home was still standing some years ago when we drove through.

Mama Prince was also active in politics, and labored early and consistently in support of women's suffrage and prohibition. She was an active early member of the local chapter of the League of Women Voters

This is what Rita wrote about Mama many years ago, when her grandmother was still living:

I call my grandmother Mama, from Honey, who calls her Mother. She can remember when she drove a horse and buggy, and when there weren't any houses here. Her horse was named Nellie, and she had a white cat called Mutsie. Now she has a car, and takes long trips in it. She is slightly old-fashioned, and very sweet about it.

To me, Grandmother and Grandfather Prince were as different as black and white. His criticism was Mama's love. She was soft and loving, kind, understanding, funny and fun-loving, but in an understated way. She giggled where someone else would guffaw.

Mama was dependable and overly cautious. She worried about colds and wet feet, and never drove over 35 miles an hour. She was afraid to drive near other cars, so the policeman would stop traffic on Main Street when she came, because she would drive down the center line. They finally asked Honey not to let her drive downtown. She dusted her car every day, though, whether she could drive it or not.

Mama had tea every afternoon, and napped with our cat, Ginger. I can't imagine her with an axe, but she used one like Carry Nation one time, smashing a bar in a saloon during Prohibition. She was also an active Suffragette and was one of the founders of the Downers Grove League of Women Voters group. She had a will of iron, and faith, and led a loving, Christian life.

In among papers that Rita saved were some writings that appear to have been composed by her grandmother. The first looks like a prayer:

> May I keep a gentle voice;
> May I be impersonal and self-effacing;
> May I have an open mind;
> May I be a vehicle to express Truth.

The next is a poem *The Little Town*:

> I like the little town:
> The farmer's wife who drives the team to do her
> early trading;

The easy going swing of business men of portly habit
        and gentle mien
Who open doors of banks and stores, and call to friends
        familiar nicknames
Jim and Joe, "Fine weather. How's the wife and baby?

I like the little town:
The little children swinging books as off to school
        they trudge;
The spires that point above,
And call the worshippers to friendly services
        on the Sabbath;
The women who keep community spirit at the boiling point,
And work their wonders for the common good.

I like the little town:
The village green, the quiet tree-lined streets;
The low-roofed houses with time worn steps;
The distant cow bell in the evening,
The sound of which comes blurred with bird song and the
        voices of children;
And sleep at night which shuts out the sound of day
        in perfect stillness.

I love the little town.

The third tells something of Mama Prince's faith:

    I enjoy the "Some One Prayed" column and am glad to add my testimony. I have always been sensitive to the inner voice and have sought to be guided by its teaching. I thank God for the wonder and joy of divine guidance.

My first leading which I recall as a marked illustration was when I unaccountably insisted on changing my wedding day. It came to pass that the date first selected was the day of the death of my father's foster-father, and the family group was at his bedside at the hour of what would have been the wedding.

I have always thought that God, in answer to my prayer, gave back to me the life of my blessed baby [Honey], when she lay in my arms in a coma, given up by our physician.

Last summer we were motoring though Canada and lost one of our suitcases off the rear platform of our car. Motorists were flying in both directions. What should we do? We went back to the town through which we had just passed. A kindly, benevolent, white-haired policeman located us for the night in a lovely Christian home. We went to bed praying that the suitcase, which contained the labor of several months' preparation for our eastern trip, might be restored to us.

In the morning, contrary to his custom, our host went to his neighbor's for the milk. There he found a Michigan man who had gone to the oil station before it was open and was passing the time by calling upon the neighbor who happened to be a former acqauintance. Several present were comparing notes and our host mentioned the State licenses which he housed the night before. The Michigan man, hearing an Illinois State license mentioned, stated that he had found a suitcase belonging to an Illinois woman. That was enough. Our host brought the suitcase to us to identify and we went on our journey rejoicing, after thanking the kind policeman who, I shall always feel, was a link in the chain of circumstance used by the Divine.

Rita's Mother
Sarah Harriet Prince Parrish (Honey)
1889 - 1967

We have to begin this section with Rita's high school biography of her mother. She gave it the title *Biography of Sarah Harriet Prince Parrish*.

All the loveliest traits and virtues in Heaven were brought together in one small mite of a baby who made her first appearance in this world on the morning of December 27, 1889. She was moved from the Chicago hospital where she was born to her home in Downers Grove, a suburb about twenty-four miles west of Chicago. Here she grew fat and chubby until her third month, when she became rather sickly. She took the "thrush", a disease caused by a fungus, and went steadily into a decline, which her parents did not notice because it was so gradual.

One day while Mr. Prince was at work, she became so much worse that her mother took her to the doctor in town, who said that her condition was very critical. After a consultation of doctors it was decided that she had Cholera infantum, and after a few days she was given up. At last she was not expected to live through the night, and a minister was called in to baptize her before she went.

However, she lived through to the next morning and took nourishment. To the surprise of everyone, most of all the doctors, she became steadily better as the days went on, while it was declared that only the New England blood in her pulled her through. She was put on different diets, and at last became her sweet rosy self again, although she was not nearly so chubby. She had a large lawn to play on, and the sunshine helped her greatly.

When she was four years of age, a baby brother, baptized Earl Samuel, was born. Straight-way she became the soul and embodiment of a big sister, mothering the baby in a way lovely to behold. She hardly ever quarreled with him, and helped him out of a good many scrapes as he grew older. Apparently she never got into many herself, for she was a "prunes and prisms" sort of maid. She was the one who pounded him on the back when the peanut brittle got stuck in his throat, who persuaded him to confess to mother that he had been sailing his boat on the forbidden lake, and who ate her turnips in order that he might follow her example.

At this time Mr. Prince was in the real estate business and had bought up land all around Downers Grove. Once he could have had his choice of this land or the land on the "North Shore", both at the same price. However, he thought no one would ever want to live on the shore, where it was so cold and barren, while the land around Downers Grove was well-wooded and had rich soil. Just think! If he had bought the lake shore property, we would all be rich enough to go through the moratorium with banners flying. Ah me! However, he didn't.

Mr. Downer, whose lands touched his, Mr. Blodgett, Mr. Rogers, and Mr. Prince subdivided the newer part of town together, laying out streets and the avenues of trees which bordered them, and selling lots. Mr. Prince was quite a naturalist, and so very interested in a project which he was carrying out at this time. This was the sinking of the "North Pond" as it is called now, and the laying out of shrubbery around it. Besides this he set out numerous kinds of bushes and trees around his own home.

In this way the two children had a great many playgrounds. Horses were kept in the barn stalls, and later a cow was bought so that the two could have real milk. Earl had his morning chores to attend to daily, while Harriet had her bed to make and room to clean. Mrs. Prince was very religious, and brought her household up as such, taking the two to the Congregational Church each and every Sunday to hear the stories of Goliath and David, Moses in the bullrushes, etc. Of course Mr. Prince went too.

Harriet entered the school, and four years later so did Earl. Harriet, or "Rita" as her father called her for a pet name, was quite a serious child. Though a good many photographs were taken of her, not one of them is smiling. However, this doesn't mean that she wasn't happy. I imagine (though I didn't know her at the time) that she was pleased in small things, and besides, there were the Church Picnics twice a year.

When Harriet was twelve the family moved to Northfield, Vermont, and here they stayed four years. It was here that "Rita" gained her aptitude for ice-skating and the rest of the winter sports. Winters are winters there.

However, at the end of the four years they came back to Downers, good old Downers. Harriet entered high school, and took three years of work there. However, as the Downers Grove High School wasn't accredited at that time, she took her last year of high school work at LaGrange, or Lyons High School.

She had decided that she wanted to major in sociology. Therefore, hearing from a friend that there was a splendid course of this at Northwestern University, she went there the following two years. About then Mr. Prince decided that his family should have a short trip, so he sent Mrs. Prince, Harriet and Earl Jr. over to Europe for six months. While in Europe they visited all the old ruins in France, England, Germany, Italy, and Switzerland. They sent back "pistol picture" postcards and varied the "Having a fine time. Wish you were here." by telling about the old wrecks and using different adjectives.

When they came back from this short jaunt, Harriet took a year at the Graham Taylor School of Civics and Philanthropy, because she was interested in sociology, and got her degree there. She took two years at Wisconsin University at Madison, and majored in sociology there, too. During her first year there she won her white sweater with the big W, for being on five varsity girls athletic teams. These included baseball, basketball, hockey, tennis, and bowling. In all these sports she was good because she liked them so well. In her senior year she was vice-president of her class. She was also a member of the Red Domino Club, the highest club a girl could then join.

She was not long out of college before she took work (carrying out the Sociology) in a placement bureau for college students. Through this she got her first job, selling Lecture Courses in communities. She was out of school about four years, when—since I guess she could stand it no longer to be away from him—she went home and married Bill Parrish, a boy whom she had met while she was still in high school. And so, on the afternoon of September 15, 1916, Sarah Harriet Prince and William Mallow Parrish were joined in the holy bonds of wedlock, at a lawn wedding at the home of the bride.

And here is more of what Rita wrote about her mother. There are some contradictions between this account and the above 'official' biography; my inclination is to trust the biography for the details:

My mother was Sarah Harriet Prince Parrish, and we called her Honey. It was a loving name that Bo called her in the south, and when Kay was learning to talk, she said *Honey* instead of *mother*, and it stuck. Honey had been a 'high-spirited' young girl, and since her mother was a soft personality, Honey thought for herself most of her life.

She truly missed her father and idolized him. She took her important decisions to him; when he didn't live up to her ideal, she was crushed, and after his death her brother Earl took his place.

Honey was brought up in the old school: speak when spoken to, don't impose, don't contradict, be ladylike, ride horses well, play tennis well, be a good Christian, be frugal, honest and loving. She learned all of it well.

When Mama and Daddy Prince were divorced, she and Mama and Earl went to live with Grandma and Grandpa Jones in Montpelier, where she went to school. Then she attended high school in Downers Grove, and went to the University of Wisconsin at Madison for her degree in sociology. She was vice president of her class. She had lots of beaux and an active social life.

When Grandpa Jones died, Mama used her inheritance to take Honey, Earl and a bevy of other girls on a grand tour of Europe. Bo surprised her somewhere there with a visit. When she read her diary years later, she said that she certainly had been silly, writing mostly of the boys she was meeting. But the art and architecture and differing cultures had impressed her, and she was interested in them all her life. She had an active curiosity, like Bo, and studied, noted, watched, and always learning about people and places.

She was very pretty, with brown hair that turned gray in her twenties. She had hazel eyes, and was always slim. She was very creative, too. For a long time, she sewed all our clothes. She was frugal, too. She went to Marshall Fields to see the best clothes, and then made the same clothes herself. She loved entertaining, and never set the table the same way twice for guests—colors, china, theme, flowers—all changed.

She was strict, demanding that Pete behave like a gentleman and Kay and I like ladies. And she was a devoted mother. She loved having fun with her children, and she carefully watched their education. We <u>knew</u> she loved us. She showed it in so many ways. She was always compassionate, always understood our troubles and joys over the years. She and Bo were very different initially, and they grew more alike over the years.

She worked in Chicago's Union Station for Travelers Aid, where she would meet trains to assist people who needed help: children;

handicapped; and foreigners i.e., non English-speaking. During World War II she also worked at the USO.

Honey rode horses well, and had one called Ned, which she rode before cars came to Downers. Then, when cars were here, she learned to drive right away.

Honey loved fun and doing gay things, but by nature she was rather serious. She was frugal and quiet, and never bragged. She was a worker—a *doer*—and busily got things *done*. She was generous with her time, love and money.

Bo had worked in Chicago for three years. The year after they were married, he and Honey traveled down to Louisiana where they worked on Daddy Prince's plantation. Three years later they moved back north to Downers Grove and lived with Mama in big old Princeholm.

In Rita's papers I found another description of Honey:

The reason I admire "Honey" so is because of her character. She seems to me to be the ideal companion-mother. She makes her own clothes, Catherine's, Rita's [mine], Myrtle's, Mrs. Prince's, and occasional dresses for [my] cousin Patricia and Aunt Marion. She always looks smart and neat, and has an enviable good taste about things, along with a good sense of balance. She entertains frequently, but gives more attention to the effect than to the details.

She loves golf and tennis, besides all the other things she did in her college days, and has learned to swim in the last two years. She has always loved the water but could never swim, an old trait dating back to the sailor blood in her, I suppose. The house is noted for all the old get-togethers in it, and the "gang" knows the house as well as the people who live in it do. She is often asked to write up some meeting, and has been writing all her life.

She has no special hobby that I know of, although lately she has been interested in setting out the dinner table in glass, and is often bringing home plates or cups or something which she has found on sale. She is quite economical, and has learned to tell the best of everything. She hates doing things just like everyone else does them, and likes to put her own individual touch in everything she does. She is quite optimistic, saying, "It takes all kinds of people to make a world," and has lately been trying to convince her daughter [me] that you cannot please everyone at once. She says that since she learned this, the world has been different for her.

The thing I most admire in her, though, is her thoughtfulness. She is forever doing something for someone else, never thinking of herself. If she is going anywhere she usually tries to take someone along who otherwise would never get there. She has just called in to me that she thinks it is absolutely crazy to write "that stuff", because it makes her so embarrassed to think anyone else knows of her goodness, and she thinks I'm overdoing it greatly. However, I just want to add that I'm at my happiest when someone says I'm my mother's daughter.

Among Rita's papers I also found the following prayer, which was probably written by Honey:
> Lord Thou knowest that I am getting older.
> Keep me from getting talkative and possessed with the idea that I must express myself on every subject.
> Release me from the craving to straighten out everyone's affairs.
> Keep my mind free from the recital of endless detail;
> Give me wings to get to the point.
> Seal my lips when I am inclined to tell of my aches and pains;
> They are increasing with the years and my love to speak of

them grows sweeter as times goes by.
Teach me the glorious lesson that occasionally I may be wrong.
Make me thoughtful but not nosy; helpful but not bossy.
With my vast store of wisdom and experience, it does seem a pity not to use it all,
But thou knowest, Lord, that I want a few friends at the end.
Amen

When I first met Honey in 1949, she was almost sixty years old, but still trim and athletic. My initial impression of her was that she had a patrician demeanor, ala Ethel Barrymore: a trifle brittle and judgmental, but very sincere. To me, she seemed to have a tendency to observe people and analyze them. She was always polite, though, and seldom let people know what she was thinking. She had a soft and romantic side, too, but almost seemed to try to conceal it. The following letter that I just found in Rita's papers was written by Honey to her brother Earl, and shows clearly what a loving and caring person she was.

July 14, 1942

Earl, dear –

Another birthday….thinking of you and your birthdays all the years when we were children, then youngsters and now adults not welcoming them too heartily….my mood is very tender, Earl. You were such a plump sweet (I mean *sweet*, just that) little boy and I remember imposing on you even when I would have fought for you any instant. Then you were awkward and you teased me about the boys, getting even. But it never seemed obnoxious or mean but just a game. Pulling my false curls off and leaning over the roof to listen…. you certainly had plenty of ideas. Better that your Earl hears about them later.

Then the college years when I wanted you to have all there was in it because I knew I missed some of it....and then the four years began to make less difference and we had many of the same friends.

How I cried and cried because I could not be at your wedding. It seemed so terrible not to share all the important events. The visits into your home since you have had one, loving Marion as fiercely as I have you. And enjoying your children; sharing Mother and those last years with Dad. The void after he left us gradually less hurting. And gradually, more or less unconsciously, finding that you are filling that void in so many ways, Earl.

With all the tough spots, we have had much for which to be deeply thankful all along the way. Just because we lived in a big house and had a trip abroad and went to college I guess it looked like a soft spot that we enjoyed. They didn't know all we had to meet. They didn't know how it hurt to have our mother and father apart and no family like the other youngsters....nor that we were almost cold in the big house sometimes, running from fireplace to fireplace....that college wasn't all a lark....that apparent successes have to be moved up to and met with level heads.

Oh sometimes I wonder. But of course one keeps plugging even when they wonder. I guess I know as well, better perhaps, the road you have come along and I have only the deepest respect and admiration and love, Earl. I am so thankful, too, for the joy both Mother and Dad have had in you. If you never did another thing worthwhile in your life, that in itself would be something you could feel satisfaction enough to rest on. You were just the right combination to afford them both that happiness that parents crave and deserve from their children…. Different as they are, Mother and Dad, your different sides were the answer.

Well….I just wanted to say these things that come to me off and on during the months….It seems a right time for the saying. I will write a family letter since Mother is to be there, telling of what we are doing. This is my love, and I doubt whether you know how deep it is and how constant.

H

Gerd Ragnhild Oie Myren

A vivacious Wisconsin native who traveled the world and lived abroad for many years, Gerd was a teacher and active in many theatrical productions in Fairfax County while residing in McLean and then Leesburg. Proud of her Norwegian heritage, she spoke English, Norwegian and Spanish. Gerd died on Friday, December 2nd, and is survived by her husband, Dr. Delbert T. Myren, three children Krista M. Hayman, Gregory A. Myren, and Eric T. Myren, her grandchildren, Christina, Jeffrey, Kara, Kyle, Ariel, Amber and Hayley Myren, and her brother Otto Oie. A memorial service was held on December 10th in Vienna, VA. Memorial contributions may be made to the Sjogrens Syndrome Foundation.

"We were sitting in the tent, talking about my departure, Paneak said: 'We will give you the mountain which stands at the beginning of the Giant's Valley. It shall bear your name, and we will remember you. Our people remember such things for many generations.'...I knew it well...a fine mountain indeed."

Since that day in 1950, the 4,880-foot peak that overlooks the village has been known as Ingstad Mountain...but it cannot be found on maps. Residents petitioned the US Board of Geographic Names when Ingstad died in 2001, at age 101....but such names cannot become official until five years after a person's death.

...US officials say the submission meets the board's criteria and will likely be approved,...a formal dedication ceremony may take place in the spring of 2006—and Ellen Vollebaek may get her wish to once again see the spectacular Midnight Sun of Alaska.

(Photo and much text by Arild Strømmen and Grant Spearman, from 1/8/06 edition of "News of Norway")

Rita's Father
William Mallow Parrish (Bo)
(1888 – 1967)

Bo was the opposite of Honey. A hearty Midwesterner, he was as volatile as she was reserved. When I went to Downers on a weekend visit with Rita while we were students at the University of Michigan [you'll read about it later], Bo went to great lengths to make me feel at ease. A top sales executive for International Harvester Company for many years, he had just retired and was starting his own executive recruiting business—a pioneer in that field. Bo's memory for names and his vast repertoire of stories were legendary at Harvester. In all the many conversations I had with him over the years, I can't remember his ever repeating a story he had told me.

When Bo retired from Harvester, they gave him a great going-away party, and this was what his "friends of Harvester" wrote about him:

> "The captains and the kings depart"—but they leave an indelible impression on the minds and hearts of those with whom they wrought their triumphs. And so, you too have left the indestructible image of your twenty-four years of achievement at Harvester. You've been one of us for so long that no separation of time or distance can ever dull the remembrance of our association.
>
> Like everything human, your official ties with us are disappearing. But how can we forget the dazzling radiance reflected from your gold-plated, "off again on again" spectacles? Or what can the veil of time do to hide your famous motorcycle belt from our view. Can we ever forget your suitcase, which, when opened, revealed only a pair of socks? No, Bill, whatever the future holds, the past held too much to forget.
>
> From the time you severed your ties with Henry Ford, 'way back in 1924, you have been a tireless instigator of improvements at Harvester. You put I-H in the industrial power business by converting

the old 10-20 farm tractor into what looked like an industrial tractor. And unless memory fails us, your efforts on behalf of the 15-30 in the same direction were a mighty stride toward today's I-H tractors. We never knew how you did it, but you did.

We do know that, in the course of your career, you made friends without number. How you remember so many names and faces is something known only to yourself and Jim Farley. We're pretty sure those notes you made on the backs of envelopes were not of much help. Threw most of those away, didn't you, Bill?

But remembering names and faces is just one of the mysteries about you. How you ever managed to operate without voluminous reports of your travels and conferences is indeed worthy of intensive investigation. Somehow or other, although you traveled from thither to yon and from yon back to thither, you always knew exactly what took place everywhere you'd been. And we'll wager a bob or two you can still tell us all the details.

And then there was that eventful year of 1942. Dollar-a-Year Parrish, you were known as in those days—Dollar-a-Year Parrish, the dynamic doer of deeds for the War Production Board. We never really suspected that your dollar-a-year salary had anything to do with a desire to lower your income taxes.

These have been highlights in your life, Bill. They are, after all, just a few of the little things we remember about you. But life is a collection of little things, and together they make a big man. Little things like your kindness and consideration for everyone who knew you, your honesty and straightforwardness in all your dealings, your readiness to create a laugh when merriment was needed—all these things added up to Bill Parrish.

We are going to miss your presence around Harvester. We hope that you will not dissolve your friendships with us even though your future plans keep you busy. You see, Bill, you have done a tremendous job of salesmanship. You have sold I-H products everywhere and sold them well, but far more than that, you have sold all of us on "Bill Parrish," sold us so well that we know there isn't a better "product" made on this populous planet.

As you begin this newest phase of your career, you have the heartfelt good wishes of all of us who knew you. We hope they will be an inspiration to you as you have been to us.

March 1, 1949

One thing that Bo didn't realize was that corporations are not like families. When you leave a corporation, you really are not missed, and soon are forgotten. No one could be like Bo, but no one at I-H really remembered him or really cared about him for very long, and that hurt him.

Rita was Bo's special girl, and her love for him is apparent in the way she described life with him.

Bo was excitable, pugilistic, terribly strong, tenacious, considerate, actively helpful, domineering and generous. Imagine; put all of these qualities in a man with a huge barrel chest (46 inches) and small hips. He had a square face with brown hair and square lower lip. His blue eyes had laugh-wrinkles.

Bo loved to laugh, and at times would laugh until tears rolled down his cheeks. I loved to go to Joe E. Brown movies with him, just to watch him laugh. It was a big event to go to a movie with him when I was little. He traveled so much and worked so hard and DID so much that he could fall asleep in an average film. Only the comedies would keep him awake, so that's why we went to see movies with Laurel and Hardy and Joe E. Brown.

My earliest memory of Bo is of a big strong man carrying me and loving me. He called me "my little Choctaw." There was no doubt in my mind that he loved me and would do anything for me. He never punished us, never even reprimanded us. He would tell Honey to do it.

Others remembered him for his generosity. He seemed to know instinctively when others needed help and would call or write to them or go to see them or send things, so that you always felt that he truly was there to help. I remember being given a phonograph in the thirties, though we had no records, as repayment of a loan he had made. His generosity was one of his finest qualities. He *did* the good deeds that many of us might think about but never bother to do. When he died, Honey had many letters telling of his kindnesses that he had never even mentioned to her.

He was very emotional. He would cry over the problems of others; tears would stream down his face as he talked with someone on the phone. He worried about his friends and loved ones. He was compassionate. At the other end of his emotional side, he could also get extremely angry. Then he was frank to the point of causing pain. When his spell was over, though, he was his own sweet self again and never seemed to hold a grudge.

When you were with him, though, knowing how low his boiling point was could keep you on edge! I have driven with him when I thought that he was going to pick a fight with drivers bigger than he was over some mistake they may have made.

He would growl at the offending car, "I'm going to give that guy Hell!"

He could also be unpredictable. He could arrive home with flowers for no special reason, wind his watch very loudly during a long sermon by the minister, or suddenly pile us all into the car on a Sunday afternoon to go for an ice cream cone. That quality made life exciting, but also led to excruciating embarrassment.

You never could tell what to expect with Bo. After you had met his train at 7:00 p.m. and were on the way home to dinner, he might stop to

give a stranger with luggage a ride to his home on the other side of town. We could understand that, but other things were difficult to adjust to. He did things in unconventional ways, like:
- changing the oil in the car in his best suit;
- driving to Indianapolis to fight on the sidewalk with a man who had cheated his niece Louise out of some money;
- going on a vacation to New York City and leaving his family sitting in the car for four hours outside a tractor factory that he decided to visit on the way ;
- bringing a crowbar to do the work of a key;
- building a closet (not requested) in a room of Kay's house while she was away at work one day;
- starting a trip at 3:00 p.m. that should have begun at 8:00 a.m.;
- Regularly arriving at trains and planes with only a minute to spare.

I could go on and on. Bo made life uncertain. One never knew what the day would hold.

One of my strong memories is driving with Bo, because I knew how accidents could happen and people could be hurt. It didn't matter that Bo never had one. That was sheer luck. He had a violent objection to ever being passed on the road. This was in the days of no turnpikes and very few four-lane roads. There were generally two or at the most three lanes. Trucks, all traffic in fact, used these roads, coast to coast, and over mountains and curving hilly roads, and through the middle of all cities and towns. Driving on a long trip with Bo meant being very alert all the time.

I was always in the back seat, usually in the middle, being the youngest. I would watch what I could see of the countryside out of the high window of those early cars.

Suddenly, Bo would cry out, "I got it! I got it, I got it!"

That told me that something dangerous was happening. He would hunch over the wheel as though he could pick the car up by it, and we would pass a truck too closely or take a sharp curve too fast, or whatever, and there was always the fear that he might stop and get into a fight. We would look for 'nice places' to eat, and he really hated the long wait before he could get back on the road.

He always had his own plan for where we would stop for the night, but didn't necessarily share that information with us, so that as dusk came we would begin looking for tourist homes in each town we came to. In those days there were no motels, just houses where you could rent rooms. They would have a lighted sign outside saying *Rooms* or *Vacancy*. He always gave a reason for not stopping: didn't see it; too dirty; too many stairs; no parking, etc. He and Honey would have words: she would say how late it was getting and that everyone needed a rest; he would opt for one hundred more miles. He was driving and was in control.

So, along about 2:00 a.m. we would finally stop, finding whatever was left at that time of night, and creep up to our rooms and welcome bed very quietly to avoid waking others.

Of course, the net result was that we got off later the next morning. I never could figure out why Bo preferred night driving. He must have been a night person, or maybe he liked driving when traffic was sparse.

When Bo came to cities, he loved to stay in good hotels, eat marvelous food and go to night clubs where we could see a show by Victor Borge or Hildegarde. When he worked, he would send us out to shop or visit museums. So traveling with Bo was always an adventure.

When Mama traveled with us, though, it must have taken all his self-control not to complain. He tried his best to drive so she felt secure (she never drove faster than 35 mph) and we never could dine where beer was served (she was a Prohibitionist). He also stopped early, sometimes.

Bo worked hard for International Harvester, using his knowledge of his machinery and his instinctive understanding of human nature. He truly enjoyed being with all sorts of people, and they knew it. So he was a good salesman, and set an individual record for sales for Harvester that now [1986], forty years later, has never been broken. But Harvester never knew where he was or what he was doing.

He would disappear and then turn up at the office with a sheaf of orders. He was his own man. When he disagreed with company policy, he said so, and I guess that that in the end led to his early retirement at sixty.

He hadn't saved much money. He had cared for his family, put three children through college, lived life well, and then started his own management consulting firm. It was hard sledding, because he was a pioneer in the executive recruitment field. It was discouraging for him.

Bo was too poor to go to college, or maybe his brothers didn't guide him that way. He worked all his later life with men who were educated, and sometimes wealthy. He felt no inferiority.... He learned, he watched, he read, he was always improving himself, and he knew that he was important to the Company. His confidence was born of hard work and enthusiasm, and original thinking. He thought of things that no one else did, and was willing to pursue them. "Lateral thought" is what it is called. He was confident he had the right answers, and would work hard to prove it.

Bo was born when the family traveled to town with horse and wagon. He saw the earliest automobiles, and owned early Buicks. He saw the uses of the earliest tractors and the first road building equipment. He traveled on the earliest planes, getting a plaque long before he retired of 100,000 miles traveled. Those were the old propeller craft, and I remember some pretty wobbly landings in the wind in Chicago at the old Midway Airport. He saw the first television, and I remember the day we were all sitting together listening to a cousin in the Air Force tell us that we were planning to go to the moon. We were all thunderstruck, laughed and said it would never happen. He lived to see it.

When Bo and I were driving to New York when I was in my teens, he told me of some experiences in the south.

This is what Rita remembered of Bo's account:

Honey and I were on the plantation, and I worked every day with some grand Negroes. I just don't understand how people down there thought.

There was a big young Negro who was seeing a girl down there. She was white trash but she knew better. They drove a wagon into town together one day. Well, that was too much for the men there.

I heard that they were going to go after the boy and went to their meeting place to talk them out of it. They had a rope and they were going to lynch him! I couldn't believe it. I pleaded with them, and got into a fight. They knocked me out, and I woke up in a field later. They had taken that poor boy out and hanged him. I never will forgive them.

You know that E.H. Prince was a real miser. We spent more than three years on the plantation improving it and making it worth selling. Then he sold it, making a profit of $33,000, and do you know we didn't see a dime of it! Honey idolized him, though. He could do no wrong. It was just sad, and I don't think Honey will every forgive herself, that when Daddy Prince died, she wasn't with him.

We went over to Dixon every weekend, you know. This one time, there was a bad snow storm and I wasn't even sure the car could make it. Honey had phoned him, and he seemed better, so I started off alone. He took a turn for the worse, and when I got there, he was failing fast. He asked me to hold him in my arms, and said, "Don't let me go! Don't let me go, Bill." [Bo was crying as he remembered; then he sighed a long sigh, and went on.] Then I had to go home to tell Honey.

We drove in silence for awhile.

Before he died, Bo dictated a condensed version of his life's story for Rita, Peter, and Kay, and here it is.

My father, Jessie Mallow Parrish, was born in 1844 and died in 1888 just two months before I was born. My mother was born in 1844 and died in 1896, and we moved from the farm into Colfax where the boys finished high school and my sister went to Chicago for some training in pre-medicine. After that we moved to Indianapolis in 1900. When Rebecca finished medical school in 1901, the home that we had with the four brothers was broken up and Rebecca went to an internship at Wesleyan Hospital.

Then one of my brothers, Frank, was selected as a good guardian for me and I made my home with him all of my early adult life. I had six brothers, one who died in infancy, but the other five were Lew, Quince, Frank, Chester and Joe. They continued to live in Indianapolis all their lives.

My brother Quince died in 1930, Joe in 1933, Frank in 1935, and in 1955 Chester passed away, and the next year Lew died. You see, they were all older, and they had reached the ripe old ages of seventy years, and in those days that was a ripe old age.

I was thirteen when I went to live with Frank and Pearl, and he was an engineer with the P and E Railroad, a division of the Big Four, which is now the New York Central. We lived on the west side of Indianapolis, and I went to Public School #16, out on White River.

After graduating from there in 1903 I went to the North Manual Training High School in Indianapolis and graduated in 1907. That was the first manual training high school in the country, and the four years that I spent there in woodworking, foundry practice, machine shop, mechanical drawing, etc. qualified me for manufacturing, which I later pursued with International Harvester.

In Indianapolis, streetcar fares were five cents, shaves were ten cents and haircuts were twenty-five cents all the time that I was in high school.

My sister Rebecca (Bebby) continued her internship at Wesleyan Hospital in Chicago and then at the Northern Indiana Hospital for the Insane at Logansport until her health was such that she could go out to Manila. In 1905, she founded a clinic that later developed into [Mary Johnston Hospital,] the first maternity hospital in the Philippines.

I had some very understanding teachers in high school and they remained my firm friends over the immediate post-high school years. I was a husky lad, probably a little fat, but played guard and center on the high school team until in one strenuous game I got kicked in the back and dislocated my kidney. After that my folks made me stop playing football, after only four games.

After I finished high school my brother Frank insisted that I learn a trade, so I went to work in the P and J roundhouse at night to work on repairing engines. Because of my training in high school I was able to do the work of the machinist, who slept all night long. I made ten cents an hour.

It would have taken me four years to finish my apprenticeship, so after ten months I left for Chicago to live with Uncle George and his boys Frank, Jay and Bennett Allison, and I learned to be a salesman. Uncle George was a very capable salesman. A cousin of mine, Clem Meander, had an automobile agency in Manchester, Indiana, and I went up there to help him rescue his investments. I left, however, in 1913 because I had the wanderlust and had been promised a job in England

I crossed the Atlantic on the liner *SS Arabic*, and enjoyed the early glimpse of England very much. I lived in Warrington, about twenty miles outside of Liverpool and found work there in the north of England, then later on moved to Southampton, where I worked until the outbreak of World War I. I thought that the war would be over in two or three months, and did not want to come home until I had wandered a little more, but after some time I decided that the war could last a long time and I had better start home.

Through a personal friend, Billy Voutaw, I was able to get on as a cadet in the mail room of the United States Lines, but unfortunately my bunk was in steerage, though I could take my meals with him in the mailroom during the crossing. When I arrived in New York, I had not stood inspection, my passport was lost, and Billy had left the ship at quarantine with the mail, so I had absolutely no friend to vouch for me. I was taken out to Ellis Island, and after a day there I telephoned Billy to qualify me to come back to the mainland and I arrived at the Battery with an English sixpence in my pocket. I walked from the Battery uptown to 14th Street where there was a YMCA. I was waiting there to ask for a bed for the night, when the man at the counter looked around and said, "Why didn't you take the job I sent you to?"

I said, "Well, I'll take it, but where did you send me?"

"The American Seamen's Friend Society, at 507 West Street," he said, "They wanted a night clerk."

"I'll go there," I answered. And I did. In an hour I had a job that lasted through the winter. You see, I didn't want to let Chester, Frank, Lew and Quince know how disastrously my wanderlust had turned out and didn't want to ask them for money to come home.

By spring, however, I had saved enough money to look presentable and I returned to Indianapolis, where I resumed working for International Harvester, selling motor trucks. This was in 1915, and on the spur of the moment I sent a valentine to Honey, whom I had not seen in years. Shortly thereafter, I got a letter from her and her friend Jennie Ericson, and that summer I went up to Chicago to see her.

We were married in 1916, and I left Harvester because they didn't pay enough for selling motor trucks and I went to work for Ace Motor Truck in Newark, Ohio, a much better-paying job.

Shortly after that America was in the war, and E.H. Prince, who had bought a plantation in Louisiana, was able to convince the draft board in Wheaton that I would be more useful in reclaiming this old plantation, which was a good commercial investment for him. Honey and I moved to Faraday, Louisiana when our daughter Kay was six weeks old. There we gradually stocked the cabins with colored people, repaired the cabins, got the equipment, of which our Sampson tractor was an integral part.

Sampson was the first small tractor in that part of the country, and I used it for everything on the plantation: road building, ditch-digging, and stump-pulling, as well as the standard agricultural chores.

We lived on the inside of Lake St. John, which was an old bed of the Mississippi River, and each day we had to row across the lake (nine and half miles) to get our mail from the box in front of the Chandler residence. They were friends of ours from Evanston.

We made satisfactory cotton crops and after two years, with the war over, we decided that we had better go back to Chicago, where the opportunities were much greater. Returning to Chicago, I went to speak to the sales manager of Sampson Tractor. He told me that they had three men in the South for six months, and they only had written three contracts. I told him that I would can them if I were their boss.

He said, "Could you do better?"

"Give me two weeks," I said, "and I'll send you eight contracts."

I went down there and did send in seven contracts, written in Jackson, Mississippi, Natchez, Alexandria, La, Lake Charles, Kipido, La, and New Orleans before I was called up to Janesville where the sales manager said he couldn't believe that the contracts were real—even though checks for $500 and large orders for inventory accompanied each order.

After two weeks in Janesville, which was really a face-saving thing for their marketing men, I returned to Louisiana and worked Mississippi and that state for the balance of the year, with Honey remaining in Chicago with her mother. Then based on my record with Sampson, I was sent into Arkansas. When we knew that a new baby was coming in 1922, I returned to Chicago and started to work for the Ford Motor Co. in their industrial tractor department.

The baby arrived in August, and Peter's birthday is August 15, 1922. He certainly was a funny looking little kid, with no hair, but a good head, and Honey and I have loved him as if he had been the most beautiful baby in the world.

Kay was four years old at that time, and we had taken a little girl from Chicago from the Children's Home and Aid Society to be her companion while Honey was pregnant. This girl, Myrtle Bower, was such a sweet little twelve-year-old that we kept her in our home until she was through teachers college, married, and once or twice a year we still see her very happily to this day.

In 1925 I returned to International Harvester to start their industrial tractor division. You see, with Ford I had introduced the Fordson industrial tractor and I did the same thing with I-H, going with them when they had built 43 tractors but had not sold any. I left Ford making $400 a month and went with Harvester to make $3,000 a year, and Honey couldn't understand my taking a cut in salary.

The years with Harvester were eventually rewarding and certainly satisfactory from the point of view of human relations.

Rita came along during our second year with Harvester. My business trips with them were combined with excursions for the family, so we had many vacations in various parts of the United States.

During the Depression, things got pretty tough, so that in 1933 I was happy to have a job with $2,000 coming in from the Advertising Department for working the Century of Progress at night and the Harvester display at the World's Fair, and $2,000 from the Sales Department during the day for working my own sales activity with manufacturing and the industrial tractor branches.

I drove down to Indianapolis to get Rita and coming back with her in the back seat, I drove alongside a fellow who tried to run me into the ditch. Just as I was about to give the other driver Hell, Rita, who was about four, spoke up, "Don't say a word, Daddy. Don't say a word."

That's been her attitude all during my life. She counsels me wisely, and has loved me to the nth degree, which is far beyond what I deserve.

Harvester became more interested in the industrial tractor, and during the 1930s I introduced the first diesel tractors to the manufacturers of America. Through that association I became president of the manufacturers division of the American Road Builders Association. I had many fine friendships develop in that association, and I am indebted to them for a Swiss 'perpetual motion' clock they gave me in recognition of the work that I did twenty or thirty years before.

My own business with Harvester gradually increased in volume and got to the point where I did $13.4 million a year with these manufacturers. Later, when the defense effort was turning into a war effort, I was called down to Washington to discuss a peacetime job in the old Supply Board, and when the appointment didn't come through immediately, I called up Andrew Stevenson and told him I needed to go on a sales trip to the West coast and he said, "Go ahead."

I was in Los Angeles on December 7 when the Japs attacked Pearl Harbor. We were clustered around the radio all afternoon, and I remember that my idol of the movies, Humphrey Bogart, was there. On Monday morning we were still on the train, to arrive in Chicago at 1:00 p.m., and heard President Roosevelt's message asking Congress to declare war on the Axis. I arrived back at the office at 1:30 and at 4:00 was on a Liberty Limited going into Washington to begin a fifteen-month stint with the government.

During the two winter months I got the situation in hand in the War Production Board, and I was made the assistant chief of the manufactured machinery division, and this was a spot that allowed me to use all my acquaintances in staffing the organization.

Prior to this WPB, Roosevelt had used all of the professors, PhDs and longhaired boys to evolve his policy of government, but I hand him this respect: once he saw that we were in the war, he let industry take over, and while we were a year doing any sort of a job, we finally got everything in shape and of course eventually went on to victory in two or three years.

During that summer in Washington, Honey and Rita and Peter came down, Peter going to night school and trying to decide whether to join the Air Force and ask to stay at Texas U until March or quit right then and take his chances on enlisting. He finally decided on the former and was in boot camp and fortunate in having 29 weeks at Yale in Aircraft Engineering etc....Later he was at the Army aviation flying camp at Grand Island, Nebraska and then had a year in Paris at Bourget Field after the European war had ended.

What Rita and Honey really remembered from that year in Washington were the chocolate sodas and hot fudge sundaes that they walked over to buy on 15th Street every night of the week.

When Rita was a baby we approached the Fourth of July one year without any invitation to a picnic, and it made me so sore that I inserted an ad in the *Reporter* asking anyone who was as unpopular as we were to come up and picnic on our lawn at Princeholm. That started our annual Fourth of July picnics, and in the 37 years since that time, we have missed having one only two times, both of these when we were in Washington. Once 22 years ago, and once just now on July 4, 1964.

We had various types of entertainment, Mexican, hayrides, stores from Uncle Edmund's New England background, a 49er demonstration and to me the highlight was two years ago when we played the movie of man's orbiting the earth. Our guests varied from the original 27 to 189 people, and of course we had Prince Castle ice cream with all of these picnics.

During 1942, when I was with WPB in Washington, of course, Kay and John were married. Then when I was back in Chicago with Harvester, Peter had returned from Bourget in Paris and we had Peter's wedding in 1947. Following that, Rita and Kay were in Japan and they came home and when Rita resumed her studies at Michigan she met a young chap named Eric Youngquist and after that she could see no other man in the world. They were married in 1950, so that our three children, in the years since 1942, have presented us with 12 grandchildren: three girls and nine boys, of which we are very happy.

In 1949 I retired from Harvester Co. I was sixty years old.

This is probably the best place to describe how Bo became so successful in selling Harvester products. He said that his solution was not to be consciously selling, but instead to make potential customers feel a need for the products he sold. This is how he described it:

> I believe that I sell goods differently from other fellows I have known. There is none of this handshaking "I'm Mr. Parrish" stuff. I simply state whom I am with and chat a moment; then—if I sense a possible "prospect"—I give him just enough to interest him in <u>actual facts</u> until I "drop in" again.
>
> Some times I call and there is never a word of selling talk. But he thus feels more friendly and when the time comes to get down to "brass tacks" why he feels a confidence in me that is genuine. He gets the stability of the company back of me—he knows that I am agreeable and rather capable of knowing what I am selling and he believes me when I advise this or that.
>
> Really I look back on some of the sales I have made and wonder at it all. I like selling for the mental exercise it gives—for the satisfaction it brings in physical pleasures made possible from the fact that you are your own boss. And then too it is decidedly remunerative. I had to laugh at what you have been noticing or rather I can't recall when you have had a chance to notice anything. I bet the other fellows talk always. You have noticed that from our being together. I have grown so accustomed to listening that I do not wonder that you occasionally ask "Just what are you thinking?"

One thing, though, absolutely – I <u>never</u> worry! It vexes me when the sales don't come with regularity. But I have proven to myself that I <u>can</u> sell goods so that, if I work, the results are bound to come. Worries or business cares would not help matters so <u>why</u> have them? I confidently expected the beginning of the year to save a good several hundred. But business men, and conditions, are so below normal that I do not know exactly how the year will end.

Another thing, too, in my "selling ideas." I try gradually to let the purchaser see that we are doing him a favor by specialising and thus producing just what he needs—to <u>not</u> allow him to think that, simply because he is spending his <u>own money,</u> he <u>rules</u> the situation. That fifty-fifty idea applies very generally to a good many of the ideas I have—it's a good way to view them too.

Harvester was burdened by unbalanced inventory, and I felt I was the only Harvester man who felt any compunction at all about taking engines away from my manufacturers and giving them to Harvester's own production of crawlers. Naturally I was living too close to this situation and so I decided to quit and get into a consulting job with all those manufacturers and I found a little office in the Railway Exchange Building in Chicago. For fifteen years I had a very happy experience among all my manufacturer friends. We made films for Maytag. We got various assignments for material on Okinawa and Guam and a survey in South America that Johnny Nelson helped to the nth degree.

I'd like to tell you about my father's family. There were three brothers and one sister. All of the older brothers had died when I was born. One sister, Aunt Sally, lived for many years in Colfax. One thing I remember about her was that she smoked a clay pipe, and one time when she fell down, before she would allow anyone to help her up, she said, "Put out that fire," because the pipe had set fire to the grass.

In my mother's family there were many sisters and one brother, Oliver, who died just last fall at 99 years old. Another brother was a very famous lawyer at Lafayette, Indiana—Uncle Willie...and I was named for him for when there was a fire in Battleground where they all lived, our Mother, who was the oldest sister, dashed in and saved Willie's life.

Of my own brothers and sisters, I was the seventh son, five of whom lived to a ripe old age. Being a seventh son in those days there was some scuttlebutt about my being able to breathe into children's throats and cure them of Flash – which was the hoof-and-mouth-disease of the late 1800s. I had two other sisters besides Rebecca: one who died of heart condition in 1920 and the other a very pretty girl who died of pneumonia in 1924. However, we were a very long-lived family as you can see by my 76 years, which comes up on July 13. I probably had a dozen different jobs before settling finally on working for the Harvester Co. when I found that I couldn't get rich quick.

Rita

Childhood and Early Years

Rita wrote the following description of growing up in Downers Grove as she remembered it:

When I was born in 1926 there were fewer than 7,000 people living in Downers Grove. It was the end of the line for many steam engines and commuter trains that came out from Chicago. On quiet days, and at night, we could hear the trains chugging through town if they were headed for the coast or New Orleans, and we heard the trains switching, and going on and off the roundhouse to be turned around.

The switching yard was seven blocks away from where we lived, and it included a tall water tower made of black wood that fed the steam engines. It leaned, and in the winter it had the most phenomenal icicles hanging from the base of the barrel. They were larger than I was, and certainly longer. The tower seemed huge to me. It had to be high enough to give pressure for the water to flow into the boilers. The day that the first Zephyr went through town, trying to set a record, all the classes in Avery Coonley went down to the tracks to watch, and the engineer threw out commemorative coins. That engine is now in the Museum of Science and Industry.

My home was one of the largest in town, since Daddy Prince thought the world would stand still and all his children and grand-children would live in it with him. So it had twenty-six rooms. It was in the center of a four-acre oak forest, and was carefully designed to be gracious and spacious.

Our garage now was a barn when I was small. There were rickety steps, and it was an adventure to go up there [on the second level] to prowl around among the moose heads and old furniture and trunks of antique clothing, and one trunk of clothes that we could use for 'dress-up'. I liked dressing up like a gypsy best, because then we used a long gaudy skirt with a red sash.

Gypsies had come many times to the edge of town, and I had seen them with their wagons. As soon as they were spotted, the word would go through town, and the women would rush out to take down clothes that were drying on their lines, and children would be taken into the houses. People really believed that gypsies would steal anything, even children. The police made them camp outside the town limits, and the gypsy women would tell fortunes. By the late thirties they stopped coming.

Each year we watched eagerly for the visit of the old Indian. He would set up his tools in the shoemaker's shop and we went there to order from him. I still have the silver bracelets that Honey bought. He was old and wrinkled, and wore beautiful jewelry. One year he didn't come, and we figured he must have died.

By the time I was born, we didn't keep horses in the barn anymore, and used it instead for parking our car. I don't remember it well, but the barn was converted into a four-car garage, with old doors that had to be opened. The cars in those days were tall and less comfortable. The tires were less sturdy, too, so a trip would be interrupted while we had to change a flat tire.

We had a phone; to get the operator, you clicked the hook. She would say, "Number, please," and you gave her the two or three-digit number you were calling. It was a great luxury.

There were no TVs, of course, but we did have a radio. I was allowed to listen to *The Lone Ranger* and *Jack Armstrong*, and on Sunday evenings we would listen to *The Ed Wynn Show* together. This left a lot of time for playing outside and reading and practicing piano, and some chores.

We had a maid, so I didn't do dishes or cook or wash or iron, but Honey and I helped to clean. The maid's name was Rita, too, so we called her Big Rita and I was Little Rita. She had come from southern Illinois to work in the city, and stayed with us for many years. She was heavyset and her English was a little misspoken, but she was a loving person and I loved her.

We did the wash in our basement, using a wringer/washer. That basement was scary. The walls were fieldstone, with an uneven flagstone floor. There were spiders hanging from the rafters. The wiring of the house had been put in after it was built, I think, and in the basement all the lights had to be turned on and off by pulling a cord that hung from the fixture.

At dinner, when I was sent down to the basement storeroom to get a jar of home-made plum sauce, I had to go to the farthest room from the basement steps. To get there I had to go from room to room feeling for the light cord, watching the shadowy corners. When I finally got to the storeroom I had another problem. There was a tall platform in the room to keep luggage high and dry, and boxes, and someone could hide under the platform and reach out and grab your legs when you went to the cupboard.

I always ran back with the sauce, leaving those dark rooms behind me in a hurry. And when I was home alone, I always pushed the bolt on the lock at the top of the basement stairs just to make sure it was closed tight.

We had an old coal furnace in the basement that Bo or Pete cared for. In the early morning I would hear the coals being shaken and cinders removed and coal being shoveled into the firebox. Heat came up into the house through a large grate in the hall of our dining room, and then straight to the second floor through another grate in the ceiling above. We always slept with our window-vent raised, winter or summer, and I would rush out of my room to stand on the grate to get warm after I had dressed.

Our kitchen was cozy after the big stove was working, and later in the day we always had a fire going in our living room fireplace. It was really our family room; we gathered there in the evening. I did my homework there.

When I was older, we had hot water registers so the house could be warmer in winter.

With snow on the bushes and trees, our yard was beautiful in wintertime. We had a long walk leading up to the front door, and it was my job to shovel it. Shoveling the drive itself was a group effort, though, and all of us helped.

In our yard there were large areas that were a mass of spring beauties. Grandpa Prince had developed a lily of the valley with a strong stem and thirteen bells. Then he had propagated them, so we had huge beds of lilies around our trees and in one large square area.

Every spring, picking lilies was a family effort, and I loved that time. We would pick each day for a week or more, putting flowers and leaves into pots and buckets of water, and then after dark we would sit together around the kitchen table, tying the flowers into bunches of two, with three leaves. Then at 5:00 each morning Bo would take them to the flower market in Chicago to sell them to a flower wholesaler. During the Depression we probably lived partly on the money from selling those lilies. Later, we used the lily money each year to buy something for the house—a sort of repayment: outdoor lighting one year; Oriental rug another; china for teas; and painting the house.

Without any TV, you can imagine how much fun it was to go to the movies. They were always double features, a B western and a feature film, and the Saturday matinee was eleven cents. That left four cents for penny candy in the news store next to the movie. The movies look pretty unsophisticated now, but they were very absorbing then. There was a newsreel first, with all the latest worldwide events and a cartoon. I was taken to see the first Disney cartoon, and then the first feature-length animated film. They look a little jumpy now, but for us it was a marvel.

There wasn't as much literature for children then, so my reading was primarily the old favorites, like *Robin Hood* and *The Three Musketeers* and *Little Women*. There were comic books, of course, but I didn't spend my fifteen-cent allowance on them. Our heroes and heroines were Charles Lindbergh, Will Rogers, Florence Nightingale, and movie stars. I had lots of scrapbooks of movie stars and comic strips from the newspaper, like *Terry and the Pirates*.

When summer came we played outside all the time, games of tag and kick-the-can and Red-Rover, etc. We climbed trees and swung on the tall (twenty-foot) swing in our yard, roller skated on the streets and sidewalks, played marbles and hopscotch and traded cards and stamps, and played *Monopoly* and checkers and Parcheesi.

We knew little of the world far away from us. The newspaper that came to our house was isolationist, and foreign news was in the back pages. The Depression was all around us. We were lucky that Bo had a job. So we always had food. Groceries were little stores then, and they would deliver. We ordered by phone, and the grocer would say his lamb was good that day or he had a new shipment of apples. He, in turn, had to go at dawn to the wholesale market in Chicago to buy the things he sold in his store.

We grew everything we could, and canned all that we didn't eat immediately. I never tasted commercial jam until I went to college. We canned fruits and jams and crab apples. I don't remember canning vegetables or tomatoes – too much danger of food poisoning.

We had an 'ice house' attached to our back porch where we had some ice covered in sawdust to keep things cool. Meats and milk, butter and lard were kept there. We also had an icebox, with the ice in a metal compartment on the top. The ice man would come by on his truck, and we put a sign in the window showing the size chunk we wanted. He wore a leather shoulder pad, and carried the ice into our house on his shoulder. In the summer, he let children pick up chips of ice on the bed of his truck. When we wanted ice for a drink, we had to take an ice pick and chip pieces off the ice in the icebox. We still had the icebox when I was in high school.

Another man that came by was a fellow we called the *Scissor Grinder*; he would sharpen knives, scissors, and anything else that needed a sharp edge.

Downers Grove was on the Burlington Railroad line, and trains stopped there to add water to their boilers. During the Depresssion, hoboes set up a camp near the tracks. They were just men traveling from one job to another, or trying to get home. They might be homeless, but not for long. So they were just men who Bo said were "down on their luck." Hoboes passed along maps of homes that would feed them or give them work.

We were on their list. Mama couldn't refuse, so men would walk the seven blocks from the tracks and knock at our back door. We always gave them some food and often Bo would go out to talk to them as they sat on our back porch steps. He was a soft touch, and he really felt caring toward those men. I remember Bo driving us by a 'soup kitchen' line in Chicago. The men were standing quietly with tin dishes, and I knew from Bo's worry for them that this was important. I was looking at a tragedy.

During the worst years, Mama worried that I might be kidnapped, because living in a big house, with a car and a maid could suggest that we were wealthy. But we weren't. Then, too, the Lindbergh baby had been kidnapped, and there was a rash of them.

Rita's older siblings, Peter (four years older) and Kay (eight years older), appear almost as strangers in her accounts of her early years, although they did involve her in plays that they staged in Princeholm. She loved them both, but we hear more about Peter than about Kay. Rita didn't really get to know Kay until they traveled together in Japan (1947-48).

Rita's best playmates as a youngster were her cousins Earl and Pat Prince and her brother Peter. Play-acting was very important, and explains the important role that dramatics played in her life. This is part of her life story that she wrote when she was a freshman in high school:

I have two cousins that live about 75 miles from us. They are Earl and Pat Prince. Earl is a year younger than I am, and Pat is a year younger than Peter. We have had some glorious days together playing *Town, Monopoly, School, Icebox, Baseball, Blocks,* and *Spookhouse*. By far the most beloved game was *Town*. We each took an upstairs room, and had a trade. Peter had the Stock Market, Pat the Post Office, Earl was various offices, and I owned a restaurant. I served water and milk, crackers, and as a specialty, jam sandwiches. We made our own money and sent letters to each other. Peter made a surprising amount of money in the Stock Market.

Second beloved of our games was *Spookhouse*, which had to be played at night. We used the upper hall and the rooms that didn't have antiques in them. We used wet rags, worms, pillows, blankets, old boards, and electric motors. Our victims were our parents, and they were forced to walk over pillows, get electric shocks, bump into wet rags and carry worms around. They reacted as we wanted them to, and we were thoroughly satisfied with ourselves when they came into the light, exhausted.

We still play some of our games when we get together. It seems that they will never wear out.

When Peter and Pat played together, Earl and I would play puppet, or else put on a play. From the very first we wrote the plays, and then put them on in the parlor, because we would pull the curtains that go out into the hall, open and shut.

One of these plays is as follows, written when I was about six. I have not changed the spelling, so you will have to figure it out.

Explanatory notes: r = Rita
Bo = Earl
ho = oh
b = bucks
Sen = Scene

Sen 1
Rita: ho Bo
Earl: yes, r
Rita: Hery up and rerd the paper
Earl: By r (exit)
Rita: By Bo
Rita: ho, I must go Done to the stor.

Sen 2
Man(Earl): Stigm-up. Stigm-hiy. Stigm-low and away thal go.

Rita: You.you you cant do this
Man (Earl): ha – ha – ha – ha - ha

Sen 3
Earl: holo r
Rita: you seme sad a bad man tak all the muny
Earl: bont wery – my bos girs me 70 b a wyk.

We considered this our best play, and took up a collection of 33 cents.

Another of our pastimes was puppet shows. We put on quite a few of these, using doll-house dolls, and furniture, china dogs, and roly-poly men. I had a book of simple one-act plays and we read from this. Peter rigged up lighting for a rigged up stage. It was not unusual to see a hand reach down onto the stage and move a character around, when the threads proved unsuccessful. On these occasions we had a little basket for money to be dropped into, and left it in a conspicuous place.

Rita was an outgoing, happy child and a joy to her parents. Her memories of childhood were lazy days playing games, climbing trees, playing with her cousin Earl and neighbor children, walking to and from Avery Coonley School, raking leaves at Princeholm with Bo, throwing snowballs, walking with her dog, going on shopping trips with Honey, and taking long trips with her parents to visit relatives in and around Indianapolis, where most of Bo's family—Parrish and Mitchell—lived, and Vermont, where her grandparents had relatives and where the Princes and Joneses originated.

Here is another way she described those early years:

When I was growing up, our summers were all our own. Maybe there was a chore or two. For example, sometimes I had to sweep our walk, using a corn broom. It seemed like a really long walk just to get to the street sidewalk and like a big chore by the time I had swept down the sidewalks along both streets. Then I had to keep the birdbath full of water, and tried my best not to slam the screen door.

But generally we were on our own, deciding what games to play. If we had enough kids it was baseball, but generally it was hide-and-seek or Red-Rover-come-over or kick-the-can or some such. There is a tall swing hanging from a metal rod between two huge oak trees in our yard, so of course swinging was always an alternative.

In the fall we raked leaves into a huge pile and got as high as we could on the swing to jump down into it. I could climb the rope as fast as the two Wilbur twins, and we also climbed the good climbing trees in the yard. There were a few good climbers there: crab apples, apple, a willow and a pear. The oaks were too big, and the maple didn't have a good progression of branches. There were nut trees, too, and in the fall we tried to be faster than the squirrels to take home nuts.

There weren't any good places in town where kids could swim – no streams or lakes or ponds. The town swimming pool cost too much to go more than two or three times a summer (30 cents).

On Sunday I would wait for the late afternoon when Bo would say, "Let's go to the Castle." [This was the local outlet of Uncle Earl's ice cream store chain, which was owned by Mr. Fredenhagen.]

We all dashed for the car, and I could choose any flavor cone. I never could have a sundae because they were too expensive, but the trip made Sunday such an exciting day! During the week, sometimes Bo would bring home a watermelon. The system was: sit on the back porch steps with a slice in our hands, eating and then spitting the seeds out on the ground. In those days you could ask the seller to spike a piece out of the melon to make sure it was good. It was wonderful. I think we paid 50 cents for the melon.

Trip back to Louisiana and the Plantation

Seventeen years after Bo and Honey had left Louisiana, the family took a trip down to visit Killarney, the Louisiana plantation where they had lived. Rita was seven years old at the time. This is what she later wrote about the funeral of a man who had been Bo's foreman at Killarney.

We had been driving down a country road toward the plantation, the one they had improved over the years before I was born. There were friends we were going to see, and of course the plantation. We slowed down when we saw a crowd outside a small white clapboard church. I had to stand to see outside the big green Buick with its high windows.

Bo got out to talk to friends there. I have a picture of him standing with a big black man wearing a straw hat and tails. Everyone was dressed up and they were flapping fans in the summer sun. Bo came back to tell Honey that his foreman had died and we were invited to the funeral. There were four preachers, and the one he was talking with would start soon. We went into the church to sit on wooden backless benches. Honey leaned down to me and whispered, "I hope they'll pat. You remember this, Rita,"

The Church was hot.
I was little, perhaps seven years old, so I saw backs and elbows and heads bobbing, but I knew it was the preacher calling from the front of the church—talking about the body up in front and singing phrases about him.
"He was a good man."
And around me came the voices singing back, "Good man."
It wasn't like the Congregational Church, all straight and stiff and quiet. The patting started. Not like drums—one beat over and over—but syncopated. Hand on knee, hand on hand, feet on floor. Softly at first,

then louder until it was all around me and the wooden board I was sitting on seemed to pat, too. I had never heard music like this, never heard anyone call back. And the beating of the patting was all around. The voices were singing louder and faster, and the faces of the people on my bench looked so alive, glistening in the heat, mouths open, staring at the preacher.

We were the only white people there, but my father and mother had known the man, and it was right that they were singing and patting and my brother and sister and I were there.

I remember, Honey.

The only other memory of that time in Louisiana was when Pete showed me the water moccasins sunning themselves by the lake. He told me specifically that I wasn't to pick them up. I liked garter snakes and would put them in my pocket.

When we drove home from our trip to the plantation, I came down with malaria. I remember opening my eyes in the dark of the car, looking up at the roof. Then I was carried to my own bed, and a Public Health nurse came to take blood from my ear to find out why I had a high fever.

Honey and Bo knew that it was malaria; they had seen it before. But the doctor wouldn't agree. Bo probably called him when he was frightened for me, but I'm sure that Honey tried to cure me with prayer and Christian Science.

That's a thread that flowed through all our lives for years: Honey believed and Bo didn't. I remember Kay almost dying of pneumonia. She was on Honey and Bo's bed – a high one, so I could just look up to see her lying on pillows. Honey was so sure that prayer would save her, but Bo walked across the street to the doctor's home and brought him back to our house.

Honey went to the Christian Science Church and we would go next door to the Congregational Church with Mama. Bo believed that Honey had lost my sister, Patricia, because of Christian Science. Bo was thankful to have Peter, whom they received after Patricia died and soon adopted, but forty years later Bo would still cry when he thought of that baby.

Avery Coonley School

No description of Rita's life would be complete without mention of Avery Coonley School (ACS). Rita loved school, and that was primarily because ACS was so special. It was an experimental school (what one called 'progressive' in those days), and it was different from normal public schools.

Classes were small, the students were given lots of individual attention, and there were many gifted children. Students were exposed to a wide range of experiences, with field trips to offices, public buildings, and even factories. There was a constant challenge to learn, but there were no grades. Rita told me that she never received a grade until after she graduated from Avery Coonley and started at Downers Grove High School. Three of our children attended Avery Coonley, and it hadn't changed. You will read in the excerpts from Rita's letters how wonderful the school was for them.

About twenty years after graduating, Rita was asked this question: "What of real value did you carry away from Avery Coonley?"

This was her answer:

One of the most important assets that ACS gave me was an inquiring attitude—a curiosity about everything in the world. Everything was interesting. I don't believe we ever used the word *bored*. There was always something to see, to read about, to think about, to wonder about.

We were encouraged to truly look at nature, to see the wonders of science, to appreciate industry and machines, to try to understand one another and enjoy being with people. And with all the interests that were stimulated, all the creative impulses that were started, we were encouraged to think of them, to write about them, to read and create things ourselves.

So that all through life, there has never been a time when I have been bored. If I must sit by a road waiting, there is the beauty of the view, the kinds of trees, the kinds of rocks, the calls of the birds, and the endless variety of nature that we were introduced to. If I sit in a city, there is the industry that we learned about, there is architecture that we were introduced to, and there are people.

A side effect which was given us in the creative arts and sciences that we were taught has been—for me—the belief that I can do most anything at least a little. I am astounded when I see a woman sit back and say she can't hammer, or do simple shop work, can't fix a lock or a light plug. We were given the basics of using our hands and using our minds while we were working.

If I need a statue, I feel that I could make it, and wood is in my home now, waiting to be carved. I wouldn't hesitate to paint for fun, or to make anything that I wanted for my home. And in the past year, my work in shop with Mr. Teal has helped me immeasurably while my husband and I remodeled our home. I've hung doors and put up studs and molding. I know that there are many things that I wouldn't do well, but I'm not afraid to try.

This feeling 'not afraid to try' was given to us over the years. We were encouraged in everything, and praised for what we did best, so that we were given a self confidence which was not arrogant, I hope, not boastful, but enough to let us face each challenge, small ones and large ones, as adults.

There are various ways of meeting a challenge, though. I believe that we were encouraged to meet a new experience joyfully. This must have been through example, for as I look back, I don't see how this was taught, but the doing and seeing of the new was an adventure, and it has remained so all my life....

Lastly, I feel I must say something of the spiritual values that are linked with each of the other things I've mentioned above. We started each day with a prayerful thought. It was a peaceful way to start each day. It brought a loving, generous, merciful God to us - God, the Loving Father. And in the self-confidence that I spoke of above was the assurance that He would sustain me. In learning of nature and science and the world, we were always conscious of Him, the Creator. I believe we came away from Avery Coonley with a deep faith in God.

Avery Coonley was a perfect environment for Rita, and she blossomed. Without grades, there was no fear of failure, just learning and enjoying the process of learning. She mentioned often how much she owed to her years there, particularly her ability to speak easily before audiences. Every day at Avery Coonley each student would be "on stage," so to speak, and Rita took part in skits and plays. The curriculum was aimed at developing youngsters, training them to have a wide range of interests.

At Avery Coonley, art, music, drama, literature, science and history were stressed, but not as content courses. These subjects became woven through projects that the students worked on, so that the students, in a sense, learned without realizing that that was what they were doing. Rita was able to identify the music of various composers not so much by recognizing themes as by intuition—an overall reaction to sound and rhythm. She would say: "It just sounds like Beethoven," for example.

Spelling was difficult for Rita. She was not a visual learner, and spelled words they way they sounded to her, and often reversed letters. She was embarrassed at making mistakes and had to work at spelling all her life. Certainly, her grades must have suffered in high school and college, because teachers would stumble over misspelled words and not pay enough attention to WHAT she wrote.

Here are Rita's recipes for eggs and bacon (she was probably eight or nine years. old):

        Making eggs
Put batter in pan.
Berak egg put in pan.
Wen egg is cok tern it over.
Take it off
        Making Bakne
put Bakne in pan
Then tern it over later
Take it off.

Here (age nine) is a note to her mother:

Dear Huney
I hope you are havaing a good time. I have had alot of letters. I am lopsum for you. Give daddy Prince and daddy my love. Don't get hert. Love from Rita +++++++ bring home some bunchus of bnanus like this [a drawing].

Here are some excerpts from her diary when she was ten:

Sept. 29, 1936
To-day I got up at six. From 7:30 – 8 I practiced. I rode my bike to school. In serves Miss Morse read a pome.
That nighe I played with Patsy Arndt. She is going to move to-day.
    Our group is going to go to the Arboreetom To-day.

Oct. 2, 1936
    ...Daddy and I are going to the Movie to-night, it is "Joe-E-Brown in Earth Worm Tracter"

In school Our decks are chanded around.
I jest came in from play. We play scoker. To-day the outher side won.

October 5, 1936
To-day When I got up it was so gloomy, now it is sunshineing.
To-day it is monday. on Monday we chooes sides for socker.
It is 1-1 as for the score.
We had rythmes, Library, and play this afternoon.
We had our dekes changed around To-day.

High School and Music

World War II started while I was in high school. We saw boys go from our town. The girl's club that I was president of served breakfast for them at the draft board on the day they were inducted. We learned about the war through newsreels at the movies, the radio, *Life Magazine*, and letters from friends. It was another world for them. We had butter and sugar and meat rationing, and gas rationing of course. Homes were not being built because copper and metals had to go to the war effort. But that was not much to give.

Men came home on leave and then went back again. It seemed as if it would never end.

In high school, Rita was a dynamo, a doer, someone you could always depend on to get things done. She never lost that can-do approach. If she said that she was going to help with something or make something, you could consider it done. That's why the people loved her so much in the volunteer organizations she joined. She was always happy to help and never criticized others or fought to get credit for what she did. Here is a list from her high school yearbook showing her many activities.

Girls' A Capella 3d year; School carnival 1st/4th years; Junior class secretary; Dramatics 1st year; GAA 1st, 2d, 3d years; GAA sports 1st, 2d, 3d years; GR all four years, President 2d year, Vice-President 3d year, President 4th year; High Life 3d/4th years, Feature Editor 4th year; Music 1st year; National Honor Society 3d and 4th years; All-school play 2d/3d years, Assistant director 4th year; School Council 4th year; DAR award 4th year; Senior play 4th year. An efficient worker, the third Andrew sister.

Much as Rita loved art, her true forte was music. She began playing piano early, and learned quickly. From the beginning, she practiced regularly, often in the early morning. Her teacher was Adelaide Farrar. In 1938, Honey and Bo bought her a Steinway baby grand from Lyon & Healy in Chicago. Arthur Rubenstein was in the store when they bought it, and he autographed it for Rita. As she progressed, she began taking part in competitions. In 1943 and 1944 she received the highest rating (excellent), and also passed her audition at the music school of the University of Michigan.

Rita went to Ann Arbor in the summer of 1944 to enroll in the University. Her piano teacher there, and later a close friend, was Mrs. Okkelberg, who had studied under Schnabel. Although Rita and I started at U-M at the same time, our paths didn't cross until 1948, after she returned from her year in Japan.

Rita and Kay in Japan 1947 – 1948

Her sister Kay's husband John Root was in Army Intelligence and assigned to General MacArthur's headquarters in Tokyo. His supervisors decided—for reasons that are outside the scope of this account—that his family should be with him, and so orders were issued to have Kay travel to Japan with her two children, and that a nanny or babysitter accompany her. That is how Rita was able to visit Japan. She must have had some early inkling that she might be going to Japan, because in the fall semester of 1946 she took a course in beginning Japanese. She was clearly motivated to do well in the course and received an A.

Kay and Rita set out for Japan early in 1947 with Kay's two young children. The process of packing and getting ready to leave Princeholm was hectic, according to Rita's account. They knew little about what they would need on the sea voyage and for the period they would be in a foreign country, essentially cut off from America. According to the orders they received, they were to travel to Seattle by train from Chicago and sail to Japan on the *SS General Gordon*. They began organizing their luggage in March, 1947. Bo had a problem with all the things they wanted to take.

This is Rita's account:

We even get sick in a big way! When my sister and I were going to Japan with her two children, the day before while we were still packing, we all—I repeat all—came down with a bad case of flu. We could just get up to put one thing in the bags and we would have to lie down again. We ended by getting on the train with 22 pieces of luggage and baskets. That was an absolute crime to my father, who likes to travel light. We had a compartment with our mother, and the five of us just moaned all the way and stared at the cold chicken and cookies so carefully packed for us by a friend. It wouldn't have been so bad to be so sick if my father hadn't been so well. Counting my brother and his wife, there were seven of us who couldn't even see straight, and my father in perfect health.

Now this wouldn't be so bad, except that he is very bombastic. He couldn't see WHY we weren't all packed and chipper, and he couldn't see WHY we had to have so much luggage. Then we just barely made the train, which made him more explosive than ever.

Rita also wrote a poem about the voyage, perhaps motivated by her reaction to the rough sailing they encountered:

> The sea, the sea
> Cold and death you say?
> Oh, but to me its white foam flying
> And the black black depths
> And a million waves as far as the eyes could see.
> Roaring, you said – Oh music, music,
> A million kettle drums resounding from the ocean floor,
> A million orchestras beyond the horizon,
> And in each wave rushing tambourines,
> In the foam tiny castanets.
> And over it all, the conductor's breathing.
> Oh, I love the sea—its white foam flying
> The green foam underlying
> And its black, black depths.
>
> Repulsed by the ship,
> The waves flee from it in white-foamed terror,
> Blindly careening against one another,
> And the braver of the waves dash themselves
> Into white spray against the hull.
> While below the ship, the depths toss it recklessly,
> Make it creak and groan

And remind it always that the master is below,
Playful, cruel, and will claim it some day.

We drove by jeep from Yokohama Harbor, and on the way to downtown Tokyo we couldn't see a single building left standing. The street was a bulldozed lane, with people living in makeshift hovels. Fire bombs had devastated it all. Pinpoint bombing had, however, spared the buildings that General MacArthur wanted to preserve: the *Daichi* (the Emperor's palace), the Parliament, a hotel, perhaps more. In the area known as Washington Heights, buildings were put up for the wives and families of the American military and other government personnel.

During the year we were there, streets were cleared, homes went up, buildings were built, department stores began selling, streetcars moved, and factories began producing again in their bombed-out shells. And the Japanese people I met, teaching English, shopping, in church, were uniformly civil, friendly, courteous, and delightful.

At night the only lights were the lanterns outside restaurants and shops. We saw the first neon sign go up on the Ginza. There were few cars, and women wore the traditional dress.

Kyoto had been declared an open city, with no military factories, so it was never bombed. When we visited Kyoto, we saw the city as it had always been. The homes, the people's dress, their lifestyle, were all the old Japan.

It was only after I saw Japan that I understood a little of the destructiveness of war. When we went to Europe in 1951, Eric and I saw some of the wartime destruction that was visible. There were great areas of London that were still bomb-rubble, and as we traveled through Germany we saw so much destruction in cities like Munich and Ulm. Our friends in Norway are still bitter over the German reprisals, the destruction of the northern 1/3 of their country, and the export of the Jews from their country.

Sumo, Silk, Earthquakes, and Leading Families

Rita was not as diligent a letter writer in Japan as she was after we were married, but the few letters we have from that period show how keen an observer she was and how much she enjoyed her experiences.

Sumo

June, 1947
Dear Honey and Bo:

I think of you all so often and wish you could be here to enjoy some of the experiences. You would have liked the Sumo matches. There was a week-long tournament here last week....

There is a natural bowl over in Meiji near us, all enclosed like a circus. There are tarpaulins over the tiers of mats. The Allied Forces had a front section roped off so we were ten feet from the wrestlers.

The ring has a purple silk canopy over it and the judges sit on all four sides. This ring is a hard packed sand platform which is smoothed over after every fight so that the referees can tell whether either man has touched the ground outside the ring. If a man touches the ground with any part of his body other than his feet he is out, or if he steps out of the ring he loses.

They wear a loin cloth of very heavy silk which is wound round and round like a belt and tied in back. While they wrestle they try to grasp this belt and lift the other fellow out of the ring bodily by it. So it is generally the fattest, heaviest man who wins. Sometimes they win by pushing or slapping each other out of the ring.

They are not matched for weight or height but for skill and so often unevenly. They wrestle on either the east or west side of the ring and so must never leave that side. Then there are finals for the east and west side champions. Fights do not take long - two to five minutes. They are not brutal like our American boxing and wrestling.

Many women are in the audiences and businessmen in their best clothes. The bowl holds about 2,000 people. Rarely do they show excitement over any but the champions. Prizes are fans, scrolls, bowstrings, and a silver cup for the finals. The whole exhibition took from one to five each day and we never tired of it except our derrieres for we sat on mats, too.

Silk

July 23, 1947

I can't remember whether I told you about the Silk Fair we had. It was to display the methods of producing silk—the methods of dying, silk-screening, weaving, and embroidering—and we had two fashion shows also. One showing the kimonos—the brides: one that she wears for the day, a second that she wears for the ceremony, and a third that she wears for the reception—and another showing silk in Western fashions.

There was a display by the foremost designer of kimonos and one of them went right to my heart. It was the first one I have really yearned for—heavy black silk with sky rockets dyed against it. Rockets were white with color at the ends of the sprays and the edges were tipped with embroidered silver and gold. I raved about it to Mary Sawada and she told me that the designer is the man who has made their family kimonos for years. She had an aunt price it for me and it would be four thousand yen IF I could furnish the silk!

Earthquakes

I have been trying to remember to write about earthquakes - I felt my first one a week after we arrived in a seven story building. It swayed about ten seconds and I'd say about a foot back and forth. Since then there have been scads of them—lots of times you are walking and don't feel them.

There was one back at the Hotel that got everyone out of bed at 8:00 a.m. and it really shook us. But my favorite one was the other night—it shook me awake. They say it lasted twenty minutes. I was in Rick's bed because we had company and I sat up and looked at Asake (nursemaid)—she said it was a bad one—I lay and shook with it till it stopped.

The next morning I told Kay about it, thinking it was a dream, and she informed me there really had been a quake. They will be more and more plentiful during the summer and soon we can expect typhoon weather. There had been a few good storms but we are expecting to see some doozies.

Leading Families

Mary Sawada has taken embroidery lessons and is going to teach me. She is the daughter of Mickey Sawada, and Mickey is the daughter of Baron Iwosaki, who is one of the ten families who have owned all Japan supposedly. They were the aristocrats and the very wealthy—they have houses all over—many here in Japan. Baron Iwosaki's family is the Mitsui, and the ten families were called the *Zaibatsu*.

They are having terrible taxes now and are losing 90% of their property. They are not allowed to be in any business ventures either. Mary grew up in London, Paris and New York, and then returned to Japan. They are grateful for any favor and Mary comes at least once a week for luncheon and we have plans made for a trip or doing something. She is delightful and sweet and we have learned much about Japan from her.

[Mary is Rita's age and is an accomplished musician - according to a letter from Kay]

Climbing Fuji

August 19, 1947

Phewww --- we made it!! In my last letter I told you that we were going to climb Fuji—glib and cheerful wasn't I? Little did I know what was in store. Brother!!!

Pardon me if I sigh now and then and rub my aching limbs, and take a long sip of cold Coke. What a time we had. But here is the story:

Cheerfully we started for our train at 1:30 p.m. Friday carrying our shoulder bags, blanket roll, two ski jackets, two sweaters, twelve K rations..., six Hersheys, eight gums, much cosmetics, two blankets, camera, shorts, scarves, mittens, extra socks, a canteen, fans, Unguentine, BandAids, Halazone for water, salt tablets and Kleenex, sunglasses—I guess that's about all and we were traveling light! It was heavy and cumbersome and the straps went over only one shoulder. Phew.

We started for the 2:30 p.m. train, got there and found it left at 4:30 so we shopped and bummed and then found we were tired already. But we got on the train cheerfully—gaily—only to have the MP ask for our travel orders, which of course we did not have. Nobody—Including the Red Cross, John's commandant and the RTO office—told us that we had to have them. When the MP became insistent, we disembarked and went home again.

So I dashed downtown to the Provost Marshal's office and got travel orders and we started out for the 8:24 a.m. train.... When we arrived at the RTO, they told us that there were no Allied Forces cars on this train and we would have to wait and go Saturday morning at ten. By that time we were so tired shuttling back and forth with those packs that we were giddy and so we had a Coke, giggled and went to bed.

Saturday morning we dashed off again and made the train with half an hour to spare. The ride there took till 2:00 p.m. I think. We changed trains once. As soon as you leave the Tokyo area, you find beautiful mountainous country on all sides. They are like big steep hills, covered with forest, usually pine. The mountains are kind of blocked out where they are cutting lumber, farming, or letting forest grow, so the landscape looks chunky—cut up. Honestly, the hills go up at a 75 degree angle and the people live in the villages nestled in the valleys.

There are great pipe works to bring the water down to the villages and great cement troughs to bring the water down from the mountains—living depends on irrigation. Of course there are good sized mountain streams—you can see where they rose terrifically during spring thaws. The railroad is electrified. I counted twenty tunnels during our first two hours riding.

I now know why Japanese artists paint as they do—Mama would love this country—because looking down the valleys, each succeeding mountain gets mistier and bluer till the farthest you can see is a gray mist against the sky, and the hills rise so steeply and are like moss-covered jagged stones, and are weathered with great gullies. It is all dazzling and many times unreal—it isn't like any part of our country because the heights are so steep and sudden and just as suddenly you look below you to hundreds of feet into a V-shaped pine covered valley—it is beautiful.

The Fuji Hotel was the destination of many people on the train and when they heard that we were going to climb Fuji their jaws would drop and they would mumble something about "just seeing it was enough."

They would laughingly wish us luck. Few of them had ever climbed it or even wanted to climb it.

We bummed a ride from town toward the second station about eight miles away. But they soon let us off and we had to bum another ride. So a troop of soldiers and we started walking with six miles to go. We got hungry and sat down to eat. A K Ration lunch. It turned out we had 'suppers' and 'breakfasts': ham and eggs, crackers, bouillon and coffee, cereal, sugar, cigarettes, and chocolates, and that's what we lived on.

We had just finished two cans which lightened our load, then two jeeps passed us and the second picked us up. It turned out that the three troops had been told to climb Fuji or do KP and most were climbing. The jeep that picked us up was dashing up the road to pick us some men that were to have been shipped out.

We rode with them to the fourth station which was a good ten miles, and were certainly grateful. The road goes all the way up to the timberline but it is rugged with boulders and ruts and it's at a 45 degree angle - the jeep was in 4-wheel drive and still had trouble now and then. I am not kidding about the 45 degree angle - it WAS. The road zigzagged all the way but it was still an awful climb.

Honest, the forest was pine and you could look out and twenty feet away, even with your eyes, was the top of a pine with roots on down the cliff; the turns were right angles and the edge of the road all the way was a drop that was covered with pine. It was really very beautiful, with wild flowers and occasionally a peek at the valley below.

There are ten stations on Fuji, which are really just Japanese houses with one room about fifteen x forty feet. Families live in these and travelers (for a fee) sleep there under futons (like feather quilts), buy water for ten yen and have their Fuji sticks stamped. The sticks are poles about 4-1/2 feet long, and at each station (and there are many substations) they have a brand or two which they burn into your stick. By the end of the trip the Fuji stick is full of brands and certainly is evidence of a long, hard journey.

We were taken to the fourth station and there we begged sticks from some kind hearted fellows who were retreating, and I was given a coolie hat to have stamped in ink. The fellows were all over the mountain, lolling around at every stop, and generally were surprised to see us. They were friendly and generously offered to carry our packs but we held on to them because we'd brought 'em and we'd carry 'em!

At each station they had cleared the pines so we could see the valley and there were picnic benches we would stagger to. Of course we tired easily and we'd drag ourselves up the road about thirty feet and rest on a boulder and then start over again. We had decided to take it easy and we sure did. The nice thing about it was there were all these stations and sub-stations that we could see on ahead, and we'd aim for them. Many fellows would tag with us and, when they found the going too slow, go on ahead, but we were cheerful and happy and it was cool so our energy renewed every time we rested.

One of our many life-savers was that the mountain was shrouded in mist and clouds so we did not know how high we were going to have to go. Honestly, the day when we came down off it and I really had my first look at it, I was stunned - SHOCKED. It's tremendous, and we only saw the first fourth of it when we started climbing. I think that if it had been in full view on Saturday, I would have dropped dead! It is so huge and overbearing that I am awe-struck that I climbed it.

Well, we climbed on the dirt road until we hit the timber line at about the sixth station and all the time we could just see about 1,000 feet up - it's 14,000 in all, so the third station was 6,000 up. Then it was 5:30 p.m. and we stopped for dinner—K Rations—and started to the sixth. Now we were on volcanic ash and at every step we slipped back, but we did make progress. The air was getting thinner and we got winded easier so we could not go for long at a time. And this was the longest between stations; we could barely see the light of the 6th.

Here it was that we succumbed and let two gallant fellows carry our packs. I still had one on my back but it wasn't bad. It got dark as we staggered on but the trail where people had walked was plain and we plunged on—honestly, I thought we would never get to the darned sixth. We were all exhausted and hungry and tired of slipping but we stayed gay, and were never sorry we had come. Kay was beginning to get blisters from her boots by now and that made it harder for her. All along the trail there were others and everybody was fairly cheerful. The troops generally were buddy-buddy and kidding and though they didn't like it they were cheerful so there was a good spirit even though we were all tired.

Well, we finally pulled our weary selves into the sixth station and though we had planned on being on the top by sunrise, we took one look at that dark trail ahead and stayed overnight. The station was packed with men and more came shivering in all the time. The showoffs and brass would go on up with their flash-lights but we did not dare.

We'd acquired quite a few friends by then and they informed the men coming in that there were women present, so they were all sweet and didn't swear though I am sure they were feeling like it. We rolled up in our blankets and closed our eyes against the charcoal smoky air and dozed fitfully. All night long men were talking, coming in and going out, sticking their heads in the door to ask for someone or telling each other to be quiet. It was quite a night!

We started off after eight hours there at 4:00 in the morning and DID see the sunrise. There were clouds a few hundred feet up and below us and we could look down into this sea of clouds with a few peaks like islands, and then the sun rose over the clouds in a burst of peach color! It was beautiful because of the bluish clouds below us but nothing spectacular. We were very glad we had not gone on climbing the night before because the trail suddenly lurched over a great lava bed and we climbed over rocks as though they were steps—it was a huge mass of boulders that were stuck together and the going was treacherous.

There were cliffs near at hand on both sides and if you had started rolling you would have had to start from the bottom again. No kidding—we looked off to the side of us and saw that 45 degree angle and that treacherous old mountain and shuddered. The thing that really convinced me of how high we were, though, was the occasional peek hole down into the valley thousands of feet below. It was like standing on a ladder looking down; the valley seemed so near and you felt you could fall so easily the slope was so steep. All the cliffs gave you weegies, too, 'cause as you looked back out over the edge there would be only white mist.

The stations up there were made of mud-packed rocks. Unless we were climbing we got very cold. We wore our sweaters and jackets from the 6th station up and were very glad of them. Our big mistake was in leaving our packs at the station where we spent the night. We thought it would take an hour or two to the top so we took only ONE K Ration box.

I wasn't hungry and Kay ate it and the next food we had was at three in the afternoon. We climbed the lava field 300 feet and then began on ash again. Sleeping did not help us very much for soon our legs were right back to the same old state of fatigue again, so we would climb and rest and climb and rest. We went about four times the height of the mountain because of the zigzagging.

The clouds around the top would come and go rolling on so we could see to the top now and then. That was a discouraging sight cause it was so steep and ashy, and the people up there looked so small. . . .

At the topmost part was a large station and we aimed for it most of the time. It looked so far away and like such a long haul and it certainly did take long. We reached it about 8:00 or 9:00 p.m. and looking up as we climbed the cliff, we could only see a great mass of a peak rising before it. I have never been so disgruntled and disheartened. I was really angry with old Fuji for having the extra 600 feet of hidden ash. We slept at station 8 there on the cliff and at 10:30 a.m. started the long drag up. From here on up everyone coming down gave us cheerful little earfuls like this: "Don't bother going up - it isn't worth it" or "I wouldn't do it again for $100."

By now we were terribly hungry and begged a can of sardines from a benevolent fellow. We ate them with relish. Then another fellow gave us two cans of *Velveeta* cheese which we ate ravenously.

We certainly were a sorry sight but our consolation was that everyone else looked the same. We were dirty, baggy, and by now a little sunburned. There was a mist all day so we didn't get much burn. Well, I dragged myself up to the ninth station—200 feet and an hour's climbing from the top—and decided that that was it. I'd had enough.

Everyone said it wasn't worth it and we had been traveling on grim determination for so long that mine gave out. My legs were buckling under me and shaking with fatigue and I didn't think it was worth it. I was picturing my way down when I would need control of them 'cause we would have to go stiff-legged, heel down so that the momentum wouldn't get hold of us. I felt OK about staying there at the ninth station....

So a soldier we had met went to the top with Kay and they got back down about 3:00 p.m.—after I had had a nice snooze. They brought cookies they had been given and they tasted good.... They had their sticks stamped and Kay had a stamp burned into her boots, and an ink one on her shirt and they got the ribbon you get for going all the way, which sure was work....

So, still gay, we started down and that was something! For every step we took we would slide three. The ash was deep generally and all we had to do was slow ourselves down. The sticks were a help. We rarely fell down and never hurt ourselves. We started down at 3:00 and at 5:30 p.m. reached the station where we had slept and started from that morning. The only trouble was that now our legs were not very reliable.

At first, mine felt like two sticks and then two slabs of meat. The worst of the jelly-legged times was when we were walking down the steps of the lava fields 'cause we had weight to balance.... The mist was really rolling in now so after a K Ration dinner we three started off again and only met four people going up. Once we were lost in a cloud on that long ash trail but it passed and we got to about 5-1/2 station before it got too dark to see. Then we used [the soldier's] flashlight and with jelly-legs staggered down that 45 degree angle of a road.

It was really treacherous going because there was loose rubble on top of solid dirt and it was easy to slip; you had to balance perfectly. Surprisingly enough we rarely fell. We had picked up our packs. Our soldier friend was carrying everything—he had us carry the light—and he took royal care of us. The annoying thing about going down on the road was that our legs had to be bent all the time and you constantly had to stop yourself from going too fast.

We finally reached the fourth station at 9:00 that night and decided to stay till dawn. It came about 4:00 a.m. and we started off again very breezily but we were so sick of going downhill. It's an awful thing to have to hunch down constantly.

The sunrise that morning was beautiful - all pink and clear and perfect. Then we looked up for the first time seeing the whole thing and our jaws dropped. Honestly I can hardly believe it. It seemed impossible that I could have done it. Then we started the longlonglong trek into town—it took us till 9:00 p.m. walking steadily all that time. The beauty of that walk was that it was over level ground and through a shiny morning, through corn fields and tall pine forest. We got our sunburn that morning.

By this time we were walking by mechanical propulsion, and stopping was a chore that took five or six steps. Now we really began to ache and any motion but walking hurt. Kay's blisters really hurt her and I was sorry for her—she didn't have her boots off the whole time—we didn't wash either and certainly were filthy....

We no sooner got to the station than a train pulled in and we dashed to make it. We thought all the way home about hot baths, Cokes, getting Kay's boots off and SLEEP. We had a two hour wait for connections but finally pulled up here at 3:00 p.m. and were glad to flop down at home. Our muscles really ache now and we hobble around—no kidding. We are just like people with arthritis.

Sendai

...[S]o we decided to take advantage of [having Asaki, the maid] take care of the children and started off again on Wednesday night for Sendai. The train arrived at 6:30 a.m., and we went out to the 11th Airborne camp for breakfast - it looked for a while as though we'd be able to fly over the islands in a liaison plane, but the weather was bad and it didn't go through. We took the train out, and when we got there, we met a fellow who runs General Reider's motorboat for a living, and he showed us the shrine - then we rented a little skiff to go out among the islands.

It was a misty day, and gray, and certainly was beautiful on the water. The water was jade green and our little rowboat was waddling along. They row differently from us - with one oar that they push from the stern. We ate out on the water - our sandwiches.

We saw a shrine there that had a rock formation in front of it - with caves in it, where people had worshipped when the actual shrine was destroyed (four times, I believe) probably by earthquake or tidal wave... There were statues of Buddha in the caves, and some of them had been carved by hand out of the rock—really an interesting shrine—and just as we left, the sun shone, and it was so so beautiful with the sunset and the blue ocean and the green pine-covered islands....

Mary Sawada's Grandfather's Farm

September 21 - October 8

Mary Sawada's grandfather owns the largest farm in Japan—6,000 acres—and it is about to be claimed by the Government. This was one of their last trips up there before it is legally handed over, and though they could keep the house that is on the land, Mary says she thinks her grandfather will hand it over lock, stock and barrel. Mickey, her mother, is thinking of starting an agricultural school on the property and keep a claim on it that way.

At any rate we went up on a night train to Morioka.... It took about twelve hours and cost $5 with the compartment. It was very comfortable and they served in the diner. There were six of us that went up . . . .

There is so much acreage on the farm that I think it is right to divide it up. Mary was quiet on the subject but said something about how "in Russia they would have had more." As she sees it, it hurts her family to have it taken. An uncle died when his property was split up and she is bitter about that. But she is very quiet and thinks a lot when she does not say much - she is fun and interesting, though she is not a real pal . . . .

The home was a sprawling Japanese home, covering lots of ground for there were little courtyards and patios and there was a whole wing that we were never in - all the rooms were large.

The anteroom is where you take off your shoes and walk on boards to the front hall and then you walk on mats the whole time. They are soft (padded) and you feel so carefree and informal without your shoes. The only room without mats was the kitchen - sensibly.

They make their entire walls of windows, glassed, with small panels and the furniture on the porch was wicker. In the dining room and living room the furnishings were European style. The bedrooms had nothing in them but along one wall was a low window seat with cupboards inside and on the other side of the room was a slight platform where there would be a vase of flowers or an incense burner with a painted scroll above. They use wood as a frame for everything. The plaster is a grainy clay, dark and consistent and then the wood outlines all the angles of the room and all the panels of the windows. The doors, too, are of panels and sliding. Everything slides - cupboards and all!

Then at night they brought the futons in - these are quilts about five times as thick as ours. You sleep on two or three and under three. The first one above you is made like a kimono or coat but you don't get into it.... I slept in the Emperor's room - so called 'cause he had slept there three days recently. The futons are heavy but feel so good and are so warm. The poor people here stay in their beds most of the winter after the sun is down because it is warm and they have no fuel.

The house is surrounded by a pine forest, with a slight hill over at the side and there a little tea house is nestled in with a view of the valley and the horse racing track below it. This part was very well cared for and trim - all the bushes rounded and the trees clipped and rocks around - gardenish.

We got there in the middle of the typhoon season and it rained or drizzled all the time we were there. In fact the tracks were washed out the day after we got home. The first day we got there for lunch and then went out to see the property in a little railroad car - the rails were set closely and a horse pulls the car.

We saw the dairy where they pasteurize the milk for the vicinity; the school; a few of the villages; two Shinto shrines; the mills for flour and storing corn and wheat and vegetables which is a tall five story building; then we saw the great hay barns; calf barns; bull barns; horse barns, sheep and goats and the machinery. All the cattle are descended from Canadian or American lines and now they have 100 cows and fifty calves and about twenty bulls. But they are all tremendous and there are four huge barns of them—nine times the size of the Hacklander's barn. All the buildings were wood, clean and permanent looking, well cared for.

There were great fields of corn - as far as you could see, and wheat and soy beans and hay and pasture—great pastures all fenced with roads going here and there and trees planted deliberately as windbreakers. There were three race tracks that I saw, with their grandstands—one was a mile stretch straightaway! And there were forest lands springing up here and there but as you got nearer the volcano and away from the valley it got wilder and wilder....

The horses, of course, were their pride and they were thoroughbred stock. We saw three big stables with a good 150 horses. They were beautiful and spirited - and there were colts - we kept seeing colts in the pasture, and they ran like wild, following a leader, tails and heads up, feeling skittish....

Back at Michigan
1948 – 1950

Rita and Kay returned from Japan in the spring of 1948, again by ship, and were met by Honey. They had not heard about the New Look fashion craze that had hit America—the long, long skirts that were the new fashion—so Honey gasped when they came down the gangway in their mini-skirts. The first thing she did was whisk them off to a department store to buy suitable skirts for them.

At that time, Michigan was still running on the trimester system, and Rita came to Ann Arbor to attend the summer semester. She left Downers in mid-April, shortly after her sister Kay had had her third child, and went to live in one of the several residence homes, a large frame structure run by Mrs. Hutchings, very close to the League and the bell tower. Her roommate, Annette, had been in the Waves, and was almost thirty. They enjoyed the summer, but Rita had little contact with the other residents because they were from Spanish-speaking countries and she couldn't communicate with them easily. As Rita put it, "We didn't pal much."

At the close of that session, her high school beau Elmer came to fetch her, and on the way home they enjoyed eating a watermelon he had brought. She felt that he had changed during the year she was away in Japan, and she wanted to avoid getting into a serious relationship with him. She had several other boy friends at Michigan, and was very popular, but she was still looking for someone who could 'make the bells ring' for her. She was also thinking seriously about teaching, because of how much she had enjoyed teaching when she was in Japan.

We find one another

Art was what brought us together. In the fall semester of 1948, she decided to take an extension course in life drawing, and that is where we met. In my book *A Simpler Time*, I wrote that we had met earlier, when I was just a model, but I was mistaken. We met when I was taking the same course as she was, but was also modeling on alternate days. She came to her first class on a Thursday. Rita kept a record of her doings at Michigan, and I just found her notes. Here is how she described our first meeting:

I arrived with my pad and charcoal and watercolors. We each took an easel, and waited. Soon the model came in with Mr. Jones. When the model took off his coat, I couldn't help feeling a little embarrassed for him, but I had grown accustomed to models in sculpture, and soon was able to be as matter-of-fact about drawing him as he was in posing. My sculpting had all been realistic—pretty classic—and I hoped to draw the same way. But that wasn't Mr. Jones' idea. He said not to give him the exact representation of the figure, or color, but the feeling of it, the line, and the mood.

[Note: what Mr. Jones actually said was, "If it ain't got that swing, it don't mean a thing."]

I had taken up a stand near a woman, so we could talk if need be, but as the class wore on I noticed more and more a fellow who was drawing at right angles to me. He wasn't using the easel, but was tilted back in his chair, holding his sketch pad with one hand and sketching with the other. He was in blue jeans and a T-shirt, and was physically very powerful, I thought. But the thing that intrigued me was his face – so handsome...too handsome for me...Look out, Rita.

When the model took a break once, I sauntered around, talking here and there (as everyone else was doing), commenting on one another's drawing. I of course surveyed his work, and it was very experienced, I thought. One line said what ten of mine did, and he worked SO FAST. I was fascinated. He continued to work as I talked to him, and I don't think I got much more out of him than a grunt or two. I took the hint fast, and didn't bother him.

I have to interject a comment here. I was not ignoring Rita. I was just trying to concentrate on my drawing, and was not particularly interested in chatting. In any case I had no idea that she was interested in me, really. She thought that I was deliberately ignoring her, but that wasn't at all what I was doing. I was simply absorbed in the drawing, and—as always—blissfully ignorant of everything else. But Rita was curious.

The model re-posed, and I went back to my work, swearing to myself that I would stay away from him. He was dangerously good-looking, and somehow I didn't trust good looks anymore. Besides, he obviously wasn't interested in me!

The weekend went, and on Tuesday I was there, but that boy wasn't. I was a little relieved, and a little disappointed. Not for long, though! When Mr. Jones came in, followed by the model, who should it be but HIM. Mr. Jones called him Eric. I was surprised, but I soon remembered his grunts to me, and his disinterest, and became quite glad that my ideal for sculpture was now going to model for me!

He seemed serious about it all. He never broke a pose without Mr. Jones telling him to, and he rarely moved. He seemed made of iron up there...and stern. His mouth turned down at the corners and his eyes stared. Sometimes he looked at us drawing him. He would show with his eyes that he wanted to see our work, and then when it was shown he would give a facial opinion of it...generally OK. If I found him looking at me, I would smile...and get one in return. It seemed that now and then his smile about something in the room or what was said would be ironic or sarcastic, with the corners of his mouth turned down. I double-warned myself against him.

That Thursday, he was again drawing, and from then on he alternated, but after the class had been going a little while, he came over to the easel next to mine. In a while we were talking, but I have no doubt but that I let him start the conversation. He disconcerted me, so I hardly got a thing done; I was so busy thinking about what we were saying. We really had a good time talking, and I began to take back the things I had been telling myself about him. He seemed very nice now...intelligent, honest, sincere, straightforward and fun.

Here is where my recollections and Rita's own notes diverge. According to Rita, I never walked her all the way home; only from the Art School to a point just beyond the library. She wrote that that confused her, and left her wondering why I didn't take her all the way home. My own purpose was to escort her through places that I thought might be dangerous, and I left her where my own way home was most direct. I was going out with other girls, and had no romantic thoughts about Rita at that point. To me, she was just an interesting friend. She was going out with lots of other guys, too, but began wondering about me.

Rita was living in a residential house presided over by Mrs. Hutchings. Her roommate that fall was Joanne, a devout church-goer with bright red hair ("lots of it" according to Rita). They would often pal around with two other two girls from the house: Elena, a well-traveled and "absolutely delightful" Venezuelan, and Marg. The four of them formed a group and enjoyed life together. The first three were all trying to get over failed relationships with boy friends at that point.

But let's return to Rita and her account:

I don't remember if it was that time, or another class when Eric got sick of drawing the model and suggested that we move and draw anything we wanted to. He drew cartoons for me...very fast and caricaturish. We were off in the next room of the long wing...I remember I was embarrassed when Mr. Jones came by, because I had accomplished so little. I was too engrossed in watching Eric draw and talking. He asked me questions now...and when the one came about where I lived, I thought that was very encouraging.

I was right – he walked me home that night. We talked a lot...mostly the preliminary questions when you are just getting to know someone. What you're studying, where you live, sports, hobbies, etc. I looked forward to the next class.

Classes came and went, and each time I was walked home, and I liked him better. We went on in our conversations to our families and likes and dislikes. He was Swedish through and through, and I immediately bought a little dictionary and tried to learn a little. My first was *God Jul og godt nytt år* (Merry Christmas and Happy New Year). He said my Swedish was out-dated and taught me other phrases. I loved it. His middle initial was V, and he made me guess what it could be. I finally came to Viking...and was delighted to find that I had hit it. *Vikar.* I liked the name; it was unusual and interesting. It seems he had always been called Vikar until he came to college.

Here I have to digress and mention something I just found in a box, buried together with her memorabilia. It was a college workbook, and in the last pages were notes that Rita had jotted down about what I had told her about my growing up, my parents, et cetera.

Her notes filled ten pages. As I read through them, I was awe-struck, because almost all of the events that I had dredged up from my memory to include in my book about growing up were already covered in brief there. What I think happened is that she remembered what I had told her, and then wrote them down in abbreviated version so she would not forget.

But that was typically Rita. Like her father, she had an incredible ability to listen, see or hear and later recall things. I saw that on our many trips, when we would be gone for, say, two weeks and then, when she had time, she would write up an account of the trip for her parents. This account, typed as all her letters were, would go on for pages, and she would remember every place we had been, everything we had done and what people had said.

Returning to Rita and all the boys who dated her at Michigan, there were many of them. It is clear from her observations that she was assessing them. All of them seemed to have weak spots, but they were fun to be with. One—the doctor's son—was a fraternity member and had a "lecherous" buddy that Rita couldn't stand. So she wrote that he "lasted until I just didn't like him any longer." Another was so hopelessly materialistic—speaking of the cars and other things that his friends had—that she cut off ties with him as well.

The list of boy friends went on. Since she was always so bubbly and outgoing, boys were naturally attracted to her. She met a couple of veterans in an education class, and there were several interested fellows at the church co-op where Joanne worked and encouraged Rita to do the same. And there were others—one or two in speech class—and Jack.

Jack and I dated a long time, and very steadily. We always had a date every weekend and during the week, and when his family came up I entertained them. We went to football games together—doubled with Hal and Marty, and Marg came, too. He was a southern gentleman. Fun. If he ever flattered, he meant it. He was young in thoughts, still. Our talk was interesting.... He taught me to jitterbug He went to the Baptist Church, and we went to their young people's club often.

But Jack was never a thrill—just fun, and a good date. All the boy friends were interesting...most were fun, most were a good date, but none were thrilling. None rang any bells. Only Eric.

But Eric had not a clue of what Rita was thinking. He enjoyed being with her, but he was going out with other girls, still looking for Miss Right, and didn't know Rita well enough—at least not yet.

A big event for both of us was the weekend we spent in Chicago just before Christmas 1948. I don't recall how the subject arose or how it was decided on, but I offered to drive her home from Ann Arbor so we could see some plays together. I got ready carefully, wanting to make a good impression, and borrowed my parents' car for the occasion. I had no idea that Rita regarded this as a key event. Here is her account – much more detailed than mine in *A Simpler Time*, and obviously written from her point of view:

I asked Mr. Jones if I could have a little Xmas party there in class. He liked the idea, and told me of a little bakery where they made good German Xmas cookies. I ordered them, and cider, and got nuts and candy canes. The walnuts were whole, so I bought crackers at the dime store.

Eric modeled that night, and at intermission I brought in my food. He had a coat on, and we had a very happy, relaxed 15 minutes. Eric was cracking the walnuts without a cracker, and I looked: he was holding them in the palm of one hand and hitting them with the hard muscle at the side of the other hand. I COULDN'T do it, no matter how hard I tried.

After the party, Eric walked me to the library as usual, and we made final arrangements about Saturday morning. I was excited and delighted and happy...but puzzled again by his hurrying off home. A test, I thought. But I was happy. Oh, time couldn't go fast enough.

Friday went by slowly. I bought brownies and various foods for a snack on the trip. I packed the bag that I had planned so many times over. My clothes were ironed and everything was ready by 9:00 that night. I had refused a date so that I wouldn't be up late. I had a lot of stuff to take. Two shopping bags of Xmas presents, a doll for Storm, my large bag, a hat, a second coat, boots, and a blanket. He'd warned me that the car had no heater.

We were to start at 6:00 the next morning, and I turned in. I thought and thought about him and the trip and what I hoped it would all be like.

What we would talk about… I tossed and turned and thought until early morning, 3:00 I think, and then I was wide awake when the alarm went off at 5:15. I was so excited that I could hardly dress.

It was still dark outside. I didn't put on my shoes 'cause I didn't want to wake anyone. I wore my checked suit, which I considered flattering, and my new little red hat that I loved. I hope that he would like it. And my fur.

I hoped that he would be suitably dressed, but hadn't seen him in anything but Levis. I dashed about, waiting impatiently. Then I heard a quiet knocking at the front door and down I went in my stocking feet, happy as a lark to see him. He looked so fine in his gabardine overcoat, with his hair combed well and all smooth-shaven. Under it was a sport jacket and regular trousers, thank Heaven, and a white shirt with a plain colored tie. I told myself that I should have known that he would be very well-dressed, but I was a little relieved. For all I knew he could have shown up in three plaids.

I dashed up the stairs again to get the bags and stuff. He was very surprised by how much I was taking. He made a trip to the car while I brought down the other things. He seemed very amused at my lack of shoes, so I put on my high heels, thinking they did wonders for my legs when I got to the landing on the last trip down. We walked through the crisp leaves to the car, which he had left by the park. He had told me that it wasn't anything new or pretty, and it wasn't, but I certainly didn't mind. It looked like Heaven to me. I dropped my sunglasses as we went along, and we spent a little time looking for them, and then gave up and we started to the car again.

He had covered the front seat with a blanket, and soon I was happily seated beside him. I admired the way he drove, and just about everything about him. His movements were very sure, and he certainly knew the road. We drove out the familiar highway that I had been over so many times, but it all looked fresh and new to me, and we appreciated the dawn together. It was an absolutely beautiful day.

We talked and talked. I rarely noticed the passing world, except when we would comment on something in it. I looked at him as much as I could. I was immeasurably happy. I thought to myself that this was the best of all my Xmas presents. We talked about submarines, and his hitch in the Navy. I kidded him about girls, but he was unresponsive. He told me of his swim meet in Florida, the All-Navy meet, and I was duly impressed. We talked again about his family, his parents, and horses, and his sisters. And we recalled the plight of our oldest sisters, neither very happy; mine divorced and his near it. We talked about children, too.

Mostly, though, we talked about Eric, about his likes and dislikes, his life and his studies. What he would be. He rarely seemed to ask about me. I noticed, but just accepted it as part of his makeup. I wasn't anything but happy. It seemed to me that the six hours went by faster than any time I could ever think of. I put on my shoes and hat and coat as we arrived on the Outer Drive, and felt as though life—the vibrant, exciting part of it—was going by too fast.

I knew his laugh from before, but often I heard it on the trip down. It was wonderful to be able to bring it out.

We hadn't considered the time change, so we were very early for the first play *Streetcar Named Desire*. We parked the car near a theater and went looking for a movie. We found one: a double feature. One was a movie about whaling schooners, photographed up in Alaska and very absorbing. We had to leave before it was over. The first one was *The Hasty Heart*. The lead actor got an award for his acting, and we were glad that we had gone in.

We had just enough time to meet Bo when we came out of the movie, so we walked fast over to the theater. Eric went to the car to leave or get something and I went to wait in front of the theater. Bo came with our tickets just as Eric started across from the parking lot. He looked so tall, and Bo said immediately, "He certainly looks like a pitcher [I told him about Eric's pitching]—long and rangy."

I introduced them, and we talked a little. Bo was rushing off as usual, gave Eric the tickets and then pushed $10 into his hands. I hadn't expected Bo to do that, and hadn't warned Eric. He was very surprised and said Bo shouldn't do that, but Bo said, as always, "Oh, never refuse money," and in a minute he was off.

Eric was stunned, apparently, and I tried to explain about Bo: how he had had to work for everything and was so generous; and just got pleasure out of giving. The money was to be for dinner.

We went into the theater, and I was happy that our seats were in the front row of the balcony (with our family they are usually in the last). We just got settled and the play began.

I forgot to mention something about the movie we saw. That was the first movie we saw together, and gave me cause to re-warn myself against this fellow. He could twist me around his finger. As soon as we sat down, his arm was around my shoulder. I don't think he thought that it had any place else to be. But that wasn't the disconcerting thing. His thumb just came about at my cheek, and he was rubbing it across my cheek, near my ear, not exactly playfully, just caressingly. It made me tingle and warm. I finally took his hand and held it in mine, and ever since that is the way we sit in the movie, holding hands on my shoulder.

But to get to the play. I was a little disappointed that we couldn't hold hands there, too, the same way. But after a while we were in the old conventional hand-holding position and I was happy. *Streetcar* is an unhappy play—well-written, moving, depressing, a little shocking—and we left in a subdued mood. But we were looking forward to *Mr. Roberts* so much that it couldn't take us too far down in the depths.

When we came out, Eric wanted to go to the Blue Note, where Louis Armstrong had a combo. We sat at a table in the basement and listened. It was fun. They wanted us to have drinks, but we didn't.

Armstrong was fascinating to watch...he seemed to enjoy it so much. Their music was good too.

We left after a while and Eric asked where we should go to dinner. I took him by the nice places, like the Palmer House Hotel, and they seemed to scare him. Even Stouffers seemed too much of something, and after much walking we finally ended in a cafeteria. I was a little disappointed, but amused.

I had never seen him eat, either, and was a little apprehensive about his manners, but they proved to be excellent. We ate quietly and sociably, but a little stiffly. Then we walked around until *Mr. Roberts* opened. It had begun to snow. My shoes were toeless and my hair was wet. I had put perfume on it, but the dampness made the scent too powerful, and I was sorry. We enjoyed being out in the fresh air. I washed his face with snow and we played a little

Soon we went into the theater and we were in the back row of the first floor. I blessed Daddy for they were good seats, and back there Eric could put his arm around me. The man in front of me was bulky, so I had to lean Eric's way, so soon that arm lay resting casually around me and we were happily engulfed in the wonderful comedy of *Mr. Roberts*.

The best part of that evening was Eric's laughing. I had seen the play before, and knew it would be good, but I was doubly appreciative of it through his eyes. He roared and slapped his leg, and when the captain was told off by Mr. Roberts, I thought he would roll down the aisle. Some of his laughs puzzled me, and I asked later about a few of them. It was a wonderful evening. I felt as though an angel had been favoring me beyond my deserving. I didn't want anything more than to see Eric so happy. It filled me all up and I was in a wonderful world.

When we left the theater the snow was deep—quite a few inches—and very wet. We didn't mind. But when we got to the car, it had a flat tire, and Eric wasn't going to pay anyone to change it. I held his coat while he changed it right there in the parking station. He was in a white shirt—a novelty for me—and I enjoyed watching him work. He was powerful and so strong. I didn't mind having that tire flat.

When the tire was changed we got in and were ready to leave, but the car wouldn't start. The parking lot attendants weren't too sympathetic; they just pushed us out into the street and left us there in the Loop. After a while someone gave us a push for quite a ways, way away from the parking lot, and then we were alone. The snow was getting deeper and deeper, and it was late. There weren't many cars out, and all of the hauling trucks seemed busy. Eric left for quite a while trying to get help. But while I was waiting in the car a jeep-hauler stopped and asked if he could help. I gladly accepted, and he said he would be right back.

Eric returned downhearted, and frustrated about the whole situation. I tried to convince him that it didn't matter. Soon the jeep driver returned and hauled us to his garage. He looked the car over and found that water was frozen in the gas line, or some such, but soon we had paid him and were on our way. Then Eric was in much better spirits.

The route home wasn't too well-traveled that night, and the snow was getting deeper and deeper. There was no wind, and the snow all stuck to the trees and twigs, to the grass and the weeds. The world seemed absolutely beautiful. The ride home was fairyland.

As we got nearer I decided that I had better prepare him for Princeholm. I'm not sure how I did it, but I got over to him that it was a large old farmhouse, and I told him about its history. But even at that, when we finally turned up Oakwood and saw it, he was surprised. He seemed a little awed and uncomfortable when we walked in.

I have to interject a comment here. What impressed me most was the sheer size of the house. Three stories high, it could have held three homes the size of our farmhouse in Dixboro. It was grand in a Victorian sense, and I loved its setting among the snow-covered oaks. In retrospect, I believe that *awed* would be more accurate than *uncomfortable*.

   I was happy as always to be home. The yard was beautiful and peaceful all blanketed with snow. The moon was out now, and all was clear and sparkling. When we got in, I went around and drank in the beauty of the house. Then I asked Eric if he was hungry. We rustled up something in the kitchen, and then I just was too excited to go to bed, so I asked him if he would like to dance. We put on some slow records and danced a little. His chin hit my forehead as we danced, and I went off into a dreamy world. I think he kissed me; I'm not sure, but I know that fairly soon we thought that it was pretty late and he had better get some sleep, 'cause he was starting out at 6:30 in the morning. and it was already 3:00 or 3:30 a.m..
   So we turned out the lights in the house and got to the last one— the hall light. I left him at the stairs while I turned it out and came back and took his hand. He seemed as though he would go right upstairs, but I definitely wanted to be kissed goodnight, so I held him back and asked him to. He did, in his very effective way, so that I was still in my trance an hour later as I tried to make myself go to sleep. I liked that kiss, but we started up the stairs and said goodnight at the second floor and he went on into Pete's room. I sat on the edge of my bed putting up my hair, and just thinking and thinking. I didn't want to forget a minute of the day.

   This record by Rita illustrates—at least to me—what a huge difference there is between men and women in the way they react to situations. Men tend to be so one-dimensional, and seemingly unconscious of the emotions that they are arousing. I was acutely aware of Rita's happiness and bubbly personality, but I was completely unaware of the impact that my actions had on her. I'm not sure how I could have coped with them at that point. Now on to the rest of our odyssey.

I woke with a start the next morning as I heard Eric go down the stairs. Honey hadn't wakened me. I threw on some clothes and took my hair down and got to the kitchen just in time to see Eric get up from the table and thank Honey, preparatory to leaving. Oh I hated to see him go. I walked out in the snow with him to the car and wished him a very merry Xmas, and waved goodbye. I slept a good part of that day and dreamed the rest away.

Bo went with him to show him the best roads in the snow. He liked Eric and they talked about the hitch-hiking Eric had done.

Elm of course called me, and we went about the business of fun together. We made plans to see the Ice Follies with his family as usual, and he asked me for New Year's Eve in Chicago. I had never done that, and we agreed.

I thought a lot about Eric, and waited and waited for a letter. It came and kidded me about not paying my debts, and there is a story to that. On the trip here, we played Cockeye, but only briefly in the morning because it was soon light. That night, though, as we drove west from Chicago, I was too interested in Eric to keep my mind on the game and get some points, so it ended 9-0 in his favor. I was a little ashamed. I had never had trouble like that before! And that's the debt he said I hadn't paid.

I caught a bad cold, and once Elm insisted on seeing me and asked me to go out dancing with him that night. I was really sick, and I forgot and called him Eric that afternoon. I excused myself, but he kidded me in a hurt sort of way about other fellows. Then that night of dancing was interminable. Oh was I miserable. I was so glad to see home again. As I thanked him, I called him 'Mr. Youngquist' and that made a big hit, too. I had a hard time explaining. He asked about the other fellows, and I told him he had always known there were fellows at school, and pleaded that my cold had caused my confusion.

Christmas was a happy occasion, with everyone at home and baby Billy growing. That night we went to the Follies with Elm's family, and he was growing more and more serious, now that he was graduating.

Finally New Year's Day came, and we went into Chicago on the train to see it in on the busy corner of Madison and State. There was a big crowd, confetti and streamers and drunks and stuff. It really wasn't much fun. I had asked him about trains and we thought we could catch the last one home. When we got to the station, there was no train because it was a holiday, so Elm called his family and they piled into the car to pick us up. An hour's wait in the station.

While we sat there in the wee hours, staring ahead on one of those hard benches, Elm asked me to marry him.

I said no, and explained. I also said that I had tried not to encourage him. He was quiet and moody, and drove home quietly. We all chatted, but the chill was on. About a month after I got back to school I got a burning letter from Elm, saying that I had led him on and hadn't been fair. I wrote a scorcher back, saying to grow up, and that I hadn't led him on. When I got home the next summer, he picked up our friendship as though nothing had happened.

I was ever so glad to get back to school after the Xmas vacation 'cause I wanted to see Eric. NOW, I thought, after such a pleasant time together, he would surely date me!

I went to art class full of hope. We talked about the fun we had had, about Xmas, and how his family liked their presents. Over the vacation, I hadn't been able to resist making him a pair of gloves. I thought that navy blue would go well with his Navy pea jacket and made them large. That night as he walked me toward home, I gave them to him.

He was very surprised. I explained that I didn't like seeing his hands cold. He told me then that it was his birthday. I was delighted. We celebrated by his walking me home, and even kissing me goodnight. He kidded me about my unpaid debt, and I think that I paid a good part of it that night. We sat on the steps of the house, as I furtively looked for cockeyes in the passing cars. No luck. His kisses left me in that same state, and I was sure that everything was going to be rosy. But he said nothing about a date.

Tuesdays and Thursdays came and went, but never the mention of a date. He walked me to the library, or sometimes home, and then I didn't see him till the next art class.

When that term was over, he decided not to pay for the art lessons, so I only saw him on the days when he modeled.

His lack of attention had to be adjusted to, and though I liked him so very much, I decided that he wasn't the one, and not to think any more about him. I would be successful for a while and then I would see him again, and he would be so natural that I couldn't help liking him, and would have to start all over. I was a little bitter.

I didn't understand what was wrong with me. I knew I was no beauty and left a lot to be wanted in the figure department, yet I was hurt. I liked him too much. He continued to dwarf the other fellows. None of them rang any bells – only Eric. I deliberately went out of my way to avoid him sometimes, but more often I didn't have the will power and succumbed to looking for him and went to places where I thought he might be.

He was working at the League, pouring coffee very early in the morning. He looked pale and sleepless, often. I was eager to just pass him with my tray and smile and exchange a word or two. Elena and Marg went with me. Then we would sit where we could see him, and I would get jealous if some other girl made a fuss over him or someone else made him laugh.

Then I could see him at Art class, and did. Always with the casual talks, happy, generally intelligent, I thought. Sometimes we talked a long time.

Besides that, I went to the campus functions where I thought he might be. Louis Armstrong came, and I went, but no Eric. I missed Danny Kaye, but he didn't. I saw some movies that I thought would attract him – in the art school where the auditorium is small. I went to see *Romeo and Juliet*, and heard his laugh near me! I puzzled it out and finally saw him a few rows down, but I couldn't bump into him on the way out.

We compared notes about it afterwards; not too flattering ones, either. The old nurse was saying, in an unfortunate tone, "Oh woe is me, woe is me" and we have joked about her ever since.

Then I walked along the parts of the campus where I thought he might be—slowly—but only occasionally did we meet.

Once I was coming out of the arcade when all of a sudden a book shot out in front of my eyes, and when I realized what it was, there behind it was Eric. We stopped and talked and I brazenly hinted that I wasn't going anywhere, but he didn't ask me to go for a Coke. I kicked myself afterwards for being so forward. Often as I came out of the arcade, I looked around for him. Silly.

He worked in one of the bookstores, too, and when I could do it legitimately I went in for something.

Eric worked a lot and he studied a lot. I felt that maybe he thought I was just a loafer, so I was glad to tell him that I had a job, too.

That spring I took Shakespearian Tragedy, hoping that we might be in the same class, too. We weren't. I had talked about liking Rowe, and he had mentioned liking Bredvold. I took Bredvold's section, but he took Rowe's. A fitting turnabout. I did enjoy the course, and when we met in the library we were often able to talk about Shakespeare and compare teachers and comments. We did a little reviewing together, and went over final exam questions together. I went to the library a lot, because I found that I often bumped into him there. He would come up behind me, and touch my neck or tilt my chair, and then we'd whisper a while. If he was walking somewhere, sometimes I would find an excuse to go that way, too. I found that he often studied in the basement library, and I frequented it, too.

That is, I looked for him when I wasn't trying to make myself dislike him. I never saw him at a dance.

I was hoping that spring would bring to his blood a new surge of romance, and he might look my way. Then when he didn't I would go farther into my admission that I was inferior to some other girl and I would just have to forget him.

When Valentine's Day came and all the cute cards came out, I just couldn't resist sending him two that were cute. Then one day I met him on the street and he had one in his hand and was just going to mail it. He seemed delighted to be remembered, and gave me mine. It was something like this: lots of girls are so-and-so, but none of them are as swell as you. I was pleased.

The next part of Rita's account is about the Kentucky Derby and her accurate prediction of Ponder as the winner and my failure—using my 'expert' discretion—to place her bet on her horse. That was always good for a laugh between us, for years after we were married. Summer vacation came, and our paths diverged.

I hitch-hiked out West, thinking that I would work in the oilfields of Alberta. Because I didn't have enough money with me when I reached the Canadian boundary outside of Sunburst, Montana, the Canadian border guards wouldn't let me in, so I continued west. I reached Seattle, and ended up working for the Army Transport Service, helping to refit worn-out ocean-going tugs just outside of Seattle in the little town of Renton, on the shores of Lake Washington. We promised to write, but Rita did not expect much from me. There she made a mistake, because I did write.

After getting Eric's letter, my summer was spent thinking of things I would write, writing them, waiting for letters, and thinking about Eric. I gardened and took care of the cooking and the children, and Bo and Honey thought I was abused, but I was perfectly happy. As long as Eric and I were corresponding, I enjoyed it all. I saw Elm...the usual fun but more careful on my part. The other fellows wrote, but I didn't answer them. There was only one letter I was interested in, and that was Eric's. I continued to write and try to make my letters the best, most amusing, most original and most intelligent that I was capable of. We talked of books we were reading, plays, opinions, children, things we were doing, plans...

Bo took me to New York, where we did some business and saw Bo's friends, and just enjoyed the city. I got in to see *South Pacific*, and Bo and I stood through *Kiss Me, Kate* and saw Carol Channing in *Lend an Ear*. We had a great time and I really felt as though I had been on an exciting trip. I wrote long letters to Eric, about the trip and the plays and New York, disgracefully long ones. I was sure he wouldn't read them, but I couldn't contain it in me, and I thought he might understand about the plays, and the city, 'cause he had been there, too.

Again, Rita didn't know what effect those long and interesting letters she sent had on me. I believe that they, plus the wonderful times we had discussing the *Bible as Literature* class we both took in the fall, played a key role in my falling in love with her.

Fall soon rolled around, and it was my senior year. I was glad to go back to school. I don't know HOW I was feeling about Eric. He had written so faithfully, and seemed eager to see me at school. Yet I didn't dare pin any hopes on his strange "courting." I WAS eager to see him, though.

I fell right into the old dating routine with Jack, and we arranged to see football games together. I knew where Eric was sitting—rather standing—and looked for him once in a while.

I was actually selling programs, and after the game started I generally stationed myself on the top row of the stadium so I could see the entire field.

During the Ohio State game, when my uncle Frank was supposed to be in the press booth, I wanted very much to see Eric so I excused myself to go "look for Frank."

Eric and I watched halftime together, holding hands, and he fondled my hair. I couldn't help thinking that THIS was the thing that I would remember the day for. This was the thrill and the person I wanted to be with. I was encouraged, too, as always, that maybe he was glad to have seen me, too.

Now we come to what I regard as the crucial period in our relationship. That fall, we both signed up for Professor Weaver's course on the Bible as Literature. We sat together on the couch in her residence, studying together, playing chess, and just talking and sharing ideas. In the process I came to know so much about the things that mattered to Rita—her dreams, her ideals, and her family. This is how that semester was for her.

I had signed up for Bible as Literature, and was pleased to hear Youngquist called on the roll. I made sure we saw each other that day, but after that, Eric came and sat with me. We talked now and then and wrote notes, and thoroughly enjoyed and learned a lot from Mr. Weaver. He seemed to offer us so much. There was always something to think about or marvel at or discuss when we left his lectures.

I hated the day when they finally seated us—alphabetically. Then Mr. Weaver asked for members of a committee, and he chose Eric because he knew him. Eric suggested me for the committee and so the committee of six was formed. I sat very near the back of the room because I had started by auditing, but liked it so much I decided to take it for credit.

They didn't have me up front, so I was in the last row, across the room from Eric. I passed him as I came in, and we talked, and then he usually waited for me as we left. I was glad to be on that committee with him, but soon was glad because it brought me into real contact with Mr. Weaver. He was inspiring. We talked of the student-teacher contact that was lacking at Michigan, and of the course. I liked him very much.

Professor Weaver was equally impressed with Rita. He saw a fire in her, and we kept in touch with him by letter for many years, until he passed away. The Bible course was a watershed in my relationship with Rita, because I discovered how wonderful she was. This is from the final chapter of *A Simpler Time*:

> We talked a lot about our plans and what we wanted out of life. What attracted me to her was her smile. It seemed to bubble up from inside of her, making her eyes sparkle.
>
> Then we began dating. Often we would sit together on the sofa in her residence house, playing chess or just talking. As I got to know her better, my ideas about looking for a wife changed. I had started by looking for someone I adored, like Peggy, but over time I realized that what I ought to look for was a woman who wanted to share her life with me as much as I wanted to share mine with her. Small wonder that I was drawn to Rita....
>
> Once I got to know Rita, I decided that she was the perfect girl for me—someone I would always enjoy being with. In fact, she was the only girl I ever took home to meet my parents or even mentioned to them....
>
> Mine was not the weak-kneed kind of love, though—not like with Peggy. I thought about what my father had said and realized

a fundamental truth: Rita was intelligent and talented, and so full of goodness, happiness and energy; who wouldn't want to spend a life with her?

My proposal was not conventional, but it was direct and from my heart. After walking together one frosty night and kissing on the sidewalk outside her front door, we talked about future plans, and I asked her, "Do you think we can make a go of it?"

She nodded, and we sealed it with a happy kiss.

The Rita I married was a truly inner-directed person. She was raised in a home that stressed Christian virtues, and where tobacco and liquor were not tolerated. She held to those principles all her life, and she never compromised them to gain popularity in school or elsewhere. She realized that by rejecting smoking, drinking, and premarital sex she might make herself an outsider, but that did not trouble her. She made a conscious choice to be true to her own beliefs no matter what others thought. She was comfortable in her position, and did not feel at all defensive about it. At the same time, she never embarrassed others by making an issue of her beliefs.

There are givers and takers in this world, and Rita was a true giver. She was always ready to help others—without being asked or expecting gratitude. She had an infectious enthusiasm, and was ready for any new experience. Nothing daunted her; she felt that she could handle any situation that she had to face. For example, when she had to return to the U.S. from Finland alone with our children (The State Department had run out of travel funds so I had to remain behind), she didn't just fly directly to Chicago. She wanted to take the children sightseeing through Europe first. It never occurred to her that it might be difficult to manage six children (our five plus her 13 year-old nephew, who had lived with us for a year), one of them an infant in arms. She took them on a trip to visit museums and shops in Copenhagen, Paris, and Rome, all before finally flying to Chicago. They all had a great adventure, and somehow things worked themselves out. But that was Rita: CAN-DO.

Marriage

Our wedding was a typical Parrish production: seemingly chaotic yet somehow coming together just in time. We had several chores to take care of aside from greeting arriving guests, relatives, etc. We had to pick up the minister, who had headed the local Congregational church that Rita attended but was now living in Michigan. We also had to

- pick up chairs and tables rented from a local funeral home,
- go into the outskirts of Chicago to pick up the wedding cake, and
- buy lilies-of-the-valley and peonies at a local florist, since the ones at Princeholm had long passed their peak

Meanwhile, people there at Princeholm were bustling about without much semblance of order. Rita was still ironing her wedding dress upstairs less than a half-hour before she was supposed to walk down the staircase with Bo. And Bo himself was nowhere to be seen, because he was pushing the speed limit and ignoring other rules of the road on his way back with our wedding cake. My good friend Jimmy Dickey was with him, and said that their trip was a 'white-knucker'—a very descriptive comment coming from a fellow who had been known for having a heavy foot on the gas pedal when he was younger.

The weather that day was ideal—warm, sunny and clear—and Princeholm's grounds were in perfect condition. The only problem was noise. A new home was being built almost next door, and we couldn't escape the sounds of loud sawing and hammering. But someone thought to tell the workers about our wedding, so just before the ceremony started everything fell silent.

Rita's childhood piano teacher, Adelaide Farrar, played a few of Rita's favorite piano selections, then accompanied Frank Parrish, Rita's cousin, who sang *Because*, and finally went to the small old organ in the dining room to begin *The Bridal March.*

At the opening strains, the procession started down the wide staircase from the second floor, led by Rita's niece Storm Root, Kay's daughter, and my nephew Johnny Ivory, who came down the wide staircase together, scattering petals. The staircase was decorated with strands of ivy and huge white peony blossoms. Next came Rita's nephew

Ricky Root as ring-bearer, followed by her sister Kay as Matron of Honor, in a long dress of lavender organdy.

And finally Rita, on Bo's arm, descended the staircase to join me at an improvised altar decorated with white peonies and backed by two tall candelabra. She wore an ivory satin gown, with a small collar of pearl beads. Her pearl tiara held a short veil.

After Rev. Pitman read the service, Rita and I kissed and Frank sang *the Lord's Prayer*.

Rita tossed her garter for the young unmarried women to try to catch, and then we had a grand reception that was attended by friends and relatives of both families. Rita's two best friends, Mickey Carpenter and Mary Ellen Foley (E-Flat), and my sister Mae served punch, coffee and wedding cake to the guests.

In due course, the festivities moved onto the lawn, where an assortment of different foods was spread out on large banquet tables. As he always did for the family's annual Fourth of July party, Rita's uncle Earl Prince brought large containers of different flavors of ice cream from his plant, along with bags of cracked ice and commercial containers of various soft drinks.

All in all, it was a wonderful occasion, full of good cheer and best wishes from everyone. The two families met and friends and relatives mingled. Everything was quite relaxed and 'homey.' We couldn't have asked for a more perfect wedding.

Just as soon as we could gracefully take leave of the party, we drove away in Bo's car and headed west for White Pines State Park, where a cabin had been reserved for us. Several tin cans were attached to our rear bumper, so we had to stop fairly soon to remove them. The drive took longer than we had wished, but we arrived at our cozy cabin well before dark.

We were greeted by a crackling fire in our large stone fireplace. And then our life together began.

Our honeymoon was not what I had originally planned. I thought first that we might take a camping trip, but Bo—very wisely—suggested that staying in or near civilization would be better. He was right, of course. But we did do a lot of driving.

After three deliriously happy days at White Pines we headed north into Minnesota. Our objective was International Falls, where I thought we might find an outfitter and go canoeing on some of the lakes in the area. As we approached it, we noticed a sign for Lake Kabetogama, and decided to stop there to see what it was like. We parked near the beach and thought it might be nice to take advantage of the sunshine and go for a leisurely swim.

Not a good idea. We waded out into the water to swim but gave up on that almost immediately. We were freezing cold below the water line and being eaten alive above it by swarms of starving mosquitoes. So we gave up on driving north and instead headed south and then turned east into the Upper Peninsula of Michigan, stopping on the way to visit Fort Wilkins at the point of Keewenaw Peninsula and then the canal at Sault Ste. Marie. We took the ferry across the Straits of Mackinack and another ferry over to Mackinaw Island so we could see the Grand Hotel. We couldn't afford to stay there, of course, but we did ride bikes and collect a few small stones while we sampled the sun.

Finally, we headed back to Downers Grove, stopping briefly in Dearborn to see my parents, and prepared for our adventure at the University of Wisconsin.

Part 2
Photographs
Wisconsin
Rita's class and brood hen in cage
Rita's students with hatchlings
Norway
Bo and Honey saying goodbye at NYC
Bergen - on the funicular railway
Rita in the heather (Sweden)
Rita at lake by Rjukan
Our apartment on Nordstrandshögda
Honey with Vikar
Rita with Vikar
Eric with Vikar
Cornell
Rita at Vikar's christening
Vikar being christened
Our home in Ithaca - 131 E. Spencer
Vikar with Pip at Christmas
Vikar helping Eric study
Vikar with Pip
Reading to Vikar
Rita with baby Tor
Honey with Tor
Daddy playing chase with Vikar
Vikar and Tor
Vikar on horse, and Tor watching
"Pick me up," says Tor
Tor hiding from us
Into Foreign Service
Vikar and Tor before departure

Wisconsin

Rita's class and brood hen in cage

Rita's students with hatchlings

Norway

Bo and Honey saying goodbye at NYC

Bergen-on the funicular railway

Rita in the heather (Sweden)

Rita at lake by Rjukan

Our apartment on Nordstrandshögda

Honey with Vikar

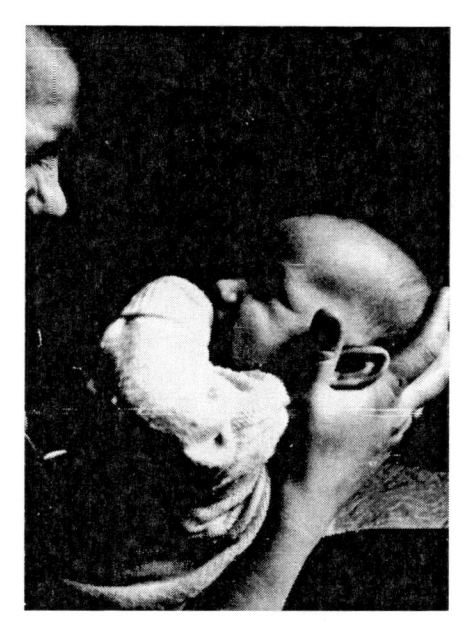

Rita with Vikar

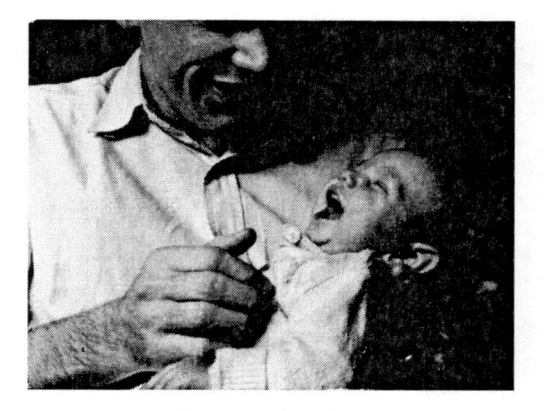

Eric with Vikar

140

Cornell

Rita at Vikar's christening

Vikar being christened

Our home in Ithaca - 131 E. Spencer

Vikar with Pip at Christmas

Vikar helping Eric study

Vikar with Pip

Reading to Vikar

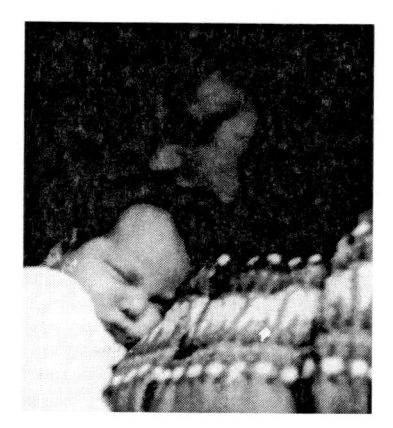

Rita with baby Tor

Honey with Tor

Daddy playing chase Vikar

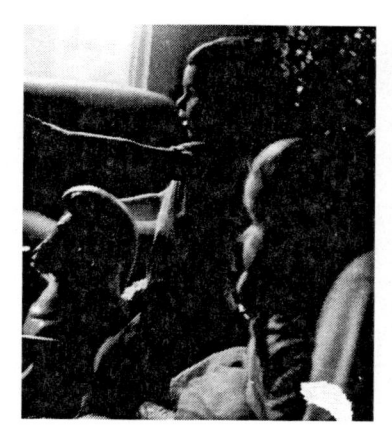

Vikar on horse, and Tor watching

Vikar and Tor

"Pick me up," says Tor

Tor hiding from us

Into Foreign Service

Vikar and Tor before departure

Part 2 – Our Life Together – From Academia into the Foreign Service

You've already read in the preceding pages about Rita's life before we were married; this next section—which includes many of her letters—tells about our experiences: while we were at the University of Wisconsin; in Oslo, Norway, on a Fulbright fellowship; in Ithaca, NY, as a graduate student at Cornell University; and finally as we prepared for our entry into the Foreign Service.

It is important to know about Rita, because much of the material from this point forward was written by her. Her letters reflect the wonderful qualities that endeared her to everyone who knew her: the joy, the optimism, the enthusiasm, and just plain goodness that bubbled over in her.

Some of what I have written here may be familiar to those who have read my earlier book on my own growing-up years: *A Simpler Time*, and I apologize for the repetition.

Rita had more than a unique personality. She had a wealth of talent, skills and learning, in areas that helped me as well as our children. Her grandmother was a skilled painter, and fostered a love of art in her. Rita went often to Chicago to visit the Art Institute; she loved the Impressionists.

I enjoyed art, too, and many happy memories from our marriage were linked with trips that we took and places we lived, when we visited galleries such as the Prado, the Hermitage (in 1959 we were among the first Westerners to be admitted to its 'decadent' western European art section), the Tate, the national galleries in various countries, the Uffizi, the Bargello, and the several fine collections in Venice and Rome, the Dutch Rijksmuseum, the Metropolitan, and our own National Gallery.

Rita was not just an observer, though. She had a fine eye for shape, and worked easily in clay or wood, and she made several very lifelike sculptures. From time to time, she played around with acrylics (she did many seascapes when we lived in Miami Beach) and had a keen sense of color, even though she insisted that she was not good as a painter.

She was a super performer on the piano, able to capture the soul of the music she was playing. But she was not a student of music, and at Michigan had stumbled in her course on theory. She was also intimidated by all the music majors who had 'perfect pitch' and an encyclopedic memory of themes. I think she was made to feel inferior, and that discouraged her. The experience led her into music education and teaching, however—a field for which she was so perfectly fitted.

Rita was an absolutely inspired teacher, and fostered in all of our children a deep love of learning. She made learning fun, so that our children (and her other students) were always eager to read, figure out puzzles, and explore new fields and ideas. They learned without realizing it, just as Rita did at Avery Coonley School (ACS).

Rita had many other talents. Having given talks and helped on programs in her classes at ACS and in Girl Reserves in high school, she was completely at ease speaking before groups small or large, and was active in drama as well, and was very good. She excelled at handwork (this is another legacy from ACS), and always had a knitting or weaving project going. Whenever we watched movies on TV she would be knitting, sewing, embroidering or some such. She knitted many handsome sweaters for all of us as well as for other relatives, using patterns that she had collected over the years, beginning when we lived in Norway.

She did elaborate hand weaving as well, making five large ryijys (Finnish hanging rugs), and she learned to cane well enough to do it professionally.

Her sewing may not have been elaborate, but she was able to produce repairs and new items (e.g. kimonos and children's clothes) at a phenomenal pace. When chairs or sofas needed to be recovered, she was called in and she would measure, cut and sew up a storm, producing great results in double time. She did not place any limits on what she could do, and I had to struggle at times to keep her from doing handyman projects around the house that I felt were in my bailiwick, such as installing shelves, putting up molding, caulking, etc. She could do it all.

Rita was also great at flower arranging. Shortly after she passed away, I wondered why the house seemed not just empty, but lifeless, and it suddenly struck me: there were no flowers anywhere. Rita had always kept fresh flowers or dried arrangements in our home, and she changed them regularly.

She never just stuck flowers in a pot or vase; she took care with each arrangement. She selected the appropriate container (she had more than forty of them, including several crystal vases that she had bought in Japan), and then she made her arrangement, usually following the *Ikebana* principles that she had studied during the year she spent in Japan. The type of arrangement she chose would depend on the materials she was working with but also on her own mood at the time.

She could produce arrangements almost as fast as she could sew. At our daughter Heather's wedding, for example, in one morning she single-handedly did all of the flower arrangements for the church as well as for the tables at the reception.

Rita was a fine cook, with a real flair for desserts. She was able to organize large dinners without any apparent effort, an essential talent for the entertainment obligations that we had in the Foreign Service. Our kitchen may have looked like a disaster area while she prepared meals (making was more important to Rita than cleaning up), but everything was delicious and all the dishes were ready to eat at the appropriate time. That kind of organization came from meticulous planning and years of experience.

She planned her table carefully as well, matching the colors of the foods with the colors of the dinnerware and her flower arrangements. Unfortunately, during our last years together she was not able to display her talents very often, because my low-fat regimen ruled out most of the foods that she really enjoyed making. Now and then we would break down and have Swedish pancakes, but she stopped making the cookies, cakes, and puddings that she enjoyed so much. From time to time she weakened and made a half-recipe of brownies, but ate only one or two and threw the rest away.

Note on Reading Rita

To appreciate Rita's letters, you need to understand how she wrote them. She wasn't trying for deathless prose or writing for publication; she had so much to tell her family and wanted to record and convey impressions and memories just as they unfolded for her. That's what gives such spontaneity to her prose. What you see are in a real sense first drafts; she didn't spend time honing language or searching for choice words or phrases. She wrote or typed rapidly as thoughts occurred to her, without stopping to edit. Often, one or more children would be climbing on her lap and playing around with the keys on her typewriter.

She didn't worry about consistent punctuation, mostly because that would have interrupted the flow of ideas. As a result, her prose is delightfully direct and honest—just the way she was. She wrote exactly as if she were talking to the person who would get her letter, and she developed a free and easy punctuation that suited this writing style. When she was typing I often heard her chuckle or laugh out loud as she wrote about some funny incident. I'm sure you will be able to sense the smiles and laughter in her stories.

In reading Rita, be prepared for some words that don't appear in any dictionary. When she wanted to describe something and a word didn't come to mind right away, she didn't run to a dictionary; she would just make one up on the spot rather than take the time or give a longer description or explanation. Her Rita-isms are designed to tell you in one or two words what she thought of something, and they do.

Rita-isms are basically shortcut descriptions. Many of them are words to which she simply added '-ish', but ones that you normally would not see thus extended, such as 'Pagoda-ish', 'gauze-ish', 'stonewall-ish', 'Wedgewood-ish', and 'palace-ish'. What the 'ish' means is that whatever she was describing reminded her of the thing she mentioned, i.e., 'something like a pagoda', 'reminds me of gauze', 'kind of like a stonewall' 'makes me think of Wedgewood' and 'looks kind of like a palace'. If she was unable to remember the exact word to use, she didn't stop to consult a dictionary; she simply coined her own word. The result is no loss of clarity, but sometimes a surprising word.

Here is a list of typical Rita-isms:

Happifying - adj. Whatever makes a person happy.

Indianed-up - adj. Deep into a study of Indian ways - or all dressed up like an Indian.

Flappy - adj. How else would you describe a giraffe's lips?

DDT'd - verb (p.part.) Sprayed with DDT.

Pillboxed - adj. Description of people who are stationed in a pillbox.

Viney - adj. Full of vines or covered with vines.

Unkept up - adj. Not maintained or cleaned.

Snakey - adj. Looks or moves like a snake.

Cowboyed-up - adj. All dressed up like a cowboy.

Ding - verb What a samlor driver does to make his bell ding. The bell doesn't ring; it dings, which makes a different sound than a ring. I can't explain the difference.

Listening - adj. "He was kind and listening with the children."

Stretchily - adv. How our kitten walked on the stairs.

Springiest - adj. The most spring-like day, for example.

Sit-stilly - adj. Not fidgety.

Unjumpy - adj. This is how a jack-in-the-box is when a child is not playing with it.

Frostinged-up - adj. What cookies are like when they have lots of frosting.

Snowy under foot - adj. What a night is like when there is snow to walk through. "It was a lovely, clear snowy under foot night."

Lie resting - verb Rita couldn't remember *fallow* so she said that the fields were 'lying resting' instead. The meaning is crystal clear, and in some respects is more descriptive than *fallow*.

Etiquetteal - adj. having good manners

Chuggy - adj. Used for old trains. They chug along.

Scuff - verb To make scuff sounds as you walk.

Birthdayed-up - adj. Full of happiness because you got everything you wanted for your birthday.

The weegies – noun   A feeling of uncertainty and fright.

Skittering – adj. What a tiny waterfall looks like when it comes randomly down a cliff face.

Waddling – verb   Geese waddle, but to Rita a little rowboat going slowly in the water was waddling, too.

Something-wrong-with-her adj.   Young boys at dancing class classified girls as "fat or tall ones, or something-wrong-with-her ones."

In re-reading what Rita wrote, old memories flood over me – her descriptions are so vivid that I feel as if I were reliving them in a kind of time warp.

One more observation—a reminder, really—the accounts that follow are not complete, since Rita's contribution is limited to the letters that she wrote. Had she been alive to share our experiences with you, the record would have been immeasurably improved.

University of Wisconsin

Maple Bluffs and Summer Time

As soon as we returned to Princeholm after our honeymoon, we packed our things and were driven up to Madison so we could start summer school at the University of Wisconsin. Both of us were going to be taking Norwegian classes, and I had signed up for other Scandinavian Area subjects.

We had arranged to stay in a neat little upstairs apartment of a home in Maple Bluffs, on the north shore of Lake Mendota. It was beautifully situated on the grounds of a golf course. Rita settled right in.

We arrived in the afternoon on Sunday, June 24, but our landlord wasn't ready for us. He was driving to Milwaukee so we waited to meet him when he got back about six o'clock. We spent the time feasting in one of the lakeside parks.

Lake Mendota is beautiful, very blue and even choppy sometimes. We have a beach just a block away, and the golf course by the house is for members only, but there are others. We CAN use the tennis courts, though. We're on a hill, and it's very quiet and breezy, 'specially since the breeze comes off the lake or the golf course generally.

At 11 o'clock, I take Norwegian, and had to pay the full price, too, but we figure that we'd spend the same for private lessons ($60). We still haven't heard about Norway yet, but we'll call when we do....

I'm looking for jobs, but most of the part-time ones are gone – the only ones left are waitress work or housework, which I'm trying to avoid. I'm going to try to canvass stores tomorrow, and the bakeries, etc....

Later:

It's turning out to be worth $60 for my Norwegian! Since I'm the only credit student, I talk most of the time! I really am learning it, and can understand it very easily. He's a good teacher and lots of fun.

I have a job for Saturdays in a bakery and hope it will develop into an afternoon job, too. It's a nice bakery with young girls and a nice woman employer. Sixty cents an hour, though.

Part time jobs are very hard to find. I'm going to keep on trying....

I'm waiting to meet Eric for lunch. We pack a picnic one and eat on the lakeside. All of our classes are in Bascom Hall, Honey, and we go over by the ski jump to eat.

I had applied for my Fulbright while I was at Michigan, but we were not optimistic that I would be selected because I had done no graduate work, so we made alternative plans. Prof. Litzenberg at Michigan had arranged with Professor Haugen to give me a fellowship if I didn't get the Fulbright, so I could complete the course work for a Masters Degree in Scandinavian Area Studies.

We searched for, and quickly found, an apartment in town where we could live, and Rita also found a teaching job at a school not too far away. The school was delighted to have her, because they needed another first grade teacher.

We had no car, so during the summer we commuted to and from the campus by bus. I frequently started by myself in the morning because my classes started early.

So the summer rolled along quite peacefully, filled with classwork, lunches by the ski jump, and studying. But the most important part of the summer—for us—was getting adjusted to married life.

We had to cope with the fact that we were no longer just individuals. We had become two people living together, building the foundations of our life as a married couple. We talked a lot, we laughed, we shared, and we learned more about one another. We talked frankly about what pleased and what bothered us, so we could avoid differences. It still surprised me a bit to wake up in the morning and find that I was sharing the bed with someone else.

When I was single I didn't have to be concerned about how I looked or felt when I woke up, but now I had to be careful not to impose my disorder on Rita. I imagine that she felt the same way. She was modest and never undressed openly, so I was careful to respect her need for privacy. We had to harmonize our daily routines. Fortunately, we were young and in love and not set in our ways, so adjustments were not really difficult.

We were both thankful that we had restrained ourselves and postponed sex until after marriage, because now we felt free to explore its delights freely and without guilt or shame. We were already in love, so sex for us was a wonderful extra gift and blessing that came with our marriage commitment. Since we always aimed at giving our partner pleasure, that gift ripened and continued to improve during our forty-three years together.

As soon as I learned that I had not been selected for a Fulbright scholarship, I re-applied for a grant for the following year, i.e. beginning the next summer. We reconciled ourselves to staying in Madison while I got my masters degree. For money, we had only my fellowship and the G.I. bill, so Rita started looking for work

Later in July:

I'm going to see first about a teaching position - then about jobs here... And all the time I'll be watching for an apartment. I'll get an appointment with the superintendent of schools here on Monday....

Rita was accepted immediately and was assigned to teach first grade at Franklin Elementary School. We were able to save a good part of what she made, and we put it to good use for our trip through Europe the following summer.

Soon after we arrived at Madison, Rita made a great discovery near the courthouse there: an unusual type of store called *Sharrats*.

I have real news, though...especially for the adults. I have found an actual real pokey shop. No kidding, Kay, you'll be amazed! It's the true American copy of the Japanese real thing. There are everything from antique compotes to two penny nails and rusty hammers on the tables. It's really a big shop, with half furniture, some books, household goods, jewelry, silver, and ANYTHING in the world you could want. It's at least as big as two of our garages put together sideways.

My first thought was of you, Kay, and all the happy hours we've spent pokeying, and then of you Honey - but Bo, you'd have a swell time in there. There's probably another barber chair! So now you'll have to come up, for certain, to see it.

237 Langdon

In August, we found an apartment and Rita was so excited that she she wrote to her mother:

The big news in this letter is that we <u>have</u> an apartment! It's on Langdon - where the road turns a few blocks from the library. We're SO pleased.

It is in a house a little like Aunt Emma's - oak paneling, big stairs - on the third floor - a library or gun room once, I believe. It's oak paneled, with a <u>fireplace</u> and wall of oak bookshelves! The sofa folds into a bed for guests, too! The bedroom is across the hall—and kitchen around the corner—so it isn't compact, but satisfactory. Kitchen has a refrigerator, too - and gas stove.

Our apartment house could have told stories. It must have been a handsome home at one time, with many large rooms. During the 1920's it was owned by a professor (math, I believe) who conducted some activities that were a bit outside his academic specialty. Under a very high roof-line it contained a large, secret room (at least unknown to the local law enforcement authorities). We never knew about this room until a few weeks before we left, when our landlord showed me through it.

To reach it we had to enter through a concealed door next to our third floor landing. From there we went up a narrow staircase that opened onto a table-filled den all paneled in teak (I think) and decorated with pillars and railings covered with inlaid mother-of-pearl. It was like a Prohibition-era movie set, and I could imagine what it was like back then: smoke hanging in the air, cards being shuffled and dealt, drinks on the tables and the usual card-table chatter. No need to worry about sounds carrying to anyone below, because the floor (made of thick concrete) shielded the rest of the house from the noise.

At various times at night Rita and I had heard strange, muffled sounds. They could have come from that attic, and after we moved we wondered between ourselves whether someone might have tried to listen through the upper floor to what was happening in the three apartments below.

The house had once been quite grand, which was apparent even though it had been chopped into several small apartments. As I mentioned, there were three on our floor: two that were small and self-contained; plus ours that was largest but disconnected. Our bedroom was across the hall from our living room. To reach our kitchen we had to walk to the end of the hall and turn right. The kitchen was halfway down the hall, and just beyond it was our shower/bathroom.

On the plus side, we had an impressive dining/living room, as Rita mentioned. At least 20' x 20', it was all paneled in fumed oak. A bay window stretched along one entire side, with a long cushioned seat and a view of neighbors as well as Langdon Avenue.

I spent many hours studying in our comfortable high-backed Sheraton style cane rocker that we bought at Sharrats. I could lean back easily, resting my feet on the bay window seat cushions, and sometimes I even fell asleep in the chair.

A drawback to the large room was that the wall opposite our entry door was not really solid: a large set of pocket doors took up almost a third of it. The room beyond those doors belonged to a young couple that rented one of the small apartments, and it was their bedroom. Though the doors were kept locked shut, they were a poor sound barrier, so our living room was not the best place for privacy—for us or our neighbors.

Another negative to the apartment was that our house stood at the end of Greek row, so we were treated to the sounds of weekend revelry from fraternities and sororities. I still remember Phi Delts walking in groups by our house singing (loudly, what else?) their frat song.

On balance, though, our apartment was great for us: it was comfortable; we could live with the way it was cut up; the living room was a good place to study; and we were close to the university library, union and field house and my classes.

For Rita, however, it was not so convenient, because shopping involved a longer walk and we had no car. If she had more than one large bag of groceries the trip was not easy at all, particularly when she had to haul everything up three flights of stairs. But she didn't complain until one day when one of the grocery bags split and all her cans and jars spilled onto the sidewalk. After that, I helped, but not as much as I should have.

Most of my class time was spent in Bascom Hall, which was perched atop a long stretch of grassy hillside covered with trees and lined with university buildings and sidewalks. Walking up Bascom Hill was a trudge, but winter brought a benefit: going down the hill could be a real experience, especially after a good snowfall. The sidewalks would soon become a series of long slides, and students would see how far they could glide without falling. Here and there groups of students would gather to catch colleagues who were unable to stop, keeping them from tumbling into the snow.

The Scandinavian Area Studies department at Wisconsin was quite small. All of its activities were limited to Bascom Hall, where it had a few offices and classrooms. As Chairman of the department, Einar Haugen was deeply involved in everything. He seemed to be with us even when he wasn't, because our few instructors reflected his teaching. He was always helpful, particularly if one had questions; and he was always ready to give advice and suggestions for budding Scandinavian scholars. Those of us who continued in fields related to Scandinavia found him a willing source of support. I was particularly indebted to him for his constructive observations and comments when I was in the State Department, handling Danish and Norwegian affairs.

My masters program was focused on Scandinavia, and within that rather broad category I had a wide range of choices. Everything seemed to be relevant, and I steeped myself in history, literature and language. Some of my favorite courses combined two, and sometimes all three areas.

This was particularly true of Old Norse. The development of the Icelandic language follows the history of Iceland. Present-day Icelandic still reflects strongly its roots in the language that was spoken there around 1200. Events in Iceland, Europe and as far away as Constantinople during heathen times and early years of Christianity were preserved there in oral tradition. After Christianity brought writing to Iceland, those stories were written down and are recognized today as a unique literatary genre. At the same time they offer a clear view of the historical relationship between the Icelanders and their original home in Norway and later with Denmark.

Old Norse also gave me my introduction to Norse mythology, because the old pagan myths that were common to the Scandinavian countries were preserved best in the Icelandic stories that were transcribed there.

I worked hard on my Old Norse, using a textbook that incorporated selections from the principal sagas. In the process I developed a deep affection for the direct, understated and action-filled stories of the sagas. My project for that course was a translation of a less-known tale (Hönsa-Thoris Saga) that Professor Haugen thought I would find interesting. Other sagas and historic writings like *Heimskringla* were available to me in Norwegian translations, so I was able to enjoy them as literature and also improve my command of Norwegian at the same time.

Literature was my favorite subject, and I was able to read many of the Scandinavian masterpieces in the original, e.g. the plays of Björnstjerne Björnson and Henrik Ibsen, and works by Sigrid Undset, Knut Hamsun, and others. Given Prof. Haugen's background, it came as no surprise that the bulk of the works in our literature survey course were Norwegian, and I selected others whose writings had their roots in early Scandinavian history, such as Saxo Grammaticus. My masters thesis was a study of the Old Norse saga themes in Björnson's writing. I also translated one of Nordahl Grieg's plays.

What was most important about the courses I took is that they gave me an overall sense of the Scandinavian impact on the known world during the two centuries following the first recorded Viking raid in the late eighth century. I could sympathize with the Norwegian playwright Björnstjerne Björnson, who reached back to those times to find his true Norwegian heritage. Those were glorious years for the Scandinavian countries and particularly Norway, when for more than two centuries Norsemen sailed over uncharted seas in daring voyages of conquest and discovery, when their kinsmen in Denmark harried along the coast of Europe and into the Mediterranean, besieged Paris and later invaded England, and when their neighbors in Sweden dominated trade routes south through Russia and all the way to Constantinople, or what the vikings called *Miklegård.*

Most of my non-class university activities took place in the area around the place where Langdon ended at the base of Bascom Hill. I played handball and shot baskets in the field house with Bill Simenson. I had an opportunity to experience the joys and frustrations of rehearsing and performing in three different plays in the student union and theater building. Most of my time in that area was spent in the library, where I studied and did research.

Rita and Teaching

Beginning with the fall semester, we led divided lives during the day. Rita spent all day at her school, while I was studying, attending classes and doing other things that interested me. Her activities were vitally important to us. Without the money she earned –and saved—we never would have been able to take trips during our time in Norway.

Rita was confident of her ability to teach, but nevertheless was somewhat uncertain in the beginning. She knew very well what she wanted to give her students, though, and she did her best. Teaching was always a pleasure for her, because it reminded her of her happy days at Avery Coonley. She always planned projects and activities that kept her students interested—and learning.

Here are some of her observations about her time at Franklin Elementary School. She was trying to describe what she was doing so that her mother could visualize everything and share her experiences.

Sometimes she felt overloaded.

September 30, 1950

I'm sorry to be so slow about writing. I get home from school, make dinner, and flop into bed after making out the next day's program. This is the day they're deciding whether to go across the border in Korea - and maybe war. We're waiting to see if we can hear MacArthur from Japan at 9 o'clock. Wouldn't that be Hell, tho....

The teachers at school are more and more fun. We have lunch together each day, and enjoy it so. They are really very funny sometimes, and Anna Grace (the kindergarten teacher) is just swell. You certainly would like her. My other first grade teacher, Miss Walsh, goes out to eat, and I've seen very little of her. I'm beginning to think that perhaps she's feeling a rivalry. She shouldn't; she's much the better teacher... I've got so much to learn.

Some days I'm so discouraged, 'cause I don't think the children are getting enough, and then the next day, I can actually sit down and count up our accomplishments, and I think everything is OK. We've gone through our reading readiness books (2) and will start actually reading next week.

My worry (other than teaching the retarded ones, and a few discipline problems), is teaching the right habits and attitudes. It's just the third week of school, though, and I guess gradually we'll get everything learned.

You know that we made a house, and talked about families, and then they really got interested in stores, so for the past week, we've made our store (with a red and white striped awning) and brought empty boxes and cans from home for it... It really is full of stuff now, and we're making money so that we can buy and sell in it! The children are very enthusiastic, and bring in their older brothers and sisters to see it - and I get flowers and apples these days, too.

They're visibly improved in sharing time, too, and my problem children and I are on good terms. The little boy who cried steadily has come around to loving school, too, so all in all, I don't have many problems that are too pressing . . . .

October 3, 1950

. . . .We've now had one frog, two cats, a full grown Cocker (the boy who brought it said it was a puppy - just "laid" a few weeks ago), and a toy bulldog. We've getting along OK, with a new problem each day - which we iron out and get a new one!. . . .

January 13, 1951

. . . .My cold kept me in for a while, but I was ready to teach again. It took all this week to get back into the groove. We are really pouring on the steam on transportation, now. Bo, there isn't a factory around here that I could take them through, is there? Without too much trouble, that is. I've never forgotten, and I know that others have often spoken of the time that you took our class in Avery Coonley through the plant near home. That was a real experience . . . .

Last Friday we made a surprise trip into Milwaukee - one of the boys was driving in to see Kirsten Flagstad (the Norwegian who made such a stir when she joined her Nazi husband during the war). She was giving a concert, and there were six of us going in, finally. The concert was beautiful—with just one Wagner, as an encore. She really got an ovation, too. Then we had a smorgasbord and the Bergs—friends of Mr. Haugen—who run a travel bureau in Milwaukee - mostly air - with lots of interesting things around. They sell Scandinavian glass and silver there, and had many beautiful things. . . .

February 5, 1951

This was the end of the semester, and of a half year's work... They're really coming along all right. I thought at first that there would be so much for them to learn that I might not be able to accomplish it all, but they are learning so fast that I'm not worried any longer, except in a few cases—but I guess everyone has a few slow students. It's really encouraging to see the slow ones take a sudden spurt and do so much better in school. That's one thing about this age—they spring forward suddenly . . . .

For Easter, Rita wanted to have chicks hatching in her classroom, so together we built a large wire cage. Then she bought a brood hen and a dozen fertilized eggs. She had timed the purchase of eggs to be sure that most of them would hatch before the children went home for Easter holidays. Once we moved the cage into her classroom, she had the students spread out hay on the floor of the cage plus hay for a nest, then put in the feeder, a water container, the eggs (which we had kept at the right temperature) and finally the hen. Her students took turns taking care of the water and the feed and they all enjoyed watching the hen rotate the eggs.

March 11, 1951

.... We got the chicken picture, too, Bo, and it certainly hit the spot. It's a small miracle that you found it! I've saved it till this week, but I will take it to class on the day the chicks are due to hatch. That is Wednesday. There is a lot to accomplish this next two weeks. Little heads are full of Easter bunnies and eggs of the jelly bean variety, and I want to finish up transportation, and welcome the chicks in full ceremony with a newspaper and open house - so we'll be busy, indeed.

x x x x x

Sometime in March, Rita wrote home to announce the possibility of a huge change for us.

.... But there's big news today... Ahhh yes, it outshines the return of MacArthur. Eric and I _may_ have a baby—I have missed this period, I think—and we're anxiously hoping that we are right. So in the excitement of it all, I've been shopping for a baby, and it is such fun. So here is a list of the happy things that I bought, and what I am making . .

A day or so later.

It was wonderful to talk to you all last night, and share our happiness so excitedly. I keep thinking about it happily today, at school.

Of course, we are on clouds - and all I want to do is plan and plan. We have a lot of travel folders and are thinking more and more about the trip down through Europe.

We got the papers yesterday. 7,000 kroner, tax free, his transportation ($1,200), books, and travel, and $1000 GI Bill. We'll buy a house when we get home! Or maybe a horse....

Getting Ready For Norway

. . . .Eric has reapplied for the Fulbright—and Haugen gave him a high recommendation. Eric is inquiring about passage on the *Stavangerfjord* for Norway this summer. With a clearing of the world situation and a little push on our part, we may be on our way this summer. We plan to save $1,000 this year - passage is $190 apiece. It isn't at all definite yet - and won't be for quite a while . . . .

February 5, 1951
. . . .We had encouraging news from the Fulbright people. First we got a letter saying that the names were going before the final board and Eric was advised to start intensive study of the language (he didn't get that before), and then they sent an airmail letter asking for a recent health certificate immediately—names being considered before a national board. Then it goes to Norway, and finally we will hear.

As the time gets closer and closer that we may go, my worry about the war in Korea (impending) gets less and less. However we won't have to pay the rest of the ticket till late in May, so have lots of time to see the lay of the world. If we go on the GI Bill we will have to skimp a little, but on the Fulbright, our tour of Europe is assured. We think that we'll take our trip during the first summer, and do Norway that fall and winter. Well, anyway, it is all encouraging . . . .

It's getting near the time we should hear about the Fulbright – and we are waiting impatiently for news. No one here has heard one way or the other. Of course, the only difference it would make is more money for travel and living. We are anticipating more and more the trip through Europe, planning and replanning....now it stands at:

To Paris and Switzerland - skip Germany. I'm hoping for Rome - but definitely to England and up through Scotland and Ireland - boat over to the Scandinavian countries - cover Denmark, Belgium, Sweden, and up to Oslo again....and we'll see Finland for some of the Olympics. You knew, didn't you, that the Winter Olympics are to be in Oslo in '52!! So we'll be able to see them. Kay, a fellow from Finland talked and said that they are VERY theater-conscious—that his town of 10,000 has two permanent theaters and one summer stock! WOW.

> In early April we received an official letter dated April 5 that began:
>> The Department of State is pleased to award you a United States Government grant authorized under. . . the Fulbright Act. You have been selected for this grant by the Board of Foreign Scholarships. This grant is effective under the 1951 Annual Program . . . .

The letter and its attachment described all the terms of the award, which included transportation to and from Norway (we had to pay for Rita's boat trip), maintenance payments, tuition and fees, books and incidentals, etc. We were told that the United States Educational Foundation in Norway would also pay our tuition and incidental expernses during the six weeks we would be spending at the summer school at Blindern.

We had classes scheduled for us there in language training and orientation.

May 21, 1951

There are just four more weeks of school now - 19 days to be exact. I'm counting them now... I've pretty well accomplished the things that I wanted to, and am just finishing up now... Too, I'm tired these days, and getting up seems so hard some mornings. But I'm not at all sick - lucky me! Everything points to being sure about the baby—and I had "good" news today.

One of my children came down with measles. Here's hoping it was over the weekend. Miss Walsh's room had four or five cases, and I was so happy that none had turned up in mine, and then this arrived. Honey, would you call RoseMae and ask her if I should get that shot against measles?....

Summer is practically on us up here. It has been hot during the day, and the foliage is very thick. Tulips are gone, and the lilacs are at their peak; fruit trees are about gone, too. I feel as though these last weeks are going too slowly, I want to get packed and out of the apartment, and the trunk off! I'm only 5 weeks premature!

At Princeholm there was a large bed of lilies of the valley, which had been planted and cultivated by Rita's grandfather E.H. Prince. Mama Prince, helped by Honey and Bo, had nursed the flowers along and cared for them carefully for decades. The flowers were particularly good, in that the stems were long and sturdy, with many large bells. In the spring, the whole family picked lilies and bunched them for sale to a wholesale florist in Chicago. Rita told me that it was a family fun experience for her, and made money that was used for the house. She missed helping with the lilies and wrote home.

May 27, 1951
Dear Honey and Bo,
I certainly was remorseful when I realized that I really could have helped with the lilies, and didn't. You know that I enjoy it, and nothing here was pressing so that I couldn't get down... I guess I was thinking that I wasn't needed, and that it was time for me to be especially careful since I was passing the second period. I certainly am sorry though that I didn't come; we would have had fun doing it together, Honey... I guess the only consolation is that maybe they wouldn't have sold....

June, 1951

    Nothing much else from here. Eric just went off to take his last exam from Haugen, and then we will begin to pack up here. The children were demons yesterday—I slept 16 hours last night!

Later in June,
Dear Honey and Bo:

    Always remember that I love you very very much - and that you've made me <u>SO</u> happy. I've had a wonderful childhood -- all happy memories, and now we'll have an even happier grown-up-hood together.

On Stage

Staying at Wisconsin to complete my masters degree also gave me an opportunity to do something that I had never done (or had time to do) at Michigan, and that was get involved in extra-curricular activities. The Wisconsin Players, a university group, was casting for *Murder in the Cathedral*, and when I heard about it, I thought, *Why not try reading for a part?* Rita encouraged me; she had been deeply involved in theater both in high school and at Michigan. She thought that I would enjoy the experience—and I did.

I went to the reading and was given a script to follow. When all the readings were completed, those who had been chosen for parts were told, and I was delighted to learn that I would be cast as the Third Tempter. We went through the long list of activities preparatory to getting a play ready for an audience: studying the text and our parts; learning lines; rehearsing with others in rooms at first and then on stage; learning blocking and stage directions; working on gestures and projecting my voice; getting 'into' my role so I would feel believable; plus everything else that actors do in order to perform well on stage.

I was only a minor character, of course, and how I performed would never make or break the play, so I simply enjoyed what I was doing. Along the way I learned a gread deal about stagecraft from watching and listening to others.

For me, at least, the best way to appreciate the ability of professional artists and artisans is to try to do what they seem to do so effortlessly. It is almost always a humbling but ultimately rewarding experience.

Came the day of the first performance and I felt reasonably ready and not very nervous. We had rehearsed so thoroughly that I knew my lines and the words came naturally to me. I could concentrate instead on timing and delivery. The play was well-received, and everyone—including me—came away happy and satisfied. One of my fellow Scandinavian Area students, Erik Bye, played the First Tempter. He went on to become an icon on the Norwegian cultural scene, as a poet, writer, troubador and commentator.

During the rest of that semester I appeared in two other productions: Strindberg's *There Are Crimes and Crimes* (as one of the principals); and *The Purification*, by Tennessee Williams, a one-acter in the Union's intimate theater, where I played The Rancher.

My exposure to acting and the theater led to a life-long love for both of us. Whenever we could afford it, Rita and I tried to attend plays: in Oslo (repertory theater), in Finland, and in NYC, Chicago, London and wherever else we traveled.

Norway (1951-52)

Trip Over On SS *Stavangerfjord*

In July, Bo and Honey drove us to New York and the pier of the Norwegian-American Line, where Rita and I boarded the old liner *SS* Stavangerfjord. We waved to them from the deck as they stood on the pier waving back to us. Longshoremen lifted the lines off the bollards on the pier and our ship eased gently away and then picked up speed as it set course for the open sea. Rita wrote to them about the trip.

July 17, 1951 (Aboard the SS *Stavangerfjord*)

Dear Family,
    You have all been on my mind so much - and now, since we are docking at Bergen tomorrow, I will get this letter off - to tell you all that I love you very much. I'm homesick, but I suppose that will pass once we are in Norway - so don't worry.
    We were wrong, Bo, about the stateroom's being hot... It has grown steadily cooler as we go north, and we're using our blankets - it's too cold for many of the clothes that I brought, and I really could use my winter coat.
    The sea has been calm all the way - I'm amazed. I never thought that the sea could be calmer than Lake Michigan. I don't know of a soul on board who has been seasick... The ship rides very smoothly and has just a little side-roll, and none of the forward pitch that the *Gordon* had! The *Oslofjord* passed us yesterday, and we could certainly see IT pitch and roll - it is larger.

Tourist is almost all Norwegians returning home after many years, and they're all so glad to be speaking Norsk again that I hear no English at all. Luckily, the menu is in both languages, but our crew all speak Norsk, even understand little English... So I'm learning my Norsk very fast. Eric has his troubles but is managing, anyway. We, neither of us, can understand our waiter! I never know whether he's asking me if I want something, until he brings it!

We've had a funny menu - smörgåsbord morning and night. Here it is:

Breakfast	Lunch	Dinner
Cold table	Beef soup	Cold table
Apples	Meat and potatoes	Meat and potatoes
Oatmeal/corn flakes	Dessert - usually a	Coffee/tea
Coffee/tea/milk	funny pudding	

Then there is coffee in the middle of the afternoon. I like it because the smörgåsbord has vegetables and fruit on it, so my meal is well rounded - but the table is mostly cheeses, hard breads, meats, relishes, jams, tomatoes and cold unseasoned vegetables....

We were assigned a table with four Norwegians - two farmers returning home after maybe thirty years, a carpenter going back after forty years, and an MIT research man going back to get his children after spending two years in America. They are perfectly content to sit for 15-20 minutes without saying anything - and even after seven days, they are just beginning to unbend. The carpenter is a lean religious man whose humor completely confuses me - The MIT man is young and pleasant, and we have seen quite a bit of him - playing chess and talking....

Our stateroom, which was located on absolutely the lowest level of the ship, was quite small and only had berths, a closet and a sink with a cabinet and mirror. We had no private bathroom, so we had to go up one deck to use the large facilities there. But we didn't spend time in our stateroom except for sleeping. We were either in the dining room, the library, or strolling about on deck.

Every day we went to the ship's library to look at the map on which an officer had extended a red line to indicate our progress toward Norway. We spent lots of time lounging on deck chairs, reading. It was so restful looking out over the vast expanse of the sea.

As Rita wrote, the religious member of our table group was a puzzlement to both of us. He quoted passages (just phrases like *the pen is mightier than the sword* and *The sins of the fathers are visited upon the children*), often from the scriptures. He confused Rita because he told her what he apparently thought were jokes, but she didn't recognize them as jokes because they had no obvious point. The awkward part of it was that he looked as if he expected Rita to laugh, and she didn't know what to do because she couldn't tell whether he had said anything funny. What he apparently considered a joke would have about as much point as "I went out to buy a dozen eggs" or some such meaningless thing.

The whole atmosphere of the ship was similar to my memories of the Vasa Club parties at Lapeer. The band played Scandinavian dances, and all the people were dancing, drinking, and playing cards.

As I mentioned in my letter to my folks, "Two of our table chums were farmers, and seeing them bears out what you have said about farming being a dangerous occupation. One has only a thumb on his right hand, and the other has 2-1/2 fingers missing (I forget which hand)."

One of the things we enjoyed most on our trip was the sea, with its changing colors and shapes. We put our deck-chairs on the after deck, so that we could watch the water as we lay down and rested. Other times we would go forward and watch the waves crash against the bow, in beautiful leaping humps of green, turning into the whitest foam on top and the strangest shapes of bubble-clouds beneath the surface, as if we were looking through a Mason jar at cotton batting being shot from a hose.

Rita added a few lines here.

We have been to two of the dances, and with a rolling ship it's just like being a cow on the side of a hill, with alternate legs short!
 Then there are concerts, movies, and many chess games, but no one speaks. They are all _very_ reserved. They can sit for hours on end without saying anything to anyone! Our first dinner was about as stiff as it could get. It's only now, after eight days and in the excitement of getting home, that the conversation doesn't have long pauses.

Rita wrote a short letter to her folks as we neared the Norwegian coast, and began thinking about going ashore at Bergen.

I have just left Eric up in the bow, watching the Norsk coast go by—mostly rock and mountains now. I was waiting until he wrote so that I could add to his letter, but he seems to have covered it all well.
 We haven't been sick, just sunburned.
 You would get a huge kick out of seeing Eric struggle with his Norwegian – it is coupled with sign language. It's amusing 'cause none of the Norwegians use their hands at all! He is really doing well, though, and gaining more and more self-confidence.
 He is very thrilled about the whole trip, and as you probably could guess, I haven't been able to keep up with him. I'm hoping that I won't be so tired.
 At any rate, Bergen is a few minutes away, and we'll have a big day there. We're both eager to get started, since it is quite a large city, with many things to see!

Rita wrote the next part a little earlier, when she was trying to describe the whole shipboard experience to her parents:

There is a big lounge where they almost all go to sit and think-drink-write and talk when they know each other.

There's a large crew, three hundred of them, mostly young, and underpaid, I hear. They must not have any unions, 'cause one boy that Eric talked to was only getting six hours sleep a night, with an hour off during the day... They work hard, and the whole ship is as clean as a whistle. It is mopped in the early morning, and there's not even any dust on the high pipes that Eric can reach. There's a crew that covers the ship from stem to stern every few hours to prevent fires - there's an orchestra that plays afternoon and evening, and during the dinner hour - and movies are every other evening. . . .

We had our deck chairs put in the stern, where the sun and the wind would hit us – and got a first-class sunburn. We're both red as beets on one side and white on the other. And now, as we get up north and near the continent, it has been foggy and windy, so it's too cold on deck. We'll probably stay there as we go down the coast, though... I think that we go near enough to see the towns.

We'll have about five hours in Bergen - just enough to see the sights, take a cable car up to the top of the mountain overlooking the city, and make it back to the ship....

July 25, 1951 - Oslo

We were met at the dock by a Fulbright employee, with a car, and taken immediately to meet Mr. Marcusson. He is head man here, and very busy. He seems easy-going, though -- has a huge shock of dark hair... He told us that we'll be given $100 in kroner to tide us from the end of summer school to September 1. That was a VERY welcome surprise. He gave us a check and sent us on out to the school.

School in the summer is run in a small campus called Blindern. When we arrived, we found that they had arranged for us to rent a room in an elderly lady's apartment.

Mrs. Isvald lives just off Majorstua, one of the major streets, so we moved in with her and then made all our contacts with deans and what-have-you in the first few hours! We walked around town, and saw a show that day too, so on Saturday all I did was sleep to throw off a cold.

Then ever since, we have been on the go. We eat dinner in one of the Norwegian restaurants—making wild guesses with the menus. Once we got some terrible pickled herring..ugh. But on the whole we've been pretty lucky.

Sunday there was a trip to Eidsvold, where their constitution was signed on May 17, 1814, I think, and met there a boy who had been a student at Wisconsin last year. An "important family" here—the Matthiessens—entertained the tour group, and the student from Wisconsin turned out to be Haakon Matthiessen, a member of that family!

Their home was white exterior - large, but not imposing - but the interior was all high ceilinged, panelled, with old and expensive furniture and masters paintings hung everywhere - very spacious and palace-ish... We were surprised by the feeling of nobility there—with pictures of the royal family signed very intimately—and with furniture that had been in the family for hundreds of years - and ancestral portraits everywhere.

Then on Monday I began exploring downtown Oslo, and here are my impressions. The Osloites dress as well as and better than most people in Chicago - well-matched outfits, hats, the men all in coats and ties. I haven't seen any good-looking clothes in shop windows, but I certainly have seen them ON people. I have a hunch they shop in Sweden or on the continent.

The subway is the way we get to town - in three minutes we go what takes ten to fifteen minutes in a car. They are rapid, clean, and uncrowded. AND I've never had to wait for one!

There are parks with lush flower beds all over, and streets are pretty clean, and there are window-boxes with flowers EVERYWHERE. Flowers on the corner are cheap and varied—I got a bunch of yellow daisies and one of bachelor buttons for 40 cents.

There are 3-4 story apartment buildings for miles on end. They're in great units, and seem unending as you drive around. About apartments - we have answered two ads, and are putting our ad in the paper in the paper today... The paper will have three columns of people wanting apartments and about five inches of ones to rent. Marcusson may be a help there, though. The Embassy doesn't help.

We can cook here in our apartment - but not dinners, so we have breakfast here, and snacks. Food isn't cheap - even cooking at home it'll cost quite a bit. The foods we like are luxuries here - tomatoes are 80 cents apiece - and melons go way over a dollar. Meat isn't rationed - and the sugar ration is plenty sufficient for us. I've only seen lettuce sold once, but cauliflower and broccoli and cabbage and carrots etc. are plentiful - so are strawberries.

We will have to stretch our trip money quite a bit—but we DO have gift money to fall back on if necessary.

We just figured it all out and won't need it! Hotels should be about $3 a night. That gives us two days in Copenhagen, four in Paris, and three in London. We found that we would be spending our entire trip money for tickets if we went to Italy, so that was abandoned. A Paris ticket cost 220 kroner for each of us, or 440 ($63). We'll look for our china in London -- hope that it wouldn't be more expensive than getting it here. Well, Oslo is just like Chicago, but window shopping is more fun! The streets are wide, many cars, clean people, streetcars and busses, rush hours, obliging clerks - movies in all languages....

Did I tell you that you close all doors in a house here? It is a cardinal sin to leave the front door unlatched—Mrs. Isvald is terribly afraid of burglars—and all doors get closed behind you. I left the door unlatched once while she was here, of course, thinking about my shopping, and I am still hearing about it! She is very considerate of us, however, and is always ready with advice. She must be seventy and is going to the mountains to ski next month!!!

The apartment building we are in is one of five with a court-yard—six stories and brick—all with balconies with flowers and with great maples in the yard. It's very pleasant, and quiet – everyone is off on vacation now! Even the doctors are out of town, so that the papers print which doctors are IN town!

Most meats are available—even canned chicken—and they're not rationed. Fruits canned are high but available -- and Jello and puddings are here. Chocolate bars are everywhere - I think I can get cooking chocolate, too. Milk is seven cents a quart - and rich. Sugar is about eighteen cents for five pounds.
They seem to have most clothing—just not so fashionable—even nylons!

We went to a track meet at Bislet, the Oslo stadium, which was a *landskamp,* or a country competition, between Sweden and Norway. There is a great rivalry between them, so passions run high. In back of us stood a man and his son. They were Swedish—I could tell easily by their pronunciation of *kanske*. We were watching the 10,000 meter run, and near the end the Norwegian runner began to increase his lead. Then the little boy couldn't hold still any longer.

He yelled out, *"Kom! Springa det värsta du orkar!"* (Come on! Run as fast as you can!) The words themselves weren't especially comical, but coming like clear bell-notes from a child, and carrying so far (I bet the entire stadium heard), they created quite a sensation.

To Rjukan Power Plant

Now on to the trip. We went last weekend to Rjukan where there is a large hydro-electric plant and lots of industry, and the highest mountain in southern Norway. We originally were going with a group to another town, but missed connections, and went off on our own. The trains here look brown and forbidding, and the seats couldn't be called well-padded. Some are compartmented, like in the British films, so that you sit and stare at someone who is staring at you - and some are like our old suburban trains.

It's unusual to see a bag here - everyone travels with a pack on their back, even the children. We changed trains twice, then took a ferry for two hours down a long cliff-sided lake, and another train down the valley to the city.

The cliffs were so high that the pines at the top looked pin-thick, and I couldn't figure out where the water for the waterfalls was coming from. I thought that maybe there were a lot of lakes up on top of there. None of the waterfalls were spectacular, but all thin and filmy and skittering down the cliffs. There was a rapidy river in the valley, and we found that that water was coming from the large electric plant.

The town was built like Montpelier, with just room for one main street in the valley. Here the street was the river, and factories were lined up on one side, and houses of all shades on the other. It had one hotel - which was full, and a travel bureau that placed us in a woman's home.

We had her son's room - clean as a whistle, with pictures of skiing trips on the walls, and of all of them in their uniforms. There was one restaurant, which fortunately served excellent food. We got there at 9:30 that night, and started right out the next morning to go up the mountain.

We walked up quite a ways to the cable car - eating wild raspberries and picking flowers, then the cable-car took us up to 860 meters, and a very impressive trip it was. It was an open car, and we were a few hundred feet up above the pines most of the time. As we got higher, I saw where the water for the falls was coming from. The high mountain rose from those cliffs, and there was still snow in the crevasses. We walked on up to get a better view - and we think we got almost up to the timberline.

We were going to bus back, for the fun of a different route, but found that there wasn't any place open to get a ticket on Sunday. EVERYTHING CLOSES ON SUNDAY HERE - except a few restaurants - yet they don't seem to feel very religious about it. They are 90% Lutheran, and dance and such on Sundays, but I've only seen one farmer who was working on Sunday. So we had to take the train back....

July 29
Dear family-

We're on the way home from Rjukan now—same train, same route—much to our disgust!

This train seems to stop at every farmhouse, so we're getting a good slow-motion picture of "Rural Norwegian Life!" It's all pine and birch out here – all wooded mountains. You wonder how the trees live!

Since there's so little soil, the farms are small (growing hay) and often you see a whole panorama with only one farmhouse. There is water everywhere—creeks, rivers, falls, lakes—and <u>always</u> with the water are signs of lumbering: the logs are along the edges and there are many mills.

Trip to Paris, London and Glasgow

Sunday August 5

    Here I sit, munching excellent goodies in a Copenhagen hotel. We really saw the city today. We went on a "historic tour" this morning—from the stone age to the present, including the Royal jewels—and then this afternoon we spent 1-1/2 hours on a bus, and saw the WHOLE city. . . .

    It really is a charming place—as Eric just said—and it is so cosmopolitan. Every language on the street and all sorts of people. Our poor guide had to speak in three languages today: French, English and Danish -- sometimes German!

    But the city is <u>Pretty</u>. The important buildings all have copper spires that have turned green - and often green roofs, so that there are these spires on all sides and multicolored buildings.

    The ceramic shops are all on one street - Royal Copenhagen, Bing & Grøndahl, Dahl Jensen (Porcelain) - and antiques, and crystal and paintings. Tomorrow being Monday, we'll spend the <u>whole</u> day shopping! Whooppee!

    We walked around Saturday after we got here, and it's just like New York at night! People mill about and restaurants are open 'till all hours....

    Then today we went on the tours and made a complete tour of the shops we want to see tomorrow.

    We have eaten like <u>Kings</u> here! The luxury item has been <u>salads</u>. I haven't had such good food since we left home. The salad I had tonight was <u>delightful</u>: fruit with lemon in the juices. We eat in the terraces in front of the hotels - usually facing a square. The dinners are exorbitant for a Dane but only $3.50 for us! Steak last night and chicken tonight and fruit and vegetables and shrimp and things we haven't seen for so long!

The bakeries here are Marvelous - open on Sunday, and we got a coffee cake and five goodies for thirty-five cents! There are Chocolate stores here like we have drug stores - and it is SO good!...

Have I told you that everyone goes on a vacation in the late summer - and that they all wear these back-packs? You see them on people all over in Oslo, but I haven't seen many here in Copenhagen.

You remember that exhibit in the Art Institute—with the golden salt cellar like a ship—well, this "Pleasure House" (a storehouse for the King's priceless objects) has twenty rooms packed full of similar objects - tables that took 30 years to inlay, marbles, golden desks, settings for <u>72</u> in gold service, chalices, rock-crystal chandeliers and stuff - the jewels belonging to the royal family, their crowns, and coronation chair -- thousands of objects of beauty!!! Our heads are swimming!

Now tomorrow we'll buy a few objects for ourselves!

August 18

This is the day that we go to Harwich to get a steamer to Esbjerg and then by rail to Copenhagen. We're just loafing in the hotel while my hair dries....

Our days in Paris were crammed full of sight-seeing. So much so that we are glad to come to London! The plane—my first trip in a plane—was SO exciting. It was a <u>beautiful</u> day and we loved it so much that we immediately reserved seats to Glasgow to meet Muma Youngquist.

That trip was cloudy, and we saw the "aviator's rainbow" - a perfect circle around the shadow of the plane - and a quadruple rainbow, too! It cleared so that we saw the highlands from the air... then we spent the next day meeting Muma - and <u>shopping</u>....

NOTE: We met my mother at the airport during her stopover on her way to Sweden. She was carrying extra money for us that we were planning to use for the rest of our trip. In order to give it to us, though, she had to go into the ladies restroom. She had tucked away the money in her girdle! Then we hugged her and waved goodbye.

    We like the Scotch so much - much more than any of the other people we've been around. They are <u>cheerful</u>, and so very helpful. All we had to do was look puzzled, and two or three people would ask if they could help us. We decided between Edinburgh or going into the country and, since we hadn't had your letter, we decided on the country. We went up to Loch Lomond and took a launch around it - seeing manor-houses and castles. It is really very hilly farmland - you've never seen so many cows!
    This was the date of the "Gathering of the Clans" and there were kilts and tartans everywhere you looked - even a few bagpipers!...

    There is so much to write about that we've done - I'll just pick out a few things.
    We saw Gielgud in *A Winter's Tale* here in London - and I liked it more than any Shakespeare I had ever seen. He is <u>Marvelous</u> - then we topped it all off with "whipped cream": we stood in line (a *queue* here) for an hour and got returned ticket seats to the sold-out performance of Olivier and Leigh in *Anthony and Cleopatra* - an absolutely <u>Superb</u> production. The whole cast was excellent and the setting simple and effective. Olivier was <u>excellent</u> - you knew Anthony SO WELL when he did him and Leigh was a better Cleo even than Cornell.
    London has been greatly restored - shrapnel holes plastered - but you see great sections of rubble as you drive through the city. They live by it very nonchalantly. There were 132 churches destroyed during the blitz, but not one bridge! Westminster Abbey has many white windows, but many of the stained glass are still there. They've patched and plastered very well, but their whole life is hard. Food is so rationed and

good food is scarce. They're the most highly taxed people in the world and no relief in sight.

Now we're off to Copenhagen. We'll pick up two Finnish vases we left there and look again at Royal Copenhagen china. We found a pattern of china we liked here - but it is <u>very</u> high. See if you can find it and tell me the price there - it is a single moss rose on a cream-colored plate. English Bone - Royal Worcester - and let me know as soon as possible. If it is just as expensive there, I might wait.

Apartment in the Suburbs

As soon as we returned from our trip we were advised that the Foundation had located an apartment for us. It was not in town, but in one of the suburbs called Nordstrandshögda, up above Oslofjord. To reach it we had to take the Ekeberg train all the way from the Railway Station up along the hills on the east coast of Oslofjord to its final stop at Ljabru. From there it was just a short walk along our street, which is Bakketoppen (hilltop).

Our apartment was on the ground floor of a two-apartment building; the second floor was rented to the Henriksens. Henry was a journalist and his wife Ådel worked in an office somewhere. They had a pretty little daughter called Sissel, and Ådel often took her on short walks. They were great neighbors and we really enjoyed their company.

Our landlady, Mrs. Oftenes, met us at the apartment and showed us through. We were delighted to have found a place so convenient to the train and in such a pleasant community. We had a grocery store/meat market [Kjelle's] right by the train station, just a short walk away, so we settled in for our two-semester stay.

Mrs. Oftenes was a bit taken aback by our request that she remove some of the photos and paintings on the walls of the living room, but she took them down and stored them in her little outbuilding. We imagine that she was used to walls that were almost completely covered with memorabilia or paintings, but we preferred just the paintings that we enjoyed seeing each day. I'm sure she thought we had peculiar taste, but we didn't let that bother us.

There were other typically Norwegian touches to the apartment: in one corner of the living room we had the standard raised fireplace, and on the rugs of that room we had two huge and sometimes smelly polar bear skins, with their grinning heads that could be stumbling blocks in the night. The refrigerator in our kitchen was small, so we were forced to visit the local stores more than a couple times a week.

As colder weather approached we also had to cope with heating, which was all electric. We could heat up part of the house by wood, but Norwegians expected to dress warmly enough not to need a lot of artificial heat, and the high cost of electricity made cool homes sensible. We had a problem with that, because we generally kept our homes warmer so that we could be comfortable without bundling up in sweaters and such. But there was no heating at all in the bedroom. Norwegians assumed that the heavy comforters were sufficient.

The main reason for being careful about heating our apartment was that we would be penalized if we used too much electricity to keep our apartment warm. The electric company allocated a maximum power usage for each living unit and as soon as that maximum was exceeded the occupants paid a penalty rate for any excess, or *overforbruk* as they called it. All we had to do was look at our electric meter to tell if we were exceeding our maximum: we could see the wheel rotating wildly and the numbers rising.

Rita and I had some discussions about how we could manage to avoid the excess penalties, but we essentially gave up and decided that peace and comfort were more important than saving money on electricity.

Not long after we moved in, we heard explosions starting at eight o'clock in the morning, and wondered what they were. It turned out that people were blasting rock for foundations and other structures that needed to be below ground. Here in Norway, there is precious little topsoil in many places, and bedrock is visible all around. That bedrock had to be broken, and dynamite or something simpler was used. By the time we were outside, most of the blasting was over, and workmen were moving the results.

I happened to see how they worked, and how they prevented the blasted rock from being thrown all around the neighborhood. After they had placed a charge, they covered the blasting surface with heavy layers of tires bound together by chains or other chunks of rubber held together by cables. When a charge went off, the whole covering would rise slightly, keeping all of the rock particles from being spewed out.

After that, we could set our watches by the explosions and enjoyed following the progress of all those projects. .

Rita and I often went into Oslo together to shop, visit cultural attractions like Bygdöy, the island museum with the polar steamship *Fram*, Thor Heyerdahl's *Kon Tiki*, the fabulous Viking ships and the many old farm buildings from different sections of Norway. We loved to walk along Karl Johans Gate, Oslo's main street and wander through the many stores there, or shop for meat and vegetables in the huge market building nearby. A special treat was an evening dinner of cauliflower soup (that was all we could afford) at Teaterkafe before heading over to watch a play at the National Theater. A repertory theater, it offered a wide variety of classical works by Norwegian and continental playwrights. The National Gallery and the Vigeland sculptures at Frogner Park were other favorites.

Rita loved the Norwegian sweaters she saw everywhere, and decided to knit one. As a result, she became a regular customer at Husfliden, a chain of stores that specialized in Norwegian arts and crafts. They carried all kinds of patterns, yarn, and knitting accessories. Rita began knitting a *kofte*, the traditional Norwegian cardigan sweater, with colorful geometric patterns and oxidized silver buttons.

She became intrigued with the variety of patterns she saw on the sweaters people wore, so she started a booklet in which she noted down different ones that intrigued her. Almost every ride on the train into Oslo netted her at least one new pattern. She even followed people walking in town who wore interesting sweaters, trying to write down the patterns quickly. By the time we left for America she had knitted two sweaters and had yarn and patterns for many more. Over the years Rita knitted several sweaters, each one different, for the two of us and for each of our children. She even entered some of her sweaters in the crafts competition of the Tompkins Country Fair that was held while we were living in Ithaca.

We soon became good customers of our local grocer Mr. Skjelle, whose store was located at the end of our street, just up from the railway station. Having only a small refrigerator, we were forced to make frequent trips there for vegetables, cheese, bread, eggs and milk. He had a wide selection of fresh-baked bread, and our favorite was a sweet rye. A real treat for us was a Gouda cheese sandwich with warm slices of that bread, together with cokes that we had chilled in a snowdrift by our door.

One of our daily joys was watching the different birds that came to visit the feeder that was attached to the outside of our house, right by our kitchen window. We had a chart on the wall by the feeder with illustrations of the various Norwegian birds and their names, and we enjoyed marking off the ones we had spotted. The most prevalent birds were the chickadees (kjötmes), the crows (different from ours) and the magpies. But we also saw birds that we never saw in the US, such as the blue-topped titmouse (*blåmes*), the wagtail (*linerle*), the bullfinch (*bofink*), and the chaffinch (*dompap*). One day we heard a loud sound outside, as if someone had hammered the side of the house. Looking out, we saw that it was a *hackspett* (like our pileated woodpecker), that had been tempted by the old cheese on our feeder.

We tried to keep track of all the different birds we saw, and marked them off on our chart. Most of the common varieties came, and seemed unconcerned about the fact that we were often looking at them through the kitchen window. One day we left the window open and came into the kitchen to find a friendly chickadee perched on the calfskin shade of our floor lamp. I don't know why he was attracted to it, but he was pecking away at it. As soon as we came in, he flew up and began fluttering madly around the room, trying to find its way out. We opened the window wider, used a long broom to encourage the bird to move toward to the open window and were relieved when it suddenly decided to fly out to freedom.

My weekdays followed a fairly standard pattern: I took the train into town and a streetcar to the library and spent several hours there doing research on my study topic. I was trying to find as many 19th century Norwegian writers as I could who were influenced by the Icelandic sagas and particularly by Snorre's *Heimskringa*, or the sagas of the kings of Norway. Whenever I found a likely candidate, I tried to read what he/she had written, in order to get a sense of what material had been used and how the author transformed or interpreted it.

This process took much time, and I amassed considerable material that I thought might become the basis for a critical study when I began my studies at Cornell.
Each afternoon when I finished working in the library I would either start right home (except on my boxing evenings) or Rita would come to meet me in town for an evening out.

Honey Arrives

In December, Honey came to visit us and help Rita during the days before our baby was expected and for a short while thereafter. Rita felt so much better having her nearby as the expected delivery day approached.

It's been quite a long time since I sat down to write to you all... I've known Honey was keeping you informed, but now I'll inform you about Honey!

We ran ourselves ragged the first week till Xmas, seeing shops and town and getting Honey filled up with "Xmas spirit" here. Of course you know we've had no snow at all... The Norwegians are annoyed, and we were homesick for a white Xmas! It's ironic isn't it, that last year they had ten feet here, and this year you're having a record, and we have none.

Of course, they are also beginning to be worried because of the Olympics. They have to get the courses ready. It may mean shipping some in from the North!

But enough of that... We got to the dock after the *Mormac-saga* was in. They were early and we were late...but as soon as the gangplank was down and the customs officials safely on board, we got permission to go too, and boarded with our lily of the valley plant, coffee-cake and much excitement. Customs passed Honey through very quickly, and with the trunk on the taxi off we went!

She certainly looks pretty in her new coat and hat, and cute boots... and the new purse! She still can't find things in it, it is so BIG!

As I said, we bummed and shopped almost every day... Went to hear a boy's chorus sing the Christmas songs in their City Hall and finally were ready for Christmas. It was a very happy one for us having Honey here, and you all sent so much that our tree was just crowded with packages.

A few days before Christmas we went into town to visit the *Stortorget* (the main marketplace) and pick out a nice tree for our apartment. The selection was huge, and it was fun to wander around the aisles of trees and see Norwegian families choosing their trees. It was cold, so we stopped for hot chocolate and then went back to make our decision. We found a magnificent tall fir tree, and I dragged it over to the train. Rita and Honey sat in the passenger seats during our trip back, while I stood in the wide middle area (where people board) to hold onto our tree.

We had stockings hung up and since we didn't have a big enough stocking for all of the food goodies that Honey brought, we got out Eric's long winter underwear and tied off the feet...it just held all of the cake-mixes and dates and raisins and fudge mix! Then we had pancakes and opened presents...but another letter about that...that is a real undertaking to thank you all for our books and shirts, and pencil set, and puddings, and my beautiful ear-rings, Kay. That is a perfect match, and so well made! And it is amazing to me that you got your Xmas shopping done so early! Life was probably pretty exciting there with Honey getting off!

Yesterday I didn't feel like going into town, and sent Honey off for her first day on her own. That was at noon...and she had things to do that we thought would take a few hours. It got dark about four, and no Honey! Five passed, and then six! And finally she blew in, wide-eyed and completely pooped out!

She had walked and walked, and occasionally around in circles... She accomplished the things that she started out to do...and got along without Norwegian...and was certainly excited by it all. We giggled and giggled about it all... But she knows that town pretty well by now, and that day of orientation was a help, so that when I am in the hospital, she will be able to get around pretty easily.

A Nation on Skis

Cross-country skiing is such a part of Norwegian life that I had to try it. Whole families go out walking on woodland paths until winter, and then they ski on many of the same trails. You can see them in family groups, with the little ones working to keep up with their parents and older siblings.

I went to a large sports store in Oslo and outfitted myself. They sold me basic cross-country equipment: a pair of good ski-boots and solid wood skis, heavy and long, fitted with the combination cable-type bindings used by the Norwegian ski troops. The bindings could be converted from cross-country to downhill by simply locking the cable to the heel under a projection that would keep the heel from rising off the ski. I also bought a standard *Berganser* touring backpack plus a kit of various waxes, from soft red for above freezing, green for around zero Centigrade and then hard blue for all lower temperatures. The store gave me a dispenser of special base wax. They told me that waxing was important, because if you didn't have the right kind of wax you couldn't slide on the snow and your skis wouldn't grip the snow when you tried to go uphill.

I was all set for skiing, but had no idea what I was doing. As soon as we had enough snow on the road in front of our house, I tried out my skis there and also tried going down our driveway into the backyard. I sat down a lot because I didn't know how to turn, slow down or stop.

I asked our upstairs friends for help, and Henry Henriksen immediately offered to take me out to Nordmarka on a ski-touring trip the next weekend.

Nordmarka is a huge area just north of Oslo. It is interlaced with walking trails that become ski-trails during the winter. Because of the unique Norwegian laws regarding private property, woodland and uncultivated farmland are not fenced, and the public has the right to use that land for recreation. The interlacing trails in that area are marked with signs giving distances to intersections, kiosks and other landmarks, so navigation is no problem. And the trails were always well-groomed, because Norwegians knew enough not to damage the trails by walking on them.

A great attraction in Nordmarka were the many kiosks that offered hot bouillon, coffee, tea, oatmeal and other snacks for hikers and skiers. Every week *Aftenposten* carried an article with a suggested weekend ski-outing that was always planned so that skiers could take a half-way stop for refreshments. But it wasn't necessary to follow the weekend route; you could just set out in any direction and, when you felt hungry or thirsty, you could generally rely on coming to a sign fairly soon directing you to a kiosk. When you stopped at one, you took off your skis and stuck them in the snow banks near the entrance, and clomped inside for a wonderful relaxed snack-time. Some people carried snacks in their backpacks and depended on the kiosks for coffee, tea or hot chocolate.

When we reached the first ski trail in Nordmarka, Henry showed me the basics: how to slow down on hills by snow-plowing, how to turn by snowplowing and placing weight on the ski away from the direction of your turn; how to turn when the trail divides by stepping into one different track with one ski and lifting the other ski and placing it alongside. That gave me confidence that I could handle downhill trails.

Going uphill was a different matter. If the hill was not too steep, I could continue the regular glide steps, or walk up by raising my skis and placing them flat on the surface, relying on my wax to prevent backsliding. When all else failed, I could herringbone my way up, which meant using my poles behind me for support and a little propulsion. Finally, he showed me how to side-step my way up really steep hills.

On level areas, I had to get the proper rhythm, and Henry made it look so easy. It took a while for me to imitate his long, gliding stride, but I gradually found myself shifting my weight smoothly from one ski to the other as I alternated pushing and gliding. It was necessary to coordinate arms and legs, because properly-timed propulsion from the poles was important.

I loved skiing on the flat. When I was able to fall into a rhythm, I fairly skimmed over the snow, in a zone. It was almost hypnotizing.

I went out skiing with Henry twice and returned exhausted both times, but fell in love with the sport. Almost every weekend, and sometimes during the week, I would take my ski things, catch the train down to Oslo, board the *trikk* up past the ski-jump at

Holmenkollen, and set out on a winter hike. There were times when I really felt like one of the legendary *Birkebeiner*.

During the Winter Olympics I caught a trikk to the area where the 50-kilometer X-country race was held and went out to stand by the competition trail along with many others. The spectator area was anywhere you wanted to be—except on the trail—so it appeared somewhat disorganized. I chose a spot where I could see the coming contestants far away and then follow their course for a while after they passed in front of me. They started at intervals so the many skiers were widely scattered and only bunched up when skiers were overtaking others and waiting for a convenient place to pass.
Without a radio it was impossible to have any sense of the progress of the race; i.e. we never knew who was leading and we had to wait until we got back to civilization to get the results.

Now and then on the trail I met and chatted with Norwegians. We were brothers there, sharing the same outdoor experience.

Practicing my Norwegian

Early in the fall, not long after we moved into Mrs. Oftenes's apartment, I decided that I needed some regular practice speaking Norwegian. Henry Henriksen wanted to practice his English, I felt, and I found it difficult to use my Norwegian with people who I knew spoke very good English. I wanted to find a group where no one spoke English, and decided that sports might be the answer.

Rita was not really pleased that I chose to join a boxing club, but I thought that boxing might be a sport where I could contribute something to a team and also have opportunities to speak Norwegian. I joined Oslo-Odd, and that proved to be a great choice. I worked out with them twice a week, sparring and chatting, and felt that that really helped me with pronunciation.

Our club went to three boxing tournaments while I was there. The first was in October, at Stavanger, south of Oslo, where I won. In late November we traveled to the Oslo suburb of Lilleström, where I managed to win again. My next and last bout was in the Oslo Championships in early March. I was technically a light-heavyweight, but decided to box as a heavyweight at Oslo.

My reasoning was that I had seen the only fighter in my light-heavyweight class and didn't think that he was very good, while the one in heavyweight class—Torbjörn Breiby—had represented Oslo in a *landskamp* (national meet) against Denmark. He was a bit taller than I was and probably had as long a reach as mine, but I preferred to lose to a good boxer than win against someone who was not much of a boxer.

My second, an older fellow named Torleif, had boxed for twenty years. He spent the time before my bout giving me hints about how to handle Breiby. These consisted mainly of variations of "Be careful" and "Take it easy." Breiby was wide but narrow chested, with average arms and long legs. His shoulders, added to the length of his arms, gave him a reach perhaps a bit longer than mine. He was also fairly fast and well-coordinated, but I had heard that he was rather easy to daze. After about 45 minutes of dancing around and getting warmed up, our turn finally came.

We had met before; I had spoken with him quite a while during the *landskamp* against Denmark, just before his bout, and had lent him my hand-bandages. As we were about to enter the arena, he bowed and said, "*Apres vous*." We got into the ring and I went into the far corner to get some rosin on the soles of my shoes. Then we were introduced in turn, each of us bowing to the audience. When the referee called us into the center of the ring to meet one another, he told us to avoid low blows and hitting with the inside of our gloves.

As we met in the ring after the bell, I knew I would have to get in close in order to be effective at all. I had decided to wait out this first round and experiment with counter-punching. I had all sorts of combinations that I had planned to throw in the fight, but not very many of them got used. He hit me with a couple of jabs, and I think I nicked him with a few. It was a new experience for me to box against someone who was taller than I was, and had longer arms. As far apart as we were, I kept expecting his punches to land short, but they would come right up to me and connect – not hard, but enough to feel. I had been used to seeing punches like that just fall short.

During the first half of the round we just jabbed and felt one another out. Then Breiby came at me and I hit him on the chin with my right and he went down. He was shaken by the blow, but was ready to fight by the time the referee reached the count of eight. The rule in Norway is that if a boxer is downed, he must take a mandatory eight-count, and the referee decides then whether the bout should continue or not. The rest of the first round was a continuation of the first half: nothing startling.

As I sat in my corner waiting for round two, my second encouraged me, saying that in the next round I should try to get in closer before throwing my right. Breiby started by throwing four jabs, missing with two but connecting with the other two. Then he got me with a right to the side of my head that shook me, and as I moved to my right he connected with a left that sent me to the canvas. I had the funniest warm and comfortable feeling in my head as I was going down. I didn't lose consciousness at all, though, and was up before the referee got to the count of two.

I quickly had to revise my strategy. In my other bouts, I had gotten a comfortable lead in the first two rounds and merely coasted in the third. But I had to knock Breiby down now just to even the score, I thought. We sparred about a bit, and then I feinted with a left and got him with a right in the stomach: a good blow, I thought. Then I tried a one-two and was short with my right because I wasn't close enough. I tried once more, and this time he was coming toward me, and I caught him with a hard right in his face, and he went down immediately. I could feel the impact down to my toes, and it was probably the hardest punch I had ever thrown. Breiby got up at the count of eight, but almost fell down again, so the referee stopped the fight. I was so glad to have the bout over and still have my unbroken nose.

Our fight was not highly regarded by the press, because Norwegians really appreciate good technical boxing more than power punching. The difference between the American and the Norwegian approach to boxing is pretty well summed up in the final instructions that the referee gives. In America, the referee tells the boxers, "Go to your corners and come out fighting." In Europe, or at least in Norway, he tells them, "Go to your corners and box."

Rita was in the stands watching the fight, and she didn't like the idea of my continuing to box. She persuaded me that I ought to quit, which I did.

Anyway, the newspaper article the next day called our fight a slugfest, and said that it was clear from the outset that it wouldn't go the distance.

Winter Olympics

The Winter Olympics were a major event for Norway to host. It was a huge investment for the country, and all Norway wanted the Games to succeed. It proved to be a good investment, because the country attracted considerable foreign exchange.

We obviously couldn't see everything, so we divided our schedules so we could see the events that really interested each of us. Rita and Honey went to see the men's and women's figure skating (Dick Button) and the women's slalom; I went to see the 10,000 meter men's speed-skating, the men's giant slalom at Norafjell, and the 50 kilometer cross-country skiing in Nordmarka. All three of us went to watch the men's ski-jumping at Holmenkollen.

I was first to go, and was driven to Norafjell by Mr. and Mrs. Marcusson. We arrived at 11:00 a.m., leaving plenty of time for the start, which was scheduled for 1:00 p.m. We reached the base of the hill around noon, and eventually started climbing, because the starting line was 3,000 feet up and 1-1/2 miles away. Since the others weren't enthusiastic about climbing all the way up to the starting line and didn't mind splitting up, I went on ahead by myself.

I clambered up the 40° slope as well as I could, slipping on rocks, sinking almost up to my knees in snow, and puffing all the time. If the hill is so steep that a person has a hard time climbing it on foot, you can imagine what a time one would have trying to go down the hill on skis without missing a gate or injuring himself. I stopped at intervals on the way up and took photographs down toward the finish line. After I had gone about one-fourth of the way, I couldn't see the bottom any longer, just the lake below and the mountains in the distance. By the time I was within 300 yards of the starting line, the first skier began his descent and zoomed by me. He was Zeno Colo, the star of the Italian team, who had won two world championships at Aspen, Colorado, last year. I got a fine picture of him just as he was making a turn into one of the 63 gates on the course.

I had come to see Stein Eriksen (star of the Norwegian team) start, and reached the starting line just as the tenth skier was leaving. Stein Eriksen was number 12 and the eventual winner. I got a good photo of him just as he was leaving the starting gate. Then

I started back down the hill. My idea was to see the course from all possible angles, observe the skiers on the way down in the different places and end up at the bottom of the course just before the end of the race. There were 85 skiers from all over the world, and each of them was allowed just one try at the hill. A fall on the way down and a skier was essentially out of the running, since the difference between victory and third place in the giant slalom is usually a matter of tenths of a second.

Three evenings in a row we went to see figure skating. The first night, when the women performed, I stayed home and took care of Vikar. The other two nights, when the men skated and then the couples, we were all together, because we arranged for a baby sitter. The high point of those two nights was Dick Button. He had everything the others had and more. He made everything look so smooth and easy that a person would feel that he too could go out there and do it. What we thought was so marvelous about his skating was his grace and fluid movement. His arms were part of him, contributing to the effect of his skating, and not just appendages waving around. He interpreted his music flawlessly, coming to stops at just the right times, slowing down with the music and ending exactly as his music stopped.

The pairs skating competition was more *arty* than the men's individual competition, and was most enjoyable. Afterward, Dick Button gave a short exhibition of his skating again. This time, not under the strain of competition, he outdid the best of his singles skating, and positively amazed the crowd with his jumps, twists, and turns.

Rita and Honey went out to the women's slalom competition at Rödkleiva and perched themselves rather unsteadily on the hillside. They watched Andrea Mead Lawrence make two flawless runs and earn a gold medal.

The next and last important event was the special jumping competition at Holmenkollen. We got up early and took the train into town and caught another to travel from there up to Holmenkollen. Standing room extends to all the hills that surround the jump itself wherever a person can see the competition. So we searched around for a place to stand where we could see well. We found one that was fine—a little prominence that gave us a clear view of the jump and no possibility of having someone stand in front of us and block our view. I hacked out little standing notches for our feet so that we wouldn't slip, and then we stood and waited, and waited.

Finally, at 1:30 p.m., the competition began. We saw some excellent jumping, and the Norwegian team provided a good share of it. Their men (each country is allowed only four men to compete in each event) did very well. Arnfinn Bergmann came in first, Torbjörn Falkanger took second, Halvor Hæss took fourth, and Arne Hoel took sixth.

More Skiing

The fellow who was supposed to take me to Norafjell suggested that I come out to Westmarka and take a little trip with him there, so that's what I did. I went out early and reached his station (Billingstad) at 9:00 a.m. Then out we went. He took me over the route that goes to a place called Sollihögda. He said that most skiers take a bus from town to Sollihögda and ski back to Billingstad, but he wanted to do it differently. So up we went.

My skis were very hard to handle because I had not put the right kind of wax on them. They kept slipping backward on the uphill slopes. That meant that I was using my arms most of the time, and they got tired. At times my poles would go right into the snow two feet, so that I got no support at all from them, and then all I did was slip backward. But aside from some places that had deep snow (I still haven't learned to maneuver in that kind of loose snow if I am going at any speed), I managed without falling down once on the way there.

When we reached Sollihögda, we had a little bite to eat: doughnuts and hot cocoa and Cokes. Then we started back. My feet were beginning to hurt something awful by then because the skin was wearing off my heel. But we kept up a jolly pace at first. Then he decided to swing off onto a different trail, one that wasn't so well traveled as the rest. That was my Waterloo!

The snow was deep and soft, and when my skis weren't sinking into it my poles were. I went into the snow so much that it got between my stockings and inside of my ski boots and melted. My feet were sloshing wet, but on we went. We stopped at a place on the way (the Association for Advancement of Skiing has set up snack stops all over the area) where they offered coffee, sandwiches, bullion and soft drinks and had another little bite to eat. They had some beautiful oranges there that were very easy to peel and tasted so sweet. I had three of them and could have eaten four more.

After a rest there (no use hurrying to catch our train because it wouldn't arrive for another forty minutes) we started again on our leisurely way. We got back to the station about 4:00 p.m. By that time we had covered a little more than 28 miles.

Just before the end of winter the Fulbrighters arranged a trip to an inn at Lillehammer. We had great fellowship, and some of us were able to ski on the nearby cross-country trails. We made good time through the woods and over the fields, and I felt good about my skiing, but I had my comeuppance on a hill there. I looked down the hill and saw that the trail went straight down and continued onto a wide flat expanse. I decided to go down full speed and then coast out onto the field.

At the bottom, just as I came to the flat, I had an unfortunate surprise. The snow there was very thin and the surface of the field itself was wildly uneven because it had been plowed recently. I soon lost my balance as I bounced over the furrows, and then found myself tumbling and plowing my own furrow with my behind. The final result was a broken ski-tip and a badly bruised rear end, so I had to limp my way back to the inn.

New Arrival

Rita had so few problems during her first months of pregnancy that it hardly affected our life together. There were no limits on what she could do or wanted to do. Even later she was not really limited by any pregnancy woes. She could feel herself enlarging, of course, and then the sensations of movement inside. She would put her hands on her tummy and say, "I can feel you inside there, Boom (that was her nickname for the baby)."

As soon as we arrived in Norway, we signed up for Trygdekassa, the Norwegian system for universal medical insurance. We paid our monthly premiums and thereby were assured of proper medical care for Rita during pregnancy and delivery of the baby. We were not restricted in our choice of physicians, though we had to pay the difference if we chose to work with a private one. We chose the chief obstetrician in the State Hospital as her primary doctor.

He examined Rita and pronounced her fit. He told me that it was unlikely that he would actually come to deliver the baby.

He said, "Your wife is strong as an ox. You don't even need me there. The Red Cross Hospital has good midwives; they've delivered many more babies than I have. If your wife has a problem, there's a doctor on the staff who can help, and I will also be available if you need me. But I don't think you will."

Rita was not all that consoled by what the good doctor said, but she said nothing.

Honey arrived before Christmas, and Rita was delighted to have her there to help. We got through the holidays and then the waiting began.

With each day the baby became more active, moving around, punching with its fists and feet from time to time, and that amused us greatly. Rita said that she felt as big as a house, and joked about having to waddle around. Finally, on January 12, she began feeling contractions. We timed them and when they began coming regularly I took her to the Red Cross Hospital in a cab.

The following is from a letter I wrote the next day to my parents about the big event:

About 5:00 a.m. Saturday morning, just as I had finished studying and was crawling into bed, Rita told me that very slight contractions had begun. She wasn't sure whether they were really contractions or not, but since this was the first time in all the nine months that she had felt the way she did, she and I decided that something important was happening. We weren't risking much in making that decision, because by that time the baby was already twelve days overdue by our calculations.

I went to sleep as soon as possible in order to be fresh and awake in case the baby surprised us and came quickly. I awoke at ten, but no appreciable change. We three spent the day doing much of nothing—we played some cards after dinner to pass the time and to keep Rita up and around. About 11:00 that evening Rita felt that it would be best for us to go to the hospital, so we called a cab and rode down.

As it turned out, we were much too early; Rita's cervix had not yet really begun to dilate. The nurse gave her a sedative and sent Honey and me home. We felt that even though we were much too early it was better to have Rita there at the hospital resting rather than at home, where we could never be certain what might happen. We went home, ate and slept until 5:30 the next morning. Then we took a cab down to the hospital, arriving about 6:25.

Rita was awake and feeling all right, though she was a bit groggy from the sedative. Honey and I sat with Rita in her room, which was small but pleasant, with white walls, double doors to keep out noise, a nice view of the grounds and a comfortable bed. Rita's contractions had continued all night, but were never severe enough to do more than slightly rouse her from her slumber.

We sat and talked, and then Rita asked me to read *The Green Pastures* to her (we had started on it the night before). At about 8:00 a.m. the midwife came in and gave Rita an injection to strengthen the contractions. Immediately after the shot, Rita began to feel the contractions noticeably. She tried to do her breathing as her prenatal book instructed, taking deep breaths and trying to relax. Soon she found that breathing deeply did little good, so she switched to quick panting…that helped.

All this time I was checking the intervals between the contractions, letting Rita know how much longer each one might last (to make her feel that it would be over soon and she could rest for a while), talking softly to her. I said, "That's fine" "Good girl" "Don't press," and other things that I thought would encourage her. None of these contractions made her <u>extremely</u> uncomfortable, but there were a few times when she said that her breath had caught and she had been unable to keep from pressing down and that had caused some pain, but never enough so that she was desperate.

Rita was very groggy between contractions and often said things that she herself knew didn't make sense. From 8:00 a.m. until about 11:45 a.m. she continued having these stronger contractions, and we were both doing our best to give her moral support and taking turns reading the play for her. Then the midwife and her assistant came in to see how far along Rita was. I told them that there had been no noticeable change in the intensity of her contractions and that they still came at intervals of about three minutes.

Well, Rita surprised all of us. The midwife found that Rita's cervix was fully dilated and everything was ready for her to give birth. Rita had wanted to have some ether a little earlier so she would be more relaxed, but the midwife had said that it would be better to wait a bit, because the body reacts to ether better when it is first given. They try to use the ether as close as possible to the actual delivery.

At that point, we were asked to leave and Rita was alone with Elsa and her aide. About fifteen minutes later, the aide came out with the baby and stopped to let us see him. The first thing I did when I looked at the baby was ask, "En gutt?" (A boy?).

She nodded, "Ja, en fin gutt" (Yes, a fine boy) and assured us that we needn't worry about Rita either—that she was fine.

So Vikar arrived, and he was a happy, healthy baby. His birth certificate consisted of a blank page with the name and address of the hospital at the top. All that was written on it was the Norwegian equivalent of: "Born: a boy." Underneath that pithy statement was Elsa's signature. That document was all I needed to get a consular certificate attesting to the birth abroad of an American citizen. At the same time the consul added our son's name to Rita's passport.

Because of our membership in the Norwegian medical insurance system, our total expense for Rita's time in the hospital, including three days of semiprivate quarters, and all related expenses, came to $180.

January 29, 1952

Eric says he wrote you about the baby's coming. . . . I will want to put it in the baby book when we get back. Eric was a tremendous help to me, and it really went pretty easily. I've felt fine, and could hardly wait to come home. I had purposely made Eric feel very much a part of the actual delivery of the baby—all but 15 minutes—so that it is as much his child as mine, and he really feels his fatherhood. . . .

With Vikar's arrival, our world underwent an instant, complete change. For Rita, though, it was a transforming event. She had always been creative and interested in handwork like knitting and sewing, but after Vikar arrived, he became her center of interest. He had been a part of her, and now he was a new part of our lives—another human being.

She was fascinated by his behavior and his development, as you will see in the selections from the letters that she wrote. She was at her best in writing about her children, mostly because she wanted her letters to be a record—for herself as well as for our parents—of what they were doing.

Here it is, 1952, and I am now a MOTHER! It certainly is wonderful to be a family... I can barely stand it to be away from the baby! Honey and I went to town for a few hours today, and I could hardly wait to get home and see him again! And Eric is worse than I am! He never looks at Vikar without smiling... and that's a fact! He revels in feeding him...and constantly has me come over to see him smile, or purse his lips, or do some other cute thing. And I have to admit...I've never seen a baby that was HALF as cute as ours!

A few weeks later:

Vikar is the cutest baby you ever saw! He spends most of his day trying to please us, by talking and gurgling, and gooing, and when you respond, he just shines! He likes having Eric play with him most of all, and fairly—not quite—laughs with the fun of it. He is so very well and good... We thank our health and lucky stars that he is good natured and healthy... we have no worries at all about his ever feeling bad, or even having a stomach ache! We've been taking pictures furiously for you all, and will have the reel developed soon so that you can see the prodigy....

Boom sees his feet now! He just lies there with his feet straight up in the air and stares at them... We put the rattle-boots on, and he kicks all day now. He laughs a lot now - even just because he is glad to see you! And he is very ticklish!

February

Honey and I are planning a trip to Stockholm on Monday. She doesn't want to go home without seeing some of Sweden, so she had planned to go this week. Then when Eric was going skiing, she put it off until next week, and since I'm not nursing the baby we decided that I could go too...

We're going on the train on Monday, and probably come back on Thursday. I'm not sure I'll be able to stay away from the baby that long. Eric will be alone with him, and will probably be glad to have us home again. He does fine at feeding him, but he doesn't hear him when he cries at night! Too, he is always trying to fix the holes in the nipples and makes them too big! He'll have his fill of washing diapers—but other than that it should all go smoothly. It'll be a real initiation into fatherhood, though, won't it?

As always, Rita and Honey had a grand time together in Stockholm. They went shopping all day, every day, and went to a movie every evening.

I had another session of babysitting in early March, when Rita and Honey went to Copenhagen for sightseeing, window-shopping, bakery visiting and movies again. When they returned late on March 12, Honey had just three more days before she had to catch her train to Paris. She was going to board the Queen Mary at Cherbourg March 22 for her homeward trip.

Those last three days were busy for Honey. First she went on a guided tour of Oslo, and I took her to see Vigeland's sculpture collection at Frogner Park. The last two days were dedicated to shopping. Rita went with her and helped pick out presents to take home to friends and relatives: all kinds of porcelain figurines, little dishes, some bowls, etc.

Sometime in March, after Honey left for Paris:

I'm in the kitchen, Honey, looking at the blue plant you left (which still has a lot of buds to come out) . . .and the violets that have wilted now, and I'm thinking how very fast the time flew by us. It seems as though we just wrote yesterday urging you to come. . . and now we have Boom and you have come and gone so quickly!

We certainly hated to see your train go. . . We didn't start back for a while. I thought of you so often and was so glad to get your letter from Paris that the train hadn't been too much of a chore. Then we talked about you in Paris. . . and in the rain, typical! And finally you are on the ship right now. . .just after breakfast, probably embroidering on the costume and chatting with someone. . . .

We're so glad you came, and so glad you were here for Boom, and we'll be home soon, too (we keep telling ourselves).

Our trips were such fun. . . now I'm not sure which I liked the best, but I think it was Copenhagen. . . .It's finally snowing here now, and everybody is on the way to the store on their *sparkstöts*. That certainly was a queer twist of fate. Here, you were getting rested and refreshed, and finally sleeping well, and that *sparkstöt* threw you! I hope Dr. Cochran can straighten it out soon. . . .

I bought a HEPATICA plant in the market. . .It is such a sweet little plant—in moss, with purple and pink flowers. It makes me feel as though spring is here! And the snow is flying down!

Eric's going to the library every day, early, to get his work done and get ready for the Cornell tests of Literature. So I pack Vikar up in our sheepskin bag and wheel him down to the store. He doesn't like to be swaddled, and cries the minute the carriage stops. . . then after I've shopped, I wheel him home, and the return trip puts him to sleep! So he sleeps on the porch for a while and comes in hungry as a bear.

I asked the doctor if I could "air" him at six weeks, and he said, "The baby must be outside five to six hours a day." Wow! He hasn't had that much of a dose yet!. . .

So now we are going to be old stay-at-homes . . .seeing any movies in shifts—first one and then the other. It won't hurt us. When the spring comes I want to go to their folk-museum, and we probably will ask the baby-sitter to take Vikar that day. We go for walks with Vikar every now and then—mostly on Sundays.

Spring Arrives

April 17, 1952 (after Honey had returned to Princeholm)

I seem to be a little turned around!

Eric has gone to the library, Boom is asleep, the ironing is just dampened, and I have time to write. . . .

Easter was according to the 'pace of life' here—a week's holiday for all stores and banks, including Kjelle's—which meant going three days with the same milk (he opened the store one day just to sell milk) and the whole week with the same bread. We made out alright, thank heaven . . .The snow was just left in one patch on the lawn, and Eric put it in a box, so we had an outdoor refrigerator that way. It melted on the last day.

We've had spring weather consistently - blue skies, mild breezes and even the puddles have dried. The children all had out their hip boots and slickers two weeks ago, and now that those puddles are dry every now and then I see a little boy wistfully standing in a hole, and I like to think that he is imagining where the water came to on his boots.

The spring birds are back, too, and we see new kinds every morning: their equivalent of a robin, a thrush, a brown thrasher, a chaffinch (beautiful) and a funny bird called a wagtail (*Linerle*). It's a little black and white bird that runs very fast... Eric says it is like a 'roadrunner'. It chatters all the time it is looking for bugs, and wags its tail incessantly. There are a lot of them. . . .

Tonight, Eric is speaking to a group of adults in Moss, a suburb of Oslo, on American literature. It's been a good review for him, and he's looking forward to this evening. It probably won't be a large group...but all will speak English. I'm going, too, and Sara [our baby sitter] will be here with Boom. He's cuter than ever, more cuddly, more talkative, more smiling, and more intelligent. He holds his rattle now, and plays with it . . . and plays with his hands, too.

I'm going to Kjelle's now, and will take him. It's mild these days, but there is still snow on the ground. We've had the *Dompap*s (bullfinches) in our wheatsheaf every day this week, Honey. I think they're here to stay! They certainly are pretty!

Eric's speech went very well last night . . . informal, with people responding very well. They tend to sit like stones here and kill a discussion, but a very good one got started. It was a bit of American Lit, especially Jack London's adventures, but they read the classics—or greats—too, and Eric seemed very much at ease, giving an outline of American lit., and authors, and then some selections, and finally a discussion of current works. One of the men there had been in St. Paul for eight years—a carpenter—but the Depression drove him home.

Then there was a knife-sharpener here yesterday who had been seven years on the Great Lake freighters—thirty-six years ago. The love of his life still writes to him from Bay City . . . He had the real Scandinavian accent. . . and reminded me of the Captain in *Anna Christie*.

Vikar is as cute as ever - bigger (13 lbs. 14 oz.) and plump faced. He talks in all registers now - and loves to be on his tummy and kick his feet. He went to the doctor again, and was pronounced fit and fine, and the doctor said giving him Pablum would give him colitis... but I still am. He laughs out loud now, too, and loves to play as much as ever. He really has to be pretty hungry not to smile all the time I'm trying to feed him. He watches me with those bright eyes, and the minute I look his way, out comes the wide smile and a gurgle or two. Oh he's fun. He's drooling, too, so maybe teeth may be on the way. He wakes up smiling and goes to sleep the same way, at about eight o'clock. He holds his rattle too, and is getting more and more control of his hands....

Eric has been reading to me in the evening while I finish his sweater (it just needs the buttons now). . . .It should be ready for him this evening. We started with poetry, went through a pioneer story *The Deerslayer*, and then to Sinclair Lewis's *Main Street*. We enjoyed the last most of all; really wonderful description and a good plot. Then last night we started and finished, but didn't very much like, *A Farewell to Arms*.

The two Erics are busy reading and playing. . . and I have time to write.

I'm afraid I have been wayward since I wrote you last time, for I went to town and spent a disgraceful amount on three rattles and two teething rings! I guess he didn't need so many but he is so thrilled over the string of colored rattle-balls (we stretch them over his buggy) that I have to take them away every little while. The teething rings are still a puzzle to him, though he has started to drool. I don't really think he wants them yet. His chief delight in life is still playing with Eric. . . He laughs out loud now, and loved loud kisses and bed-bouncing. They play together every evening when Eric gets home, and both love it. He would rather play than eat, still, and he watches you the whole time you are near him so that he can smile the minute you look at him.

We're having all the Fulbright students here this Friday evening – three cakes and Jell-O and coffee. We'll probably play Charades. . . .

You should see the marketplace now! All the flowers in the world, it seems – all colors, plants and cut ones—wild flowers, spring flowers, florist flowers, tree branches, fruit-tree buds –just EVERYTHING!

Some days later we had a happy goodbye picnic with other Fulbrighters. We also had another party with the Henriksens. When we finally left in early May, Karen Slaby, wife of one of the Fulbrighters, helped us manage our buggy and Vikar as we struggled with our luggage down to the waiting ship. Some of the other Fulbrighters were on the wharf waving to us as the ship pulled out.

After we boarded the *Oslofjord*, Rita wrote a postcard to her parents and sent it from Christiansand:

Hi –
We have a Wonderful stateroom – large, comfortable – with heater and fan and three beds, closets. We're <u>delighted</u> with the ship and the service. Happy as larks – second honeymoon (or third). Boom good as gold – See you soon.
      Love and 1,000 more

Except for the major events that we have described, our life in Norway was really a tapestry of unconnected memories, each one precious to us. Rita would have had her own list, but these are some of mine, not in any order of importance:

- waiting for the train at Ljabru station and, as we descended towards Oslo, enjoying the ever-changing views of Oslofjord in the morning;
- the moments of satisfaction I felt after conversations in Norwegian with strangers when I felt that I had communicated directly, without hesitation and without branding myself as a foreigner;
- standing hand in hand with Rita at the summit of Bergen's funicular railway, looking down at the city and feeling the rush of joy and anticipation at our first glimpse of Norway;
- strolling with Rita along the footpaths in the esplanade that divides Karl Johansgate;
- the swish of skis on new snow and the feeling of speed when my stride and pole movement were in complete synch;
- resting in a kiosk in Nordmarka after a cross-country tour, with my chilled hands holding a cup of hot chocolate;
- the scent of spruce and fir trees cut for sale at Christmas at Stortorget;
- browsing through the old Norwegian classics in the *antikvariat* (old book store) near the University;
- the first sight of the Viking ships in their church-like exhibition hall;
- snuggling together with Rita under the thick Norwegian *dyne* to warm ourselves in the our ice-cold bedroom; and
- holding our first-born and realizing that we had received a wonderful gift and at the same time a heavy responsibility for a new life and a new future.

Back to America

Rita wrote this next letter while we were sailing home aboard the SS *Oslofjord*. On the way, she managed to squeeze in a short shopping fling in Copenhagen.

Boy, oh boy, am I glad to be back on the ship! I was just off at Copenhagen - 7:45 to 10:00... The stores didn't open till 9, and the ship was to leave at 10. I wanted to be back by 9:30, and when I had finished all my shopping, I looked and it was 9:40 - and the cab man seemed to go so slow! But I made it with ten minutes to spare, and the ship didn't go till 10:20, but I certainly was scared.

But to be more explicit - Eric and I took the baby in the carriage and walked from the wharf through the free harbor and into the city of Copenhagen—past a beautiful park with blossoms out, and ducks and swans—then I took a cab downtown and Eric went back to the ship.

First to Royal Copenhagen—and no Christopher Robin—or any I thought you would really like... So, next door to Bing & Grøndahl - they had a nice little girl talking to her brother, which I got for you all, and a few little things. Then to the Permanent Arts Exhibition, and they only had one stoneware bird left—the female—so I took it and ran like fury to my waiting cab and we dashed to the dock... The awful thing about it was that he went back a different way and I didn't recognize anything and was afraid we were going to the wrong wharf! Eric was waiting almost as impatiently as I was! But we're here now, and we're leaving the harbor.

WE ARE ABSOLUTELY DELIGHTED WITH THE SHIP. IT'S AS NICE AS THE PINES [White Pines State Park] WAS TO US It really is about ten times as nice as the *Stavangerfjord*... Our room is inside, but large, with closets, drawers, comfortable beds— three of them—full length mirror, fan, good lighting, a heater, and pretty pine woodwork and all.

The ship is much better laid out - and doesn't creak and groan like the *Stavangerfjord*. The lounges and reading room are nice, and a pleasant dining room - movies, swimming pool, gym and all. We share privileges with the 1st class, for everything.

The baby has the bed with no bunk above it, and just fits across it so there is no danger of his rolling off. He has been good as gold for weeks and doesn't seem to mind the change to the ship and having clothes on all the time. There is a basin here to do our wash, and warm water to make his formula warm... I have a plastic bag here for his diapers, and we really are pretty well organized.

And we're happy as larks. The departing was gay and `festive, with the Slabys, Donaldsons, Lindvalds and Joe Shaw down to see us off....

The ship was indeed newer and more luxurious than the old *Stavangerfjord*, but it wasn't nearly as stable in the water. Rita didn't mention the huge waves that greeted us as we entered the North Sea. I stood as far forward in the ship as I could, watching our bow rise high above the horizon on one swell and then bury itself under the next wave, which broke heavily onto the foredeck. When the pitching sent our stern out of the water, exposing the propellers, I could feel the entire hull shudder. The ship pitched and rolled so much that our waiter had to dampen the table cloths so that plates would not slide, and lines were rigged outside the cabins for the passengers to hold onto.

On to Cornell (1952-54)

Bricks and Books

Early June, 1952

As soon as we returned from Norway, we settled in at Princeholm for the summer. Thanks to Bo's efforts, I was able to find a job with a local construction company almost immediately. Rekstad's was building a school a few blocks away, so I could walk easily to and from work.

My daily construction work routine was mind-numbingly simple. I had to arrive at the work site early so I would be there before my team of masons – the guys who would be laying the bricks. I started in by scraping their mortar boards clean and wetting them down slightly. Then I wheeled enough bricks up to where they would be working so that all of them would have what they needed when they arrived. Then I mixed a full batch of mortar, shoveling the proper mix of sand, cement and lime into the small mixer I used. As soon as my masons were ready to start laying bricks I would pour a wheelbarrow full of my fresh mortar, wheel it up the wooden ramps to where my crew of five or six masons were stationed, and shovel out some of the mortar on each mortar-board.

My job was to keep my crew supplied, and it seemed as if they were continually running out. They worked rapidly, and I had little or no time to stand around, so I was in pretty constant motion four hours until lunch, aside from a short mid-morning break, and then all afternoon as well. The work was not really strenuous, but I needed sturdy gloves to protect my hands from the rough edges of the bricks I handled.

I worked outside all the time, but that was no benefit because of the hot and sticky midwestern summer weather. Now and then we had a real storm, but weeks went by with nothing but hot, dry days and no way to escape the heat. Needless to say, every day was an upper-body exercise day, and my work shirt was soon wringing wet. No such thing as sunblock in those days, either, so any exposed skin generally got burned and then tanned.

I was impressed by how quickly the masons worked. Even though they never seemed to rush, I could see the piles of bricks I brought steadily disappearing. There were no wasted motions: lay a brick-long line of mortar along the top of the previous course, spread it out slightly by running the tip of the trowel through it; pick up another bit of mortar and spread it on one end of a new brick in two smooth swipes; and lay the brick on the mortar, moving it toward the end of the previous brick so that the joint between the two would be about 3/8 inch; and finally tap the top of the new brick so that it would be level with its neighbor and the top face edge of the new brick would be parallel to and at the same height as the line stretched between the two corners of the course on which he was working.

The final move was to take his towel and remove any excess mortar on the face of the brick. Sometimes he would shake the excess onto his own mortar pile and work it in and other times he would trowel it onto the free end of the brick he had just laid. From time to time he would take some water from a large bucket that I kept filled and sprinkle it onto his mortar supply, mixing it together so that it was always smooth and workable.

The masons kept up a steady pace during the day, never appearing to rush, and carried on a continual chatter about sports, domestic difficulties, war stories, and occasionally about the work they were doing.

So the days, and weeks, went by. But I couldn't relax after my eight hours on the job. I had to reserve as much of my free time as possible for study, because I was trying to prepare for the exam that I would have to pass in order to enter Cornell's PhD program.

That preparation was a gigantic project for me. The English Department had sent me its standard list of the novels, plays, poems, criticism, etc. about which I was expected to be conversant. The list was incredibly long, and there were so many that I hadn't read. I had made some progress in Norway, but I still had a massive task remaining. I plodded ahead, reading, and placed a check mark opposite each title as I finished it, and was pleased to see the marks begin to accumulate on the pages of my list. I was so occupied with this project that I had little if any time—or energy—for anything else.

Rita and I had some fun times together, of course, but I was not much help around the house so all in all the summer was a strain – for everyone. I pored over my books in the library room so much that I almost took up residence there. But I did make good progress with my study list and by the time we decided to head east to Ithaca I felt fairly ready for my prelim.

Moving to Ithaca

Our trip to Ithaca turned out to be a little more exciting than we would have liked. Bo rented a trailer to carry all our things: a four-wheeler with high wooden sides and a gate in the rear. We needed every bit of the trailer to hold furniture (some of the old heavy items had been stored in the basement of Princeholm for years), clothing, luggage, tools and heavy boxes of books. As we loaded in the sofa, bed, dressers and chairs and started on boxes, the pile in the trailer got higher and higher. By the time we had organized everything in it, the trailer was packed to the brim and its springs were on the verge of giving out.

This is how Rita described it:

The last big project we managed was moving to New York from Downers Grove. We wouldn't hire a van to take our furniture – it "would be cheaper to hire a trailer, and move it ourselves." So that's what we did. We got a 14-foot trailer and hooked it onto Bo's Dodge. Eric was working so I had to do all the packing myself, and me pregnant. Then he was able to help on the day we packed the trailer.

My father was there, hefting things around and getting redder and redder, saying he didn't see what we needed "this" for. They got it all packed, and then looked under the trailer and decided there was too much weight on the back, so Eric stood on top, pushing things forward. A trunk with our most precious possessions, very heavy, landed on top near the front, and my china was on the botton. They finally put the tarp over the towering mass of furniture and we started off, with my father driving the trailer car, and us with Vikar in another.

My father likes to drive fast. After a while he decided that that wasn't hard at all, and started letting the trailer push his car down hills. We got into hillier and hillier country and Eric and I got more and more apprehensive.

Bo elected to pull the trailer with his Dodge, and Rita and I, along with young son Vikar, drove separately. This was our first trip in our just-purchased secondhand 1948 Ford, the first car we had ever owned. All went smoothly until somewhere in western New York. I was staying within the speed limits, whereas Bo paid no attention to them, so that by that time Bo and Honey were far ahead of us.

We came to a stop light in the middle of a small town and had to make a right hand turn from a standing start and immediately climb a fairly steep hill. My car struggled a bit to make it, and I could imagine how much of a strain our trailer put on Bo's Dodge. When we topped the hill the road dropped sharply again, and we found ourselves heading rather steeply down a long slope toward a three-way intersection with a triangular-shaped island on the right and a tavern on the left. We built up a fair amount of speed, so I had to slow down as we approached the traffic light at the intersection.

We could see considerable activity on the island, and as we passed by, Rita looked over and gasped, "That's our furniture!"

Our sofa, dressers, bed, luggage, boxes of books and other stuff—all our worldly possessions—were all laid out on the grass, and the trailer was lying on its side. The Dodge was there and some men were just starting to right the trailer.

From what Bo and Honey told us, they had managed the uphill section—but just barely—and Bo had been relieved when he reached the top and started down. He generally felt comfortable going faster than he should, but this time he evidently forgot to take into consideration the weight that he was pulling behind his car and what might happen if he had to stop suddenly.

This is the story we got from Bo: as he neared the intersection the light turned amber, but he wasn't close enough to sail through so he had to stop quickly. When he applied his brakes, the car shuddered, the tires screeched, but the trailer had difficulty. Loaded as heavily as it was, it fishtailed behind him and finally leaned over and fell on its side like a wounded water buffalo. Within seconds, young men poured out of the tavern across the road and came over to help. They untied our tarp, took everything out of the trailer and placed it carefully on the grass.

We thanked them profusely. We were relieved to find that, despite the disastrous appearance of the scene, nothing important had been damaged. If we don't count Bo's pride, the only casualty of the collapsed trailer was a jar of Rita's peach jam that had broken and deposited its contents on some of my books.

The fellows from the tavern told us of a metal shop not far away, and we hauled the trailer there right away to get the trailer and hitch repaired. The mechanic at the shop was able to straighten the quarter-turn in the hitch and weld a plate on the hitch to strengthen it, so after an hour or so everything was almost as good as new, and we were back on our way again.

And here is Rita's view of the debacle:.

This was the third time that Bo and Eric had packed the trailer, and they were fairly sick of the sight of it all. Our furniture was a little messier this time, because my carefully canned peach jam had splattered all over most of the furniture and on a good many books. Luckily we had some rags and my mother and I spent the afternoon transferring the sticky mess from the books to us. My mother was stoical about it all. . . she had been scared when the trailer turned over, but she was more worried about things being broken than anything. Daddy was eager to get going again. . .the daylight was waning and we couldn't go after dark.

Now there isn't anything in this world that is harder to manage than my father when he is set on something, and all his life he has traveled by car and gone on until he couldn't see for sleepiness at about 3:00 in the morning. It got more and more dusky, and the trailer wavered from side to side on the road, because the hitch had been damaged, but every time Eric and I would signal to stop because we had found someplace to stay, he would say it was too expensive or not clean or some fool thing, and we kept going into the night.

We finally stopped at a duplex motel after much coercing, and spent the night there. That was the night of the championship fight between Davey and Rocky Graziano. No restaurants were open, so we opened a box of goodies we had brought from home and we finally relaxed and laughed about the fool way we were traveling, and what we would do the next time.

Aside from a rainstorm as we neared Ithaca, the remainder of our journey was uneventful, and we were enormously relieved to get to our new home.

Settling In

With help of a loan from Honey and Bo and low-interest financing courtesy of the Veterans Administration, we were able to purchase a home that had ample room for us on the ground floor and one apartment and two rooms for rent on the second floor.

September, 1952

Well, there's good news tonight. We're all rented! It took a while since all the students were already situated, and we made the mistake of saying that it was a 'share the bath' one in the ad in the paper, but today we had two grads who are instructors at Cornell, and their friend took the small single room . . . The four- room apartment then went for $85, so we have $115-120 coming in each month! The front room went last Thursday to a business-man. It's not certain how long he will stay, but it is rented for the moment. We didn't have to make any payment on the house or stove or washer this month, but had school tax of $70. Oh, we're house-owners now! . . . .

Rita took care of cleaning the hall stairway up to the rooms and the rooms themselves. What we collected as rent covered our mortgage payments, but my teaching fellowship covered little more than tuition and fees, so the only thing that kept us from galloping penury was what I was able to make from part-time jobs. Even so, Rita was hard-pressed to manage with the little I made from those jobs, so the time we spent in beautiful upstate New York was memorable as a belt-tightener, i.e. no frills. Not to mention that, in addition to all the housework and child care she had to do, she was pregnant again and due sometime in late March. But she never complained or let that slow her down.

All this is background for Rita's delightful descriptions of some of the things we did as a struggling grad.school couple.

Jobs, Jobs

Our main income was what I was able to earn from doing car and life insurance investigations for Retail Credit [now Equifax]. I was expected to interview neighbors of the people who had applied for insurance and ask them questions about the applicant, viz. what kind of person he or she was; number of children, if any; living conditions; reputation; habits, etc.—as much as I could gather. I could never have managed to drive around to interview personally all the people I was supposed to, so I phoned them instead to ask the questions. The Retail Credit office had an address-based telephone directory, so I could find the telephone numbers of people who lived close to the address that appeared on the insurance application.

All went well with my investigations for almost all of the two years I did this work, until one time I failed to discover and report that the person who applied for insurance walked with crutches and was obviously handicapped. I didn't think to ask how he got around, so I never learned that he had to use crutches. My report was not well received, because Retail Credit knew all along about the handicap and figured out that I must not have actually interviewed his neighbors.

Retail Credit and I parted on good terms; I simply couldn't take time to drive all over Cayuga County to satisfy their needs. I was productive and otherwise accurate, though.

I had several other part-time jobs because we had to take care of medical expenses for prenatal care and delivery of our expected child. During the two Christmas seasons we enjoyed while we lived in Ithaca, I worked for a fellow who cut and sold Christmas trees. I went out with him in his truck, helped to fell and then transport piles of trees which we stored behind a downtown grocery store. Then I stood on the corner by the Kroger grocery store shivering in the snow, wind and cold, waiting for customers. That got tiresome very quickly, but fortunately lasted only a couple of weeks. I didn't make a lot of money but at least we had a super tree ourselves.

I also worked in the university's rare book room, primarily typing index cards for new acquisitions and shelving books and materials that had been checked out by researchers. While I worked there I learned a lot about book construction and old leather bindings.

One semester I taught composition at Ithaca College.

Finally, I had a newspaper route that paid for all of our groceries, because the fifteen or so dollars I made was enough for Rita to buy food for the entire week. That job lasted the entire time we were in Ithaca.
There were five or six of us who delivered regularly, and we had to gather very early every Sunday morning, primarily to assemble the *New York Times*. We laid out the sections on a long table in a series of separate piles, beginning with the innermost section. One after another we would take the innermost section, slip it into the next one, and the next one until we reached the outside section and the end of the table. A fellow standing there would stack the finished papers, and we would continue that way until all the papers we had received were assembled. The other newspapers, like the local Ithaca paper, were already assembled and placed in separate stacks. The supervisor made certain that each of us had enough papers for the paid-up subscribers on our route, and then we stacked all of our papers in our cars and started out.

My helper was an energetic youngster who took one step for every two of mine; he was only fifteen but he already wore size 16 shoes and was well over six feet tall. We (my overloaded car, I mean) labored up State Street to the main entrance to the campus of Cornell to start our deliveries. From there it was almost all downhill. On the way down, we covered one cross street at a time, from one end to the other. I would take one side and my helper the other, carrying as many of the heavy papers as we could, and we generally finished at about the same time. Then I would move my car further down the cross street until we had finished it, whereupon we coasted down to the next cross street and started all over again.

No tossing papers onto lawns or flinging them in the general direction of the front door, though. We had no plastic bags to protect the papers from the elements, so we had to place them where they would stay dry, which generally meant putting them behind a stormdoor.

Teaching Fellow

I managed to pass my prelims and gain acceptance into the PhD program, even though I stepped on one professor's toes when he asked me a question about Yeats' poem *Lake Isle at Innisfree*. I didn't much like the poem at first and said so quite bluntly. That was imprudent, but how was I to know that Yeats was his favorite? He must have been more amused than annoyed by my reaction, because he concurred with the decision to admit me into the program.

I enjoyed teaching, primarily because of the interaction I had with bright and inquiring young people. Some of them were not much more than seven years younger than I was. Freshman English had not been my favorite subject as an undergraduate, and I'm not sure I brought much to my students.

I used my own Freshman English teacher as a model, and in retrospect that probably was a mistake. I don't believe any of the other teaching fellows had ever taken a course in how to teach college freshmen to write clearly and persuasively. I did the usual: assigned themes on a variety of subjects and then graded them. Many students had problems just writing complete and effective sentences, much less organizing ideas. And some of them didn't have many ideas to organize.

I believe that I could have taught them more about clear writing if I had just given them a set of facts and asked them to write about those facts in some systematic and persuasive fashion.

Daily Living

October 14, 1952

[We bought a puppy: 3/4 collie and ¼ German shepherd] Vikar is terribly excited about it . . . just sits with his arms straight out at his sides and watches it . . . now and then grabs the pup's fur or tail or ear. The puppy has teeth, and figures that arms are for biting, and so Vikar is a little puzzled by the whole thing. It'll be a real incentive for him to crawl, I think. Well, so we now have a new problem, the pup . . . but it really isn't so bad.

October 21, 1952

. . . we're going to take the pup to a 'shelter' . . . where they will hold him until he has a new home. He just doesn't learn not to bite Vikar and me . . . and those little teeth leave marks! Vikar keeps arms and legs going when the pup comes close. He sits in his bouncer, and watches the pup like a hawk . . . but when the pup comes near, he thrashes his feet like mad, so the pup can't get him on his stomach and bite his legs . . . The pup has been spanked and scared with newspapers, but doesn't learn, so we are taking him to this 'shelter' . . . and will get a dog that is a little older. That way we will only have to train Vikar to be good to it, instead of training both!

Vikar does something new every day, today he pulls himself up to his knees to see the beads on the play pen . . . and I bought him a book of animals, and when we get to the duck, I make a duck noise, and he is delighted, and then he strains his throat and gets all red and makes the noise too . . . He likes the book . . . and any other he can get hold of. I bought a set of these blocks that fit into each other, too . . . and he plays with them for long periods of time.

Vikar rolls over and sits up by himself now, and thinks it is a great joke on me; when I come in he laughs and laughs!

October 26, 1952

    We took the pup to the shelter, and Eric came back to the car saying they had a cute kitten . . . so we came home with an all black kitten that is so small and so playful . . . It stays away from Vikar, who reacts the same way he did with the puppy: watches it and tries to crawl after it. He is making some progress now, but doesn't really get the hang of it . . . .

    He rolls over and sits up all the time, but still feels that it is an accomplishment, and when I come into the room and find him in bed on his tummy or sitting I exclaim and he gets so excited that he rolls right over . . . he pounds the bed and laughs and really feels as though he pulled a good trick. We get a huge bang out of it.

Fall, 1952

    Vikar teases to sit on my lap while I type, then pushes my hands away and tries to . . . but he isn't strong enough to push any but the spacer. Eric takes time every day to play with him, and they usually have a rip-roaring laughing game of *peek-a-boo*, and *I'll-take-the-paper-away-from-you-and-you-take-it-away-from-me*!

    Vikar's on my lap, disrupting everything on the desk, having tired of working with the typewriter and not getting half as much noise as I do.

November 17, 1952

    We get the biggest kick out of seeing Vikar and the kitten play. You know that at first the kitten had the best of it since Vikar couldn't catch it . . . but now, he has found retaliation . . . The kitten loves Vikar's toys . . . all the rattles and blocks and even the scraps of paper . . . and Vikar has caught on, and now he gets a toy he knows the kitten would love to get his paws on and torments the cat . . . he plays with it, and makes noises by rubbing it on the floor, and shows the kitten every now and then. The kitten goes wild wanting the toy.

However, the kitten (which we have named Pip) is no dunce, and will lure Vikar away from the toy by running in front of him, or rubbing his tail in Vikar's face, and then wandering off to the other side of the room. Vikar follows, of course, and just when Vikar is almost touching him, Pip dashes back to the toy and plays madly with it until Vikar can get back.

Vikar is almost possessive with the toys, and doesn't often let the kitten have one for long. But they are good playfellows . . . sometimes they sit side by side and play with the same toy . . . The kitten plays endlessly with Vikar's toys while Vikar sleeps.

The kitten lets Vikar pet him now . . . and it's a pretty rough pulling and swatting he gets, but Pip goes right on purring. He hasn't scratched Vikar yet even though he gets his ears and hair and tail pulled!

Vikar and Eric are looking at his animal book and making the noises . . . mostly duck noises. Vikar knows words now: *daddy* and *mama* and *Pip, gone, water, come, no no, drink, eat, where's* . . . .

Another October, 1952 letter

I am sitting at the desk, while Vikar crawls around . . . pulling one cord then another, tipping over waste baskets, chasing the kitty, investigating plugs, tipping over the cat's food . . . and talking to me occasionally. He doesn't sleep during the day now, so my rest periods are when he is in his play pen.

The kitten torments Vikar by staying just a little too far from him to be swatted, and still looking attractive. It likes to sleep in the seat of Vikar's bouncer toy, with its head hanging out! They play together when Vikar is in the pen . . . and the kitten roving around the outside. Vikar picks up the pad and the kitten tries to catch the strings on the corner.

The kitten is the most playful that I can ever remember . . . it plays all day (when it isn't sleeping) and with anything and everything. Last night I was sorting spools of thread, and Vikar was unsorting them, and the kitten was spreading them around the room.

Halloween, 1952

The great day arrived. Vikar hauled off and crawled, and is all over the house now . . . He crawled for the first time for a glass of water that I had put on the floor. The next best reason for crawling is after the kitten and the third is to get to the lamp cord.

He suddenly stopped eating any solids, only drinking orange juice and Pablum, and we finally figured out that we wants to eat what we eat, so now it is mashed potatoes, and vegetables, and bones, and whatever we can mash up. He is vehement about holding his own glass, and won't drink if we help. He works best with the small blue ones.

November 26, 1952

Vikar is playing around on the floor. He follows me around like a puppy now, and when he is bored, he hangs on to my skirts to be picked up . . . It's hard to resist him! He knows what is no-no around the house now . . . namely the light cords, and even while he reaches for one, his mouth is forming the nooooo - and then when reprimanded, he clasps his hands together and looks so round-eyed and round-mouthed . . .

He plays with the kitten very consciously now . . . gets yarn or clothing, and flips it around him while the kitten chases and chases. Pip lets him maul his ears and fur without stopping purring. Aside from begging, it's a perfect cat!

December 1, 1952

Vikar and Eric and I play hide and seek now, and Vikar pads around trying to find us . . . he is so funny, and when he finds one of us, he sits back and laughs and slaps his knees and has a great time.

December 13, 1952

Vikar and Pip play more with each other now instead of AT each other. They spend hours batting at the same toys . . . his favorites now are a long piece of rope that's all twisted into a bunch (which he moves and the kitten jumps after) and the clothespins.

December 21, 1952

Vikar is standing now . . . I forgot to tell you in the last letter. He has been standing and pulling himself up for quite a while. Now he gets up places, and doesn't know how to get down, and stands there and cries. He spends most of his day on his feet, and we hope he'll take a step on Xmas.

December 27, 1952

The Xmas tree lights are now the big attraction for Vikar. Pip boxes them, and Vikar wants them to chew and knock against each other . . . pulling the tinsel off is also a favorite game. So far the tree has fallen on top of Vikar two times! He doesn't seem too frightened! Pip really goes crazy over the tree - the smell and the trim. Vikar is fascinated by it, but not overcome, by any means. We had stockings, of course, and Vikar's love in them was a big red ball and a siren car.

We were wakened by Vikar on Christmas, of course; now that he stands up in bed and rocks it, it is pretty hard to sleep!

Vikar likes his cuddly dog, but is most possessive when the kitten begins wrestling with it. Vikar pulls it away from Pip (who usually is dragged along) and holds it high in the air, then lets Pip get at it again, and pulls it away. They play for a long time that way until one loses interest, and then the other does.

A few weeks ago Vikar discovered that the Kleenex sheets come out one after the other, and we have kept it away from him, after putting all 200 sheets back in, but he got it again this morning. His favorite toy is still the clothespins, I think. He sleeps with his musical dog and plays a lot with the blocks that fit into each other, and of course he plays with Pip, but the clothespins always please him.

He knows most of the things we say to him now: *right back, all gone, get milk, change, hot, cold, Pip, Momma, Daddy, come, come back, eat, drink, water,* etc.

January 9, 1953

Vikar says *good* now. He nods his head and says *goo* when you ask him if he wants a cookie or is a good boy or is hungry . . . it's so funny. He is getting another tooth on the bottom.

January 16, 1953

We had a party for Vikar, but couldn't teach him to blow . . . he just laughed at us. A big chocolate cake and ice cream, which Vikar has developed a taste for already. He is fascinated by dogs, and makes a barking sound when we just say the word, so we gave him a book of dogs, which he loves to look through. He still goes to sleep with the furry dog Pete and Sarah gave him.

Vikar is helping me now . . . pushing my hands away so that he can push the spacer. I lured him away with an ice-cube. He loves to suck on them.

January 29, 1953

If you want to bring Vikar something, make it a book or music box dog. He is crazy about dogs, and woofs at the mention of one. Eric gave him a dog book, and he's been through it so much that the pages are all crumpled, and half had to be taped back in. It keeps him away from our books, generally, too.

Pip is as playful as ever, and has more and more sense. Vikar is still a lot smarter than the kitten, however. Vikar and Eric play that game of which-hand-is-it? with anything, and Vikar is so funny. He picks the same hand over and over, and finally catches on and tries the other hand. He is so delighted when he gets it . . . and he and Eric laugh and laugh. They still play *chase* a lot. . .

Ithaca Rifle and Pistol Club

I was going through the local newspaper one day and noticed an ad for a Colt Woodsman .22 Target Model—hardly used. I enjoyed pistol marksmanship from my trips to the police pistol range with my father, so I made an appointment to see the piece. It was still in its original case and looked absolutely new. A folded target inside the box showed the tight pattern made by the gun from a bench rest when it was sighted in. I fell in love with it and paid $45 for it, which was a handsome sum for us.

Rita sensed my excitement at finding the gun and buying it, and seemed as happy as I was, even though she must have been wondering about my priorities. The last thing I needed at that point was involvement in a sport that was certain to take up time that I should be devoting to study or work. But she—ever understanding—never would have thought about mentioning that.

Ithaca had a very active pistol team that practiced in the basement of one of the old buildings in the downtown area. I joined up, began going to weekly practices and traveling to the matches we had with other clubs in the area. I bought soundproof earmuffs and earplugs and rigged up a special cover for the left eye of my glasses so I would not be distracted by double vision. Did fairly well once I got used to my pistol and got back into the habit of careful squeezing and careful sighting. Sometimes I even had one of the top five scores in our team matches.

Our home range was rather spartan: an old rock-walled basement, undecorated and poorly lit. Ventilation was almost non-existent, so the smell of gunpowder was everywhere. The shooters stood behind individual benches that had room for our ammo, gun case, wipes, etc. Our targets were lit but the rest of the area was dark. We had no cables to reel our targets back to us. As soon as the rangemaster made sure that all shooters were finished, he let us walk to retrieve our targets and attach new ones, etc. We started with the .22 caliber shooters and when they were finished we switched to .38 and .45 caliber shooters. I only had my .22 Match Target.

The members were friendly and we had great camaraderie. During the competition season, we would generally gather early for dinner and drive to matches in other towns, or drive right away to the match and eat afterwards, which made for a late drive home.

Dana Poyer was the star of our team; he and Ed Melchen were regularly at the top of our scoring column when we had matches against other teams. At the end of the season, our team competed in the Northern Tier pistol championships, and did very well, thanks to great performances by Dana.

Rita was very patient and understanding about my escapades. And that's what those shooting nights were. She could see that I enjoyed the competitions and the fellowship.

Home Life

Rita was completely swamped with taking care of Vikar and, later, Tor, managing the house and the rented quarters, looking out for our pets, and doing all the other chores that come with home ownership, and she enjoyed telling her parents about the antics of the children and all our other activities.

Honey drove east to be with us when Rita was in the final stage of her pregnancy, and she was a great help. The birth of number two son went very smoothly, with no problems at all. Rita was quite relaxed, because she felt good and knew what to expect. I drove her to the hospital and, within a few hours, Emerick Torsten Youngquist made his noisy debut.

Here is Rita again, about a month after the delivery, bringing Honey up to date:

April 29, 1953

The baby smiles and talks now . . . and talks back to Vikar and smiles at him. He's really a pretty baby, and getting lots of personality. He's not as impatient as he used to be.

Vikar has rediscovered his blocks, and makes very tall buildings, sometimes very precarious ones, usually eight or ten blocks high . . . with each addition he says a very high-pitched 'gaa' . . . and he does a lot of taking something to another part of the house, then coming and taking another to the same spot and another . . . then shifting them all somewhere else.

He walked all the way home from the store yesterday with me . . . looks so funny stomping along . . . he loved it.

Rita loved working with flowers and plants, and she was delighted with the back area of our lot, which was fairly flat and perfect for a garden. Around our property we found a variety of plants and shrubs, and she added others to those while we lived there. Here is how she described the state of our plants and flowers during our first spring there:

May 15, 1953

We've just come in from looking at the garden and lawn. Both are so satisfying . . . The garden is all up but the corn and watermelons. Eric brought home more tomato plants and some cauliflower and broccoli and peppers - and those are in, and the beans up and my zinnias and peas and all . . . It is a pretty sight. Eric is madly weeding just the tiniest weeds! I have zinnias and nasturtiums by the house coming up now. Honey, those things that we thought would be daisies are now bachelor buttons that have buds - and some zinnias!!

We are very green - the grass is thick and everything is in bloom. Really our next baby will have to be later in the spring, so you can be here at such a pretty time. It is so lovely - and happyfying . . . The lilacs in front of the house are white, and on the hillside, too . . .

Then there are purple bushes by the garage and by the front porch—lovely full branches—they haven't been cut much. Then the tulips are all blooming, pink near the roses, and yellow by the house and on the hill, and up in the garden where the violets were there must be fifty yellow and purple ones . . . I've picked and picked . . . There is a bunch in Ed's room, and all over the house - and we're taking some to another couple tonight. Then by Mrs. Woodford's, the huge lilac bush is white, and that flower garden is a mass of color, red and yellow tulips and blue forget-me-nots . . . .

In the same letter:

The baby smiles and talks more and more . . . and now Vikar talks to him. They smile happily at each other. Vikar says 'hi' very clearly now, and imitates many other words, like *hot* and *cold* and *plane* and *David* and *thank you* and *please*, and also makes a try at *pretty*.

We had a nice weekend with Eric's parents. Vikar recovered nobly from the shock of having two new people in the house, and talked and talked to them and danced for them and did all his tricks.

Vikar has conquered the hill outside now, all but when he gets interested in something, or talks, then over he goes. He gets to the walk and takes off, toward the parking lot corner . . . legs going just like pistons . . . leaning forward.

Vikar is standing on a chair in front of the TV, talking to me and working his hands closer and closer to the knobs.

June, 1953

There were things I forgot, of course . . . one is the funny way Vikar sits on his little chair. He backs up to it, and then sits, and after he is comfortable, he sighs a big, high sigh, like I used to when I was pregnant! It is so funny.

Vikar talks a blue streak, and imitates our words. The doctor asked: "Does Vikar talk now?" and Vikar said: "Blubbedy did sooooosheisthe" just as though he understood him!

June, 1953

The baby is crying for attention . . . he just calls and calls. He is playing with his hands now . . . grabs them and watches as they try to let each other go . . . funny uncoordinated things. He smiles every time I come into the room, and gurgles and laughs if you just change him. He loves being held, as I've said a dozen times.

Vikar dances a lot, now. He bounces at the knee, and swings his shoulders and arms now and then . . . so funny. If he's sitting down, he bounces from the waist. And talks all the time. Did we tell you about his pool, and how much he loves to splash in it?

With Rita's energy, her love of cooking, her sense of color and her ability to organize things, she found entertaining rather easy. She loved the challenge of getting everything ready and having everything just right. She also enjoyed sharing her experiences with Honey. This is her description of a party we had for other teaching fellows and their families. We were the only ones with a TV (eight-inch screen), so we invited them over to share Queen Elizabeth's coronation. We did the same for the McCarthy hearings.

June 4, 1953

Our party was a big success . . . Fifteen came in all, and by midnight, Eric and I had seen the coronation four times! (what with switching between CBS and NBC) I cleaned and baked two cakes, and did four washings and the shopping all on Monday, so that Tuesday would be relatively free . . . It was.

Since the party was to be informal, and begin and go till midnight, I set the table with all the wooden dishes and basket tops, and the bamboo ones you brought here, Honey. The blue bachelor buttons are all out, and they went on the table . . . It had to be very long, and I put on a striped gauze-ish cloth I bought in Madison - royal blue, yellow, white and orange stripes.

Really, with the wood, royal blue glasses, and white plates, it was a very pretty table. There were many sandwich makings, relishes, potato chips, and a chocolate and spice cake. I had the breadboard and toaster on for spreading - and then there was beer and Pepsis . . . .

The baby was good, smiled and gooed, and was held by many, and Vikar smiled at everyone and talked to all, and finally was just bursting with joy when a little boy his age came, and they played.

Vikar would pick up his pull toy, and the other boy, David, would take it, then Vikar would take a train, and David would take that, so Vikar would take the pull toy again. It was all very smilingly done, and then they'd start on blocks. They ate together and followed each other around, and it broke Vikar's heart to have him leave.

Another letter in June, 1953

Vikar has begun to climb. I pushed a chair into the bathroom for him to stand on and see me wash my hair, and now he climbs on and off everything, using the chair as a stepping stone. He's been up on the dining room table, the dresser and the desk, and on every chair in the house. He now likes to stand in the rocker and rock it . . . he's braver than I.

Sometime not too long after Mother's Day, 1953

Vikar had to learn to climb up our hill and go down it . . . many falls, but never daunted. Now he does pretty well.

He is interested in the baby's feet and hands . . . tries to tickle him like he tickled you, Honey. He also keeps trying to feed him his milk . . . jams the nipple half down the poor child's throat, but Tor doesn't seem to mind. Vikar is playing with that dirty gold pillow, throwing it around.

July 10, 1953

You would have laughed to see Vikar yesterday. We went into a drugstore where the toys were low so he could reach to pick them up. He inspected cars and planes, and each time he picked one up we told him to put it back. When he came to a big red tractor, he picked it up and began running for the door just as fast as he could go. He wasn't taking any chance of having to put it back! We bought it, and he has hardly put it down. He takes it to bed, even.

July, 1953

Vikar is now saying 'Tor, Tor' for us . . . and he still loves his 'cucks' and goes to bed with two or three plastic ones every night. He says a lot now. Copies about any word that we tell him, especially words he likes, like *Coke*, and *cone* and *good* and *cookie* and *peas* and *meat*, etc. Last night we were asking him to say *Tor* and he answered just like a Swede, with a *Tore*, just like they say it.

How he loves to go on excursions in the car, or walking to the store! He races along the sidewalk with his arms close to his tummy and legs stiff . . . and then stands so straight in the car so he'll see everything. Mostly he is on the lookout for trucks and cats and dogs.

The new little tables are just right for him, and now and then we have snacks and he runs to get his chair, and I get a table, and he sits there as big as life sipping milk and eating a cookie.

He is climbing up the bookcase at the moment, using the shelves for steps. He got to the radio, and I took him down. Larkin made us a little stepladder in shop, and Vikar has that now . . . I'm afraid the bookcases will fall over on him. So we'll discourage that. He now knows how to open my purse and is working on the doors. Luckily they are lockable.

August 26, 1953

Tor is five months today! He gets on his knees and sways forwards and back now for fun. Now and then I hear him hit his head, but for the most part, he manages to get up and down without crying. He's his same lovable self. He's wearing trousers and shirt now, and those nice little suits on warm days . . . .

Vikar talks more and more. He knows his farm animals now, and transportation, and says little phrases like "uh car" which means let's go in the car . . . and "Whatssat?" and other phrases pop out unexpectedly.

August, 1953

We went to the county fair here! And all the excitement was showing Vikar the animals . . . bunnies (bunbee), geese and ducks, chickens, sheep, cows and assorted dogs. He also rode on a little car that went round and round. He sank lower and lower on the seat until he was horizontal in the car . . . not scared, just respectful. The Ferris wheel fascinated him, too.

A little girl that is just Vikar's age comes to play every morning for a few hours. They play so well together. Both get into the rocker and watch TV, or both read, or play with the various toys. Vikar tries to impress her by climbing and jumping, and talking a lot. She says more than he does, but he is learning, and they have a treat.

This baby is so strong! He gets up on his hands and knees all the time he is on the floor, and then doesn't know what to do next. He can't sit alone, and is beginning to get the idea of crawling. He loves the bouncer chair. I put a pillow in to keep him straight.

Vikar is saying a lot now . . . and copying things we say. He pesters me all day long to read with him. We have one ABC that we go through while he says the words he knows. I'll bet we read it twenty times a day! He is very interested in purses, too, and money.

This baby is sitting on my lap while I type . . . he was tired of pushing around the floor, and telling me so. Vikar is asleep now.

Sometime in the fall, 1953:

There's news from here! We have a boxer. Surprise! You knew we had gone to see some puppies at a huge boxer kennel, and said they were too expensive for us. Well, yesterday they called us to say they had one that they would like us to have. She is a female that was the runt, and the other dogs were picking on her. She was bitten on the legs, and they didn't want to have her around the other dogs any more—and keeping her separated was too much trouble . . . So we are getting her cheap and on time, too.

She may be a runt, but she is as big as Vikar if you count her ears! She is a red brindle - which means black tiger-like stripes. Her face is black, and she has a little white on her chest. She really is terribly timid now, you have to be so sorry for her . . . We're just letting her get used to us.

She walked with her head down at first, and was so scared. Now she is getting more relaxed and stays with me all the time - follows me around the house all day. She is quiet, and good - obeys commands, and lets Vikar do just about anything. I found him running his train up and down her back, and she just stood there, not minding. Her ears don't seem to be sensitive; she doesn't jump at high or sudden noises. . . At the moment, Vikar is playing with his train, rolling it around, and Tor is in his bouncer chair watching him. Vikar is periodically going over to kiss the dog's nose, and Sugar lifts it to meet him.

Next, we explained to Vikar yesterday about toilet training for the dog, and now Vikar is trained! He hasn't had an accident yet! Isn't that swell? It's wonderful to have him learn something so fast. Maybe I'm bragging prematurely, but he is a good boy about it.

October 13, 1953

Vikar is 21 months old . . . Gee, it seems as though he should be three or four years! He's curled up in the rocker, drinking milk and watching the TV . . . he says sentences now, and talks in two and three words a lot, like "Tor crying" or "Tor fall down" or "Fun go car". He uses *fun* a lot, for going out of the house, mostly. I bought him a little book of the three bears, and haven't had any peace since . . . he hears it time after time . . . the broken chair impresses him no end! He looks so serious, and almost scared, and says "brokee, brokee!" He has another new book too, of WHEELS, and it's looking mighty worn . . . it's all forms of transportation.

Vikar wants to help me type . . . Tor is asleep. He sits without falling now, and only falls from standing up and being tipped. . .He still has a craze for paper, and dashes across the floor when he spots some. Also he crawls into the kitchen every chance he gets, to go straight to Sugar's bowl and bones. No matter how many times I take him out, he comes right back and bounds over to grab a bone.

What a dickens he is. He is wearing all Vikar's old clothes. They don't look old, though, just faded a little. He sits in the carriage when we go downtown, and Vikar usually sits behind him on the way home. Shopping is pretty easy when they can both be in the carriage.

November 6, 1953

On Monday, our furnace didn't shut off, and all of the registers except one were shut, so all this heat came up that one register. Sugar was sleeping on a closed one, so I didn't know that any were hot. I was just calling the gas man when Vikar stepped on the hot one. He began to cry, and the glass of water that he was carrying spilled and began boiling and sputtering on the register, so I knew what it was and pulled him off right away.

But that little time he stood there gave him third degree burns. Poor darling. We dashed off to the doctor and had them dressed and he was given codeine for the rest of the day. He was inconsolable all day—we held him most of the time—then Tuesday he seemed his old self and crawled around with Tor.

Then on Wednesday, he suddenly began vomiting and had a temperature of 105 and scarlet fever set in. He is still sick with it.

November 27, 1953

Tor is on the floor by me here, playing with Sugar's ears and trying to get her jowls. Sugar is very stoical about it all. Tor is delighted.

Vikar is napping. The doctor says there definitely won't have to be any skin graft for his feet. Isn't that wonderful? We're delighted . . . and he stands now for a second at a time at our coaxing. The bandages are too constricting to walk, really. The doctor is amazed at his progress, and in a week or two the bandages can probably come off for good.

He shows how well he feels now by learning fast again. For a while, he hardly talked, and now he says words out of a clear blue sky, words we hadn't prompted him on. Now trucks are divided into kinds too, dump, fire, bread, delivery, coke, big, pickup, milk, and bus.

Each time we go downtown, he says 'pretty" about all the Xmas decorations and has a picnic window-shopping with me and spotting all the toys. We've begun talking about Santa, and toys and TODAY we got him his first love . . . a bouncing horse. He was thrilled to pieces when I put him on one that was in the store, and oh how he will like his.

We are going to put out the train you gave him, too, and since he has only played with it on special occasions, it will seem like new, too. He is going to love this Christmas . . . and the tree will really thrill him too.

Tor is just a little marauder . . . nothing will be safe within three feet of the ground . . . especially the paper on the packages. I'm really enjoying thinking of Christmas so much . . . the children will love it so, and so will I.

I really am so tickled about Vikar's horse . . . it's on springs, and how he will love it. And he'll also love the house all prettied up.

November, 1953

Vikar is playing on the floor with Tor now . . . he crawls around without ever touching his feet to anything . . . holding them up in back. They itch a little now, and hurt to the touch, but are healing well. Some of the third degree parts are healing, and the little toes are about well.

The Big Payoff

Late December, 1953

    Well, there's excitement here!!! A neighbor called me this afternoon to tell me that I was mentioned on TV - on "The Big Payoff!" It is a show on which a letter is read from a listener while a contestant is playing, and the letter-sender and listener get duplicate prizes. When you see the show you'll know what I mean . . . At any rate, the letter-sender got two prizes - probably two outfits of clothing and some other incidentals. The thing of it is that at the end of the week they choose from the five letters of the week - choose the best one, and that husband and wife come to New York to try for the BIG PAYOFF . . . if Eric answers all the questions, we would have a trip to Europe and a MINK coat!

    So the Big question now is: will our letter be chosen from those of the week? See it on Friday to see whether we win! It is a daily program in the afternoon . . . We sent the letter months and months ago, and I hardly remember what we put in it - living on half a shoestring in Norway and scholarship, and first baby abroad I think. Anyway it is all very exciting and I can hardly wait to hear what I've won! Because whether my letter is chosen this weekend or not, we get the prizes that my stage partner won.

    NOTE This is one of the rare cases when Rita wasn't completely candid with her parents. As a matter of fact, I never had any idea that a letter had been written. The husband was supposed to write a letter explaining why his wife ought to get the trip and mink coat, but Rita had written the letter and signed my name. The first I heard about it was when she got the news from our neighbor. On May 14 I received a telegram from Emily Jordan :

    "CONGRATULATIONS PAYOFF PARTNER FOR WINNING ALL EXPENSE PAID TRIP TO NEW YORK FOR YOU AND YOUR WIFE.

RESERVATIONS MADE IN YOUR NAME AT GOVERNOR CLINTON HOTEL ...FROM THURSDAY MAY 20 TO SATURDAY MAY 22....

After we returned from New York, she described our trip.

> Let me tell you about our glorious weekend in the big city . . .
> We flew Mohawk taking one hour and seventeen minutes. Of course, Tor and Eric fell right asleep! Vikar was frightened when the engines revved up, but after we'd been up a while and I pointed out buses and trucks on the ground, he got interested, and liked the trip. When the steward asked if he wanted to go up again he gave an emphatic NO, though!
> Then we got on a bus, and on the way to the city saw every kind of truck and bridge and taxi and building equipment, so the trip was a success as of then.
>
> Then when we checked into the Gov. Clinton (opposite Penn Station), we found a suite with TV, and right below our window was the FIRE STATION, and the boys spent their time watching the long trucks come and go. So the room was perfect for us. We got a baby-sitter—wife of the night manager—for the next day, and went out to see the trains at Penn Station and ride the escalators - both new to the children!
> We relaxed that evening, though - we were both worn out with studying, packing, and excitement. We went downstairs to dinner that evening, and since they were paying the check, I had steak! Filet mignon, to be exact! The children were amazingly good - nothing on the floor and no noise, but we decided not to stretch our luck, and had the rest of the meals in our room . . . .
>
> We reported to the station the next morning at 10:20! And we listened to a man talk loud and fast for three hours! I'm not exaggerating .

. . We just listened and he told us all about the program: fifteen million listeners, 500 dollars a minute, two million dollars worth of stuff given away in the last seven years (radio, too), what would be expected of us. No sob story, ladies and gentlemen. Have fun, no saying "Hi" to relatives - about the merchandise - coming fashions - not being cut now, give right sizes, six week wait - about the trip, give money for expenses, and so on and so on.

Then he went over what Eric would say so that it would fit into two minutes . . . By then it was 1:30 and we went right into the studio for a walk-through rehearsal . . .

All the time we were told that if we didn't talk loud enough or weren't cooperative we would be dropped from the show . . . Then we met another producer and then Randy Merriman, and learned how to stand for the cameras and how loud to talk, and were sent out to eat at 2:15 - to be back at the theater at 2:30 to get in line with the rest of the audience . . .

We were supposed to act like everyone else, hand in cards saying we wanted to be on the program, have our names called to come to a reserved section, and be chosen (supposedly cold) from the audience. All the rigmarole was so that the audience would think that we came in as cold as they did!! Actually, they DO take the next day's contestants from that group they call down, but there is an interview first and all this preparation on the next day! Well, by that time, we were excited and nervous, and then we were called FIRST.

Eric must have looked nervous, because the man who escorted him to the stage told him the answer to the first question, which was about popular music. I guess he figured Eric might not know the answer. So he got one right.

The next question was multiple choice. They asked him to name the first king of Scotland, and gave him three names to choose from. The first was *The Black Douglas* and poor Eric seized on that, because he and Jimmy Dickey used to play a game where The Black Douglas was a main character.

The emcee asked whether he was sure, and held up a card so Eric could see the correct answer and change his mind. But he didn't look because he had already committed himself. But hither, thither or yon, we missed it, and were awfully glad it was over!

The clothes they had were darling, the models New Yorky . . . The set was small - about as wide as our living room and parlor at Princeholm - and they managed the vignettes with lighting. It was all interesting - the cameras were of no concern to us, just winning! We thought we lost gracefully though . . . The producers came and apologized, and said that they had hoped Eric would be able to answer the question. I think they were sincere - so we went out and began to unwind. It took the rest of the day, and on Saturday we really had fun . . .

We took the children on the bus to the Central Park Zoo, and we saw the Whistler, Sargent, Cassatt exhibit at the Metropolitan . . . And the boys and I bought some toys at F.A.O. Schwartz on Fifth Avenue - and all in all we had a swell time . . . It was all very exciting for the boys, and certainly for us . . .

And after all, I've been given thirteen things and the trip, so I shouldn't be unhappy. But we both are such optimists that we can't get it through our heads that it is over. Somehow the only finish we expected was the trip! Ah well!

Room service certainly was a treat! They wheeled in a table with a little dutch oven with all the warm food - and it was so simple with the children to have it where they weren't distracted - and where we weren't worried about others around us. We left the room in good condition, I might add - nothing spilled. The TV company paid all hotel, taxi, tips, and travel - so we had a wonderful trip for practically nothing . . . .

Catching the Foreign Service Bug

I hadn't been teaching at Cornell much more than a semester when I realized that I had to make a career change. I could see that it would be a long time – if ever – before I would earn enough by teaching to be able to give my family the things I wanted for them. More important, I wasn't really satisfied studying literature at the graduate level, where I felt that criticism took precedence over understanding and enjoyment. Also, I got the impression that the English department was perched around the bottom of the university's academic pecking order.

Rita and I talked about our happy times in Norway and I remembered the brief meetings I had had with officers from USIS. At some point in all this I began thinking seriously of doing something similar, i.e. working overseas for the government. That led me to asking about career opportunities. The premier unit in my opinion was the Foreign Service – or the Diplomatic and Consular Corps.

In January, 1953, I sent for materials about applying for the Foreign Service and received the standard recruitment package that described how the Service selected its new officers. The process began with a three-day written exam that was given in various cities across the country (my nearest was NYC). Those who passed were then invited to an oral exam, and that took place only in Washington, DC. After passing these examinations, a candidate would take a physical exam and then wait for his/her name to come up for appointment.

By the time I decided to apply, I had about ten months to prepare for the written exam—and I felt that I would need every bit of it to feel ready. Rita and I began to get excited about the prospect of travel and new experiences, and I'm afraid my interest in teaching began to flag.

Passing the written examination was my first and biggest challenge. Scoring was a bit complicated: each exam was weighted according to perceived importance, with reading comprehension and written expression weighted 4, economics, history and general knowledge 3, statistics 2 and vocabulary 1. Each exam was graded on a percentile basis, so if you scored in the 80th percentile in general knowledge, that would be multiplied by 4 to get your weighted grade of 320. Your weighted grades were then totaled and divided by 20 to arrive at your weighted average grade. To pass the examination, you had to have a weighted average grade of at least 70.

Historically, only about ten percent of the candidates passed the written examination. Obviously it was important for me to score high on the higher-weighted parts in order to balance lower grades on the others, like statistics. For me, that meant that I had to focus on history and economics and work on vocabulary somewhat. I figured that I could hold my own in reading comprehension, general knowledge and written expression. I didn't even study statistics because I didn't know what to study and figured that on a multiple-choice exam I probably could guess well enough to avoid complete collapse.

We also were expected to pass a written exam in a world language, which excluded Norwegian and Swedish, so I chose to take exams in French and German. I had taken a one year course in reading French, which was essential for my PhD program, but had never studied German.

History was the most daunting exam for me, because it was weighted high, and I had only studied American history in high school, plus undergraduate courses in political science and English constitutional history. I had never taken any courses in world history, although I was fairly well-versed in the history of Scandinavia. The essay-type exam would be divided into four sections, and in each section there would be three general questions. One of those questions would focus on American history and the other two would cover world history.

I decided to gamble and spend my time studying only American history. As a result, I would effectively be limited to answering only one of the three questions in each section, so I had to learn enough to be able to give a reasonable response to any question that might come up.

My language exams were a gamble as well. I didn't bother studying French, thinking that on a multiple choice test I ought to be able to guess well enough to pass, based on what I had already learned in my two semesters of Reading French at Michigan.

I took an unorthodox approach to German; instead of getting a textbook, I borrowed a German edition of Thomas Mann's *The Magic Mountain* from the library and started translating it, looking up every word I didn't know. I found that Swedish helped me greatly, because if I pronounced a German word, I could often recognize a similarity to its Swedish counterpart. Here are a few examples I picked out at random in my dictionary: *Herr, Herr* (Mister); *fenstre, fönster* (window*); schmuzig, smutsig* (dirty*); fried, fred* (peace); *knopf, knapp (button); jegen, jaga* (hunt); *stopf, stoff* (matter*); kunst, konst* (art); and *rohr, rör* (pipe).

Ironically, I passed the German exam but not the French one.

During the months leading up to my written exam I had precious little free time, what with my own teaching and course work, part-time jobs, work around our house, and time with my family. As much as I could, I read on all aspects of American history and politics, reviewed basic economics, and committed to memory the meanings of many words that one hardly ever uses but should at least recognize. My freshman year of Latin helped me.

Finally the fateful day arrived. In December, 1953, I traveled to New York City for my three-day ordeal. Everything that I had studied helped me and the exam went exactly as I had planned, and when it was all over I felt fairly confident that I had passed. Best of all, I had learned enough in focusing exclusively on American history to handle the four questions on that subject, and they were crucial.

The first three went smoothly, so I was a bit apprehensive when I turned to the final one, hoping that I could handle that one as well. I could hardly believe my eyes when I read it: *Trace the territorial expansion of the US after the Revolution.* Just three days before the exam I had become interested in that very subject and read several articles on it. I knew by heart all the wars, treaties, and political decisions that entered into the nation's growth. I could have filled pages with my answer. So I left the exam with high hopes.

On the final day of the exam, Honey and Bo came down with Rita and we went out for dinner and went to see Jul Brynner in *The King and I*. Prophetic move, as it turned out, because my first assignment was to our Embassy in Bangkok.

Here we are at the dinner table:

Dinner in NYC with Bo and Honey

Several weeks after taking my written exam for the Foreign Service I received my results. I had indeed passed, with 91 in vocabulary, 88 in written expression and 81 in reading comprehension, for a weighted average grade of 76. Cheers and hurrahs all around. We were delirious with joy. Assuming that I would pass the oral exam and we would be going overseas, we made arrangements to sell our home in Ithaca and move back to Downers Grove.

That final (spring) semester at Cornell was a lame-duck one for me, but I still had to continue with my teaching, course work and all the other activities that helped us make ends meet.

Final Semester at Cornell

When Sugar came into heat for the first time we decided to have her bred. We located a local dog breeder who owned a highly ranked male and made the necessary arrangements. The breeder fee would be the usual pick of the litter. We arrived at his kennel with Sugar and she and the male had a short, sweet, and productive canine romance.

We returned home with a satisfied Sugar and waited for nature to take its course. Some weeks after Christmas, Sugar presented us with eight healthy and frisky pups. The boys were entranced by the sudden profusion of new playmates.

Sugar needed a few days of privacy with her wiggling pups, so we placed them all in a large box with papers on the bottom and a second layer of rags for warmth and left them alone. Eventually, Sugar allowed the boys to touch and play with her brood. She was a loving mother and watched patiently as the boys carefully stroked or petted them.

Tor and Vikar would howl with laughter as Sugar would get up to walk around and they could see one or two of the puppies who were still nursing get dragged along out of their box, dangling below Sugar.

The breeder came to fetch his choice, and then we ran our "For Sale – Boxer Pups" ad in the *Ithaca Journal*. The rest of our little charges were quickly claimed by eager purchasers, so Sugar became an income-making member of the family.

January 25, 1954

Oh, I might as well brag about my boys since I have some paper left! They are playing *train* together at the moment . . . they are really pretty good. There is a riot every now and then when Tor scurries off with something that Vikar wanted to play with, but generally they are all right. Tor says many words: *thank you, cookie, candy, daddy, mummie, car, bus, truck, bird, plane, boat,* and some we haven't figured out yet . . . Vikar talks a blue streak, and is a very good boy. He really tries to help. They both climb all the time, and I've given up trying to keep them from playing on the dining room table . . .

Another letter

Tor says 'boat' now (since that eventful ride in one) and *bus*, *book*, *broke*, *milk*, *coookie*, and *truck*, and I daren't set the table for dinner until the food is ready because he is so anxious to get into his chair and would be SO disappointed if there weren't anything to eat.

You would LOVE to see Vikar's eyes roll and his mouth oooooo when we talk about Princeholm and the wagon, but his first thought every time we mention it is the ride on the TRAIN. He can hardly wait. We'll take him into the airport, too, sometime.

February 5, 1954

The children are just up from their naps, and are playing with stuffed dogs . . . this is a new craze for them. Vikar takes a yellow one to bed, and Tor goes to sleep to the music from the teddy bear that you gave Vikar last year.

Tor is very steady on his feet now . . . walks all around the house. The things that throw him are a swipe from Sugar, a change of direction on Eric's or my part, or a knock from Vikar. He plays chase on his feet, walking with his feet wide apart and laughing all the way. He resorts to trips around the sofa when life gets dull, or hiding behind doors or under tables or behind the TV. He's really a character, and we're having a wonderful time with him.

Vikar says sentences now. "I want a cookie" etc. and "all right" and "It's cold outside." He carries on quite a conversation!

Now the two boys are playing on the sofa, with the cushions in front so that when Tor falls, he'll hit something soft. They have the blocks up there, and Tor rolls off now and then, on the cushions of course . . . after which Vikar falls off.

February 23, 1954

    On Sunday Tor had a high fever - 103 - and we had a doctor here. We're relieved to find out that it is just another form of measles, in which the fever comes first, then the rash. Tor was over his fever yesterday, and is fine now . . . but the shades are drawn and we're confined.

March 5, 1954

    The boys are both walking around here with their bottles in one hand and a carrot in the other. Tor carries on long conversations with Eric by telephone, and Vikar tells him what trucks have gone by the house that day.

    Tor's interest in the edibles is still foremost with him . . . be they Sugar's food, in the garbage, the wastebasket, or pages from one of Vikar's books. His next best interest is in being picked up . . . so he is an expert in grabbing trousers or skirts and hanging on . . . or getting in a doorway so you have to pick him up to get through.

    Vikar is really being pretty good . . . tells me *potty*, talks a lot, eats well (now that his molars are in) and tries to be good.

    It's after dinner now . . . Tor is in bed, but just threw his bottle overboard. Vikar is sitting on Eric's lap as he studies, drawing cars, trucks, trains, puppies . . . just scribbles, but he always has a name for them.

    It's too bad that you couldn't call earlier on the first so that you could have talked to Tor and Vikar. Tor jabbers and jabbers, and really knows what he is doing. Vikar tells you about the last trip downtown. His real interest in driving now is to go to see the waterfalls with ice over them.

    Tor has just started in on his favorite book . . . eats the corners and it really looks ragged. It was *Abraham Lincoln* (35 cents) but Eric hadn't read it so he took it back, and now Tor is digesting *Baby and Child Care* . . . the ink must taste good.

March 17, 1954

Tor has come to the stage where he can barely contain himself trying to get onto my lap when he sees we are going to read. He sits very quietly and watches the pages . . . once in a while he turns one. He only eats his baby-care book, thank heaven.

Vikar and I just went to the store for milk and he got a new book—about taxis—and he talked about it all the way home and has gone to sleep clutching it!

March 20, 1954

My attention is being distracted now and then; the children are playing on the sofa, and now Tor is taking the challenge of the bookcase and pulling out all his books (25-cent variety).

It's just a year ago now that we were waiting for a baby . . . and now he's reading a book here, studiously turning pages. Now that he is walking, he makes wild dashes for legs and clutches whatever material comes in his way . . . hanging on until picked up. We call him the leech. When we pass him by, he crumbles into a little ball and cries. All of this happens when he's hungry, you understand. Then he's most spoiled.

He and Eric and Vikar have a rousing game of chase each evening . . . sometimes Eric is after both, and sometimes he holds Tor and goes after Vikar with Tor out in front of him. Sugar comes biting at his heels, and it's riotous.

I'm having a hard time concentrating, with all that is going on at the moment: Beethoven's 6th, Vikar on the pot, and Tor taking out the pots and pans, and Eric trying to correct papers . . .

Eric is reading to Tor (picture book) and Vikar is barreling over to get in on a good thing.

p.s. I didn't tell you about our Tor . . . He says *thank-you, hot, cold, dog, baby, go, truck* and *car!* What I love, though, is the way he goes charging around the house when he sees that we're going downtown, nodding his head, and looking for his coat . . . smiling at us and nodding, trying to convince us that we should take him. He hugs, too, and kisses, and is very lovable . . . has six teeth and is precocious in general.

April 2, 1954

All has suddenly turned into confusion here . . . I started this letter when everything was pleasant, quiet—then the children and Eric started playing (it's *Troll on the Bridge over the Water* now - Eric's legs are the bridge)—and it's hard to concentrate, to say the least . . . So I'll tell you about our trip! This is Easter vacation week, and we decided to celebrate with your $10, and go for a trip. We packed the children into the car (on one of their mattresses on the back seat so they could see out, or sleep), with food, changes of clothing, and good spirits, and started off to Corning.

It had just snowed, but the roads were clear, and we had fun just getting out. Corning was the perfect choice, because the city had torn up its main street, and had more construction equipment than I'd seen before all in one block: mixers, derricks, a trip-hammer, dumptrucks, etc. - and all the time the traffic had cars, trucks and what all. Vikar's eyes just about popped out of his head!

When we ask him about the trip, his eyes get wide just remembering it! We went to the glass museum there—really a beautiful large exhibit—all the countries were represented - and there was a historical exhibit - and stained glass windows, and exhibits about the properties of glass, and blowers making laboratory equipment, and finally we saw the area where the Steuben pieces were being made.

We really enjoyed it, and the children lasted very well, with the help of a box of pretzels . . . . Then on to Watkins Glen park, which is 700 steps up to the top of a gorge, and which we had to give up because the steps were icy - but it was well worth it (the trip) and we came home tired and happy . . . .

Did we tell you about the farm-and-home-week here? There was a big week of exhibits, lectures, fashion shows, movies, etc. here for Cornell's home economics, agronomy, and agriculture schools, and they invited everyone in the State . . . There were over 18,000 before they were through . . .

We took the boys up to the chick exhibit (it's educational for the farmers and consumers) and saw baby ones, and some coming out of their shells, and some large chickens - and then to the cattle barns where we saw their prize cattle and sheep and pigs, and even rabbits! It was fun for us, but especially for Vikar . . .

Then Eric took the boys, and I went to the rose show and the fashion show - which inspired me to great efforts this spring, and I went down and got material and patterns and now am trying to find the time when the boys won't bother me so that I can cut and sew . . . I had dresses I started in 1949 that I'm finishing, and material for five new dresses . . . I went hog-wild, as you can see!

Mother's Day, 1954

Took the children on a motorboat ride (sightseeing) and no sooner got out on the lake and revved the motor when Vikar hid his head for the rest of the trip under a coat and Tor fell asleep! Vikar's talking eagerly about riding a train at Princeholm . . . I trust it won't be so noisy!

Getting Ready for the Oral Examination

As soon as I learned that I had passed the written exam, I tried to figure out how to study for the oral exam.

I had never taken an exam like that, where there seemed to be no real boundaries for what I might be asked. I knew that I would be facing a panel that would consist of senior staff members from various executive departments like Labor, Commerce, Interior, etc., in addition to State, of course, but I would not know in advance which of those departments would be represented. So I tried to figure out how to prepare myself.

Theoretically, of course, they could always ask me a factual question that I couldn't answer. But I decided that they probably would ask me questions that would probe my opinions and general knowledge about subjects that they thought I *should* know about, assuming reasonable curiosity and a desire to learn. I figured that I ought to be able to answer questions, or at least have opinions, about a variety of subjects, e.g. my own State, any other parts of the US or foreign countries I had visited, the role of the US in current world affairs, current political issues, etc. So what I planned to do was study enough in those areas to have some opinions and also some factual knowledge that I could draw on to support those opinions.

I also assumed that they were looking for people who could show that they were curious and interested in other peoples and cultures, and looked as if they would thrive in a foreign environment and be a good representative of our country.

I also decided that it was important not to approach the ordeal too grimly—i.e. not take myself too seriously—and to introduce a little levity if the atmosphere suggested it. My second rule was not to answer a question too quickly, because then the questioner might infer that I thought his question did not merit serious thought. I remembered that from reading about the American Indians, who felt that a pause before responding to a question was a gesture of respect for the questioner.

On July 26 I was notified that my oral exam was scheduled for August 24 at 9:30 AM, in Room 1338 of a temporary State Department building on 23rd Street NW. Bo was kind enough to drive me to Washington. We checked into a hotel near the State Department and I rested up for my long-awaited appointment early the next day.

I arrived at State in good time and when my name was called I was ushered into a conference room and directed to a seat that faced a long table that stretched almost the entire width of the room. What happened then—over fifty years ago—was so crucially important to our future that the memory of it was indelibly imprinted. Even writing about it now transports me back to that moment.

Arrayed before me as I sat down were six very important-looking men, all in dark suits and power ties. They welcomed me in friendly fashion, though, trying their best to put me at ease. Then the questions began.

I don't believe that they were following any script or had decided on any organized sequence to their questioning. It seemed as if my answers would suggest areas that interested one or more of the others, and the interview bounced around like that. I felt as if I were in a batting cage, trying my best to hit whatever was thrown to me.

For the first ten-fifteen minutes I thought that everything was going fairly smoothly, but then I was blessed with a huge stroke of luck. Just three days before the exam I had been looking idly through our Rand McNally American Atlas and noticed a chart in the back that intrigued me. The chart listed every state, together with its principal natural resources, industries, agricultural products, etc. I spent more than two hours studying that material very carefully. It added to what I already knew about the US from my travels: I had hitch-hiked through most of our western states and traveled through the Midwest and Northeast, and the country's geography was deeply imprinted by years of playing with our wooden jigsaw puzzle of the forty-eight states.

I forget who my benefactor was, but he asked me, with what I thought was an assumption that I would not be able to give much of an answer, "Mr. Youngquist, how would you compare the economies of Michigan, Oregon and Georgia?"

It took all the self-discipline I had to restrain myself from sticking up my hand and shouting, "I know that one, teach! Call on me! Call on me!" I forced myself to do the waiting bit, appearing to consider the question but really just organizing what I wanted to say. I started by mentioning that I had never visited Georgia but I had spent some time in Oregon, and Michigan was my home state. With that I launched into as exhaustive a comparison as I could muster, using the material I remembered from Rand McNally, without boring them to death.

When I finished I could see from their faces that I had aced that one, and from then on I sensed a distinct change in the atmosphere. I relaxed, trying my best not to look smug.

The crucial question in the exam, and the one where I think I really scored, came a bit later.

A member of the panel who had not spoken until that point said, "Mr. Youngquist, I see that you are working on your doctorate at Cornell. What are your plans if you don't pass this exam? Would you go into teaching?"

I didn't tell him the whole truth because—if I had—I would have said, "It never occurred to me that I wouldn't pass." That would have sounded hopelessly arrogant, so what I did say—after a pause—was: "Well, sir, I've left Cornell and we've already sold our home in Ithaca and moved to Illinois, so we have no real contingency plans except that they don't include more graduate work." And that was true: I had made my decision and was committed.

The person who asked the question smiled and nodded. The next question came from someone else and I took it as an indication that the examiners were now on my side:

"Mr. Youngquist, do you play cards?"

"Yessir, a little, mostly pinochle, hearts and poker, but then only low limit and with my friends."

His next question really lightened the atmosphere: "Do you ever draw to an inside straight?"

I had to smile at that one. "Not if I can help it. But sometimes I might do it for a bluff if the stakes are low and I don't think I'm going up against a likely higher hand like a flush or full house."

Chuckles all around.

A few minutes more and the exam was over. I was asked to wait outside. No nail-biting or nervous waiting for results. I didn't even have time to relax before the secretary called me over and told me I had passed, and that I would be scheduled for a physical and if I passed that I would have to wait until the Department decided to appoint me. Actually, she said that it wasn't a question of if, but when, I would be appointed.

I felt like throwing up both arms and shouting, "Yes! I did it!" I hurried out to meet Bo where he was parked and waiting, told him the good news and we rushed to a telephone to tell Rita all about it. The trip back to Princeholm was on Cloud Nine all the way.

Then the waiting began.

Waiting for the Service

After I passed my oral examination, Bo and I returned to Princeholm, and Rita and I waited eagerly for news of my assignment. The next five, almost six, months were agony for me. I couldn't help wondering where we might be sent. Whenever I looked up and saw huge Constellations fly overhead into or from Midway (O'Hare wasn't even thought of in those days) I would wonder where they were going or where they had been, and imagined what it would be like flying off to some exotic place. Weeks crept by as I went through a series of part-time, grunt jobs to earn money.

First, I worked at Arlington Race Track, sweeping day-old trash from between the rows in the grandstand, shining up the metal on the escalators, wiping off seats, and otherwise helping to get the place ready for the day's race crowd. After the races began, I was assigned an area in the grandstand, where I was directed to carry a long-handled dustpan and whisk broom to clear the area of betting tickets, Racing Forms (and parts thereof), tout sheets, and other trash that the racing public simply tossed on the floor, completely ignoring the large trash containers everywhere. The only positive aspect of the job was that if I arrived early enough I could watch the morning workouts.

As soon as the Arlington meeting drew to a close I looked around and found another job, this one at the local lumber yard. For the next month I worked long, hot hours there, unloading railroad cars in ninety-plus degree heat. The job paid marginally more than Arlington did, and I was free from temptation to bet on any horses, but I wasn't exactly fond of the work.

Hefting 2x4s, 2x6s and other construction-grade lumber from piles stacked in the burning hot boxcars, taking them outside and transferring them to storage sheds gave me a good upper body workout, but I soon tired of it. I stayed long enough to find an easier way to earn some money.

My next venture was selling Fuller Brush products. Selling door-to-door may have been less taxing for my muscles, but was far from being easier. One advantage was that I was selling products that had a good reputation, and I could vouch for Fuller Brush from personal experience. The job required an initial investment for the most popular items (brushes, cleaning supplies, etc.), a carrying case, and a supply of illustrated catalogs that we were supposed to leave with potential customers a day or so before we called on them. Each day I started by leaving copies at homes in an area that I was going to cover a day or two later. Then I would begin by calling at the homes where I had left catalogs earlier. Few housewives worked in those days, so I was generally able to find someone home when I made my calls.

I quickly developed a routine that worked fairly well. I would ring the bell or knock on the door and as soon as someone opened the door I would smile and take a half step backward. Then I would ask—always low-key—whether he or she had had time to look over my catalog or whether I could show her some of our new products. At that point I hoped to be invited in so I could make my presentation.

I learned early on that if I could make it through the front door I would invariably sell something—so that's what I aimed for. I resolved to find out as quickly as possible whether there was a chance of a sale, and not to spend much time chatting if I sensed sales resistance or indifference. Despite my plans, I ended up talking with potential customers more than I should, because I enjoyed it and because I wanted to prepare the groundwork for my next run through the territory. I wanted to build up a customer base for repeat sales, so even if a woman didn't buy anything on my pilot run I still thanked her and said something like "Maybe next time." I wanted her to look upon me as a friend when I came through the next time.

Cosmetics were popular items, and so were cleaning products. I found it easy to sell good products because I'm sure that customers could tell that I was being truthful when I praised something. If I went out selling today, I could vouch for the reliability of our line of brooms. For over forty years the Fuller Brush push-broom I bought and used as a sample served us well, and it never died on us. We lost it in one of our moves.

After two months of selling, just about when I was ready for my second trip through my territory—and repeat sales—I decided to try something else. I was making money, but door-to-door selling was far from my long-term objective. Also, I needed more immediate returns. So back to construction work.

At the end of October I found a job helping to build a large church. The footings had already been poured, and the crew I joined was unloading heavy forms from a truck and putting them together so the walls could be poured. First we sprayed the inside faces of all the forms with a kind of oily substance so that the concrete would not adhere to the forms, leaving a relatively smooth finished surface.
Each plywood sheet was reinforced with 2x4s on edge all around and on the outside to keep it from bulging when the concrete was poured. We carried the forms into position, stationed them on the footing and slipped rods through holes in their sides, fixing circular metal pieces to the rods on the inside and outside faces of the form. With a uniform distance between the two sheets, the poured concrete they contained would obviously create a wall with uniform thickness.

About this time we began receiving letters from State, letting us know how my appointment was coming along. On October 6 the Executive Director of the Board of Examiners for the Foreign Service wrote to notify me that the Medical Director had reviewed my physical and found me "physically qualified." Since I had passed all of the examinations, my name "had been added to the list of candidates eligible for appointment as Foreign Service Officer, Class 6." He added that the Division would probably get in touch with me "in the near future."
The Division did contact me less than a month later with a letter announcing that : "It is anticipated that we will be ready to offer you an appointment within a very short time."
Now we began serious planning, but we still didn't have any idea of where we would be assigned so Rita couldn't shop for clothing.
A week later the Division advised me that "We are now prepared to submit your nomination to the White House for approval of your appointment as Foreign Service Officer Class 6." They wanted to know whether I had any preference as to my area of assignment and how early I would be available to enter on duty in Washington. I replied

that I had no preference and that I would be prepared to enter within a week after being notified. Things were really looking up!

Getting back to my labors at the church foundation, we finally got all the forms in place. The architect checked carefully to ensure that the measurements were exact and everything was plumb and sturdy. Then the mixers arrived and we started pouring. The engineers wanted to finish the foundation as soon as possible to let the concrete cure before freezing weather set in, and we were already in the first weeks of November. My job was to walk on top of the forms with my shovel and poke it down into the concrete so that the concrete flowed evenly around the inside of the forms. Then I had to 'puddle' the concrete, i.e. stick a long vibrating device down into it as far as the vibrator would go and move it all around so that the agitating motion would distribute the concrete evenly in the form and eliminate any bubbles or empty spaces.

When the foundation was all in place my job ended and I moved on to work in the local post office. I had been a Christmas season worker there before, so I knew the routine. I went through piles of incoming mail for my route, 'throwing' envelopes into openings for the various homes so that when I gathered all of the mail together in my bag it would be organized in the same sequence as the stops on my route. Then I put all my mail into my bag and drove to the starting point for my route and set out. I walked from door to door, slipping mail into mailboxes when I found them or sliding letters through front door mail slots. As soon as we finished our routes, we were expected back at the post office to help sort outgoing mail.

My Christmas present arrived a few days after the beginning of the New Year: I was appointed a Vice Consul and Third Secretary, and assigned to our Embassy in Bangkok, Thailand. Cheers, celebrations, congratulations from friends and relatives, massive relief and frenzied preparations for our entry into another world.

Into the Foreign Service
(January – February, 1955)

Just before year-end 1954, I was notified that I had been assigned to Bangkok and that I was to report to State on January 5 to be sworn in and begin orientation. With the notice came a sheet of instructions for new appointees, giving me a list of the various offices I had to visit, beginning with the Division of Employment, which would administer the oath of office. The schedule included testing, scheduling of inoculations, and bonding, and when I reported as scheduled I was given names of other people to report to for such administrative details as transportation, shipment of effects, and leave. Included was a visit to the Foreign Service Institute, where Rita and I were scheduled to attend various orientation classes.

I arrived early, and wrote to Rita regularly about what was happening.

January 5, 1955

Hi, Darling,

This is 3rd Secretary, Vice Consul Eric V. Youngquist—consular officer—reporting. I forgot to give you my official title.

Here are some other things:

APPLICATION for passport – you should

1. get 2 pictures of <u>you and the children</u>, because they will be included on your passport.
2. fill out the form – do not sign
3. take your <u>old passport</u> and everything else, including a <u>duplicate</u> of the travel orders (saves paying $9 extra), to the appropriate place in Chicago.
4. SAVE the original of the travel order

As my plane turned the corner on its way to take off, I saw you on the observation roof and waved to you, hoping that the white hanky would be more visible than my hand. It would have been 100% better had you been inside the plane instead.

. . . . I walked to the State Department and asked to talk to someone who might be able to tell me about Bangkok and about my schedule here in Washington prior to departure. For the first I was directed to the Post Report, a series of articles on various aspects of life in Bangkok which is constantly updated. Here I read various things of interest:

- Foods – plenty of all kinds, though vitamin quality is sometimes low. Important to take multi-vitamins daily (available there) because of the more serious effects of vitamin deficiencies in tropical climates.
- Clothes – dress for midsummer. Leave heavy clothing at home, since woolens are exposed to mildew. Bring sport clothes. There is a whole section on women's clothing in the post report – you will want to read it. I'll try to send you one of the Post Reports so you can read it there – but it <u>must be returned</u>.
- Insurance – get some for our valuables. Also write Phoebe about cancelling our insurance for the car.
- Utensils – better to buy cheap stuff in Bangkok than bring good stuff from U.S.
- Shopping for food – good fresh fruits and meats in markets. The Embassy co-op handles canned goods and will be handling meat soon. Also frozen foods.
- Housing – junior officers get shunted off to houses that are only partially furnished. It may be that we can get one of the better houses with a refrigerator.
- Milk – canned, evaporated or powdered. Fresh milk not safe.
- Beds and Floor Lamps – are desirable to bring. Other furniture can easily be secured there in Bangkok.
- My clothes – I can buy linen suits for $20-40 there in Bangkok. I should have 2 suits for travel outside of the tropics.
- When we get there – most Americans with families stop at the American Club where, it seems, they charge fantastic rates. Anyway, that is where they stay upon arrival and until they find permanent housing.

- Clothes and Books – must be protected from mildew during the rainy season.
- Film – it does not keep well; therefore it is better to have a standing order delivered periodically instead of bringing a whole supply.
- Linen and Silver – <u>minimum dishes</u> i.e. 2 plates should be brought. We can get stainless and have any good silver shipped.
- Women – should have some formals – light – ballerina length is perfect.
- Most houses – are screened in, but that doesn't keep out mosquitoes, though.
- Malaria – not in the vicinity of Bangkok.

Bangkok has a good clinic with a nurse on duty – also a dispensary. Medical facilities for almost every emergency are available. Obstetrical facilities are "satisfactory," whatever that means.

I MISS YOU X X X X

Here is a book that you ought to get or at least look at: *Health Hints for the Tropics*, which is issued by the National Institutes of Health. . . .

After zooming through the Post Report, I went to Mrs. Selvig's office. She suggested that I be sworn in that very day, and sent me out for about an hour while she made the appropriate arrangements. . . .Then back to Mrs. Selvig, who directed me to Mrs. Fuller's office at the Division of Employment. I went there by taxi and she typed my travel orders and then – THEN – administered the oath of office to me. I tell you I had the oddest sensation in the small of my back and my right cheek and jaw as I repeated the oath – I sort of tingled all over [almost like prodrome for shingles that I contracted decades later]. I felt as if something really important was happening, and I was proud.

From there I went to the Foreign Service Lounge, where I completed numerous forms. Tomorrow I have so many things to do, dear: scurry from office to office and then report to my area officer and get set for orientation at 2:30.

I'll write to you tomorrow, Sweet.
LOVE YOU

I called Rita from the hotel and spoke to her about what I was doing, and this was her first letter to me.

January 6, 1995

Sweetheart - WHAT A DAY THIS HAS BEEN, AND WHAT A RARE POOP I'M IN! Why, it's just 'cause I'm in LOVE. All together now, sing together; now let's go, please, now, all together—et cetera, et cetera.

I hope I didn't sound too quiet tonight when we talked. I was completely pooped. . .just out from Chicago, and I fell asleep on the train while knitting!! The low after the high has set in, I'm afraid, and now comes the packing. . . and all the problems. Honey has suggested that she could take the boys while I came out to be with you.

AND HERE YOU ARE. . . QUESTIONS. . . PLEASE ANSWER

1. Do you want me to come for a week, or me to bring the boys for more time?

My answer: YES – you and the children will stay here for 4 weeks. I have an apartment for us. You will be attending classes with me at the Foreign Service Institute every day possible, so we'll have to plan on a baby-sitter. I don't dare suggest that Honey come in that capacity, do I?

2. Do we take the car? Do you want it painted?

My answer: YES – take the car by all means. We <u>might</u> get a new one here. The Federal Credit Union might help us, but <u>don't plan on it</u>.

3. May we take <u>some</u> light woolens. . . are you taking your suits?

My answer: YES – you may take a <u>few</u> light woolens for use enroute. I personally will have two suits and the cord along. Plus the formal stuff. We'll have to store the rest . . .

4. Would cotton blankets be better than wool?

My answer: YES – cotton blankets would be vastly superior to woolen ones.

5. Would the air-lines allow aluminum footlockers?

My answer: YES – the airlines will allow such footlockers assuming that they are within dimension limits.

6. Do you want your old work clothes and grey trousers and green?
My answer: Not the old trousers, but SAVE my two old work pants – not the rest.

7. Did anyone say anything about overcoats? Will you take yours?
My answer: I'm only taking my trench coat, NOT MY BLUE.

8. What about a refrigerator?

My answer: If we can purchase a small one here in Wash., at a reasonable price, we will do so and have it shipped.

I have decided to take the minimum, as we did to Norway. . . and buy anything else there. . . i.e., china, kitchen utensils, et cetera. SO, I am going to pack a steamer trunk here with things to be left, so our leavings will be easily movable for Honey

I'm only taking the necessary things from Ithaca. . . beds, linen and some utensils. . . maybe the rocker. . . Honey wants the dining room furniture. . . she's going to talk to Bo about it. . . and that will considerably lighten the storage load in Ithaca. The carpet sweeper will go (to the trash can) and some small things that it is silly to store. The buggy will be sold or stored. . . the mirror will come with us, and so on. . . But I'll make my list tomorrow and begin the BIG SORT. My lists are in Bo's car, and it's still in Chicago—I'm lost!

But so much for the whirl in my head. I was glad to hear all the news. The month sounds good—especially for you, you'll be so ready for the job. And I'll attend to passports here, and see to the shots. . . and pack. I wish you'd be as explicit as possible about how much time we have, and whether you'll be with me at all in the packing. I thought you said we'd be allowed 150 pounds each. . . Ask someone WHAT they put stuff in when traveling. Maybe an aluminum foot-locker? We'll have more than our bags can hold!

You see, I keep reverting to the whirl again. I'm calling in the boys periodically to go to sleep. Vikar is now imitating a coyote. . . .

I haven't the time to miss you yet, I will when I crawl into bed and it's all cold and unfriendly. . . then I'll know you're not just at work somewhere or studying, but really gone. I stood on that ramp and cried and cried today at the airport...silly me, when you were doing the thing you wanted to do most of all. But I couldn't help it; I hate to be parted from you. Please send for me soon.

Vikar looked very grave and clouded all up when I told him you were far far away, and sent him a kiss...poor little thing. Yet, having them in Washington is a problem. Too, I DO need time here to pack and organize. I'll see how this week goes. It may be easier than I think. And I'll need a whole day in Ithaca, maybe more, to sort and split into three groups: the things going with us, the things to remain stored, the things to go home to Honey, and lastly, the things to be sold there.

Whirl again! Here are the lyrics in that folksong *Ihashe:*

> Ihashe, come with me. You are young and you are free,
> You are rich, I am told, but I am young and you're too old.
> At your side I'd be cold for I need much more than gold.
> I am rich, I am tall. You are poor and you are small.
> Round you I will build a wall so you'll answer when I call.
> I can climb any wall and I'm not afraid to fall.
> I hear other voices call far beyond your big stone wall.

Sweet, it's hard to put into a letter all my love. You know it's yours, and how happy I am to be your wife. We'll have a wonderful life together, *evig. Evig. Evig.*

Here's a kiss for now, and love from the boys. Write soon and often, and PLEASE tell us all important developments and information on the country

                Love
[Lipstick kiss here]   Rita

January 6, 1955

    I responded as follows:

    Got your letter this morning, you little Coke and Gauda-ost darling. I'll try to answer your questions now. [They are inserted in her letter above.]

    NOW – This is what I learned today, and there is a lot of it.

    1. We can take 66 lbs. per person aboard the plane, PLUS 150 lbs. excess baggage. That means that we can take along 414 lbs. Remember that I have about 50 lbs. here.

    2. We can send 400 lbs. AIR CARGO, to arrive a day or two after we do. That will probably include bedding, dishes, etc.

    3. We can send 2,500 lbs. SURFACE FREIGHT (That doesn't include the car, which goes separately, and we can put golf clubs etc—up to 200 lbs.—in it.

    Here is how this will work:

    A. We will go up to Ithaca on January 15 and see what we want crated and sent, what we want to discard and what we want stored there <u>at our expense.</u>

    B. A bill of lading will arrive at Dean of Ithaca authorizing the crating and shipping, so that we will not have to pay anything except the charges we already owe.

    C. <u>Sometime</u>, you have to contact the Mayflower office in Chicago (send me the address) and tell them when to pick up the stuff which will be crated and shipped from Princeholm. NOW – I will have to know the date (say in 2-3 weeks) because I will have to notify Mrs. Davidson here so that she will be able to send a bill of lading to them in time—that is, <u>before</u> they come to pick up the stuff.

    If you have questions, send them to me. There is no real rush about this, except that we must be in Ithaca on January 15.

NOW, about our stay here. I have called the place and extended our reservations for another two weeks

January 6, 1955
Darling mine

    Another lonely night ahead – oh me! I'll certainly be happy when you and the boys finally come. . . .

I went to see the apartment so I could prepare you for it. It has twin beds, a large bedroom, a furnished living room and kitchen with refrigerator and stove. Dishes, silver and linen are all supplied. We should be pretty comfortable there. It is located in an apartment building between 14th and 15th on Euclid Avenue. The name is Hilltop House and the address is 1475 Euclid. . . .We are expected to move in on the 12th and stay for 3-4 weeks. You might go there right away as soon as you come to Washington, because I'll be at the Institute until 5:30 Wednesday.

Another letter, January 7, 1955

    Hi, my little turtle dove! From your Jonathan

    My Snow White:

Some more headaches for you—as if I haven't given you enough already. Here are some instructions about shipping. . . .When you have established a contact with Mayflower and they realize that they are going to be our shipper, give them the following instructions (which are official):

    1. Pack for export shipment.
    2. Mail packing list in triplicate to Despatch Agent, indicating the gross weight and outside dimensions of each shipping container.
    3. Await instructions from the Despatch Agent for export marks and inland routing which is furnished upon receipt of the packing list.
    4. They will receive a bill of lading from the Despatch Agent which will inform them that they will be paid by the Government.

Now, as for timing on this maneuver, remember, first, that I must have the address so that I can begin proceedings here. As soon as I have done that, the goods must be made ready for shipment. When they are ready, tell Mayflower to pick them up and give them the above instructions. The idea is to have the goods in the shipper's hands about the same time as the Despatch Agent sends the bill of lading to the shipper.

If this isn't entirely clear, for gosh sakes tell me in a hurry so that I can clarify.

There is nothing new since I wrote last night. . . .Office hours here are from 8:45 a.m. to 5:30 p.m., with an hour off for lunch. Apparently, they work on Saturdays, too.

Most of the offices are in temporary buildings clustered close to New State, where all the big brass are, like Dulles, Hoover, Jr., and others of similar stature. The street car line runs on Pennsylvania Ave., not more than a couple blocks away, soit is fairly simple to get downtown.

    The first couple days, I took cabs because I had to get places in a hurry, and I didn't know where most of them were. Just like the underground in Paris, and all our baggage—remember? I am still in my little Höivang a few blocks from the Department. It is a clean but thoroughly run-down place, but it is inexpensive. I can afford to stay here for a week, because I have already paid the week's rent—they demand rent in advance, which should tell you what sort of clientele they cater to. . . .

    Try to keep a record of the questions you ask me, so that you can tell immediately whether or not I have answered every one. Any questions that I get at noon on Monday I will call you about before 1:00 p.m., or before you plan to leave, whichever is earlier. . . .

    I love you, love you, love you…xxxxx
Your little Stinky

    Since Rita's role overseas would be fully as important as my own, we attended some of the orientation courses together, mainly those dealing with cultural differences and the various do's and don'ts for Americans abroad. She had a good idea of what she wanted in order to be able to entertain properly, and probably was quite frustrated because we didn't have funds to buy the things she felt we really needed. She had to return home to Illinois to shop for clothes (difficult to find summer things in mid-winter) and organize what we would need for daily living.

    The first week we spent together, and here are the topics that were covered in our lectures and discussion sessions. We began with a description of how the Foreign Service is organized, and the various duties of Foreign Service Officers. Then we wee given a review of usual dos and don'ts while abroad, or cross-cultural sensitivity. Next we attended a lecture on the various benefits available for Foreign Service families, such as hospitalization, home leave, annual leave, and retirement plan. Finally, we learned about the important role played by families serving abroad.

The second day was full of information and advice about daily living concerns such as health, travel (vouchers, accounting, advances, customs, passports, etc.), mail, shipping personal effects and a car, handling finances and allotments, etc.). The afternoon session covered the way performance was measured and how the promotion system operated.

The annual efficiency report and promotion panel system in the Service is based on the one used by the Navy. All of the efficiency reports are gathered in Washington and arranged by grade, and reports on all officers in each grade who are eligible for promotion are reviewed by a different panel of senior officers. Their job is to rank those officers based on the ratings they received from their supervisors. The number of officers who are actually promoted depended on the funds allotted by Congress.

Even if you rank high on the list, you might not get promoted if there are insufficient funds available. In that case, your file goes back in the pot for consideration the following year. That is a change from the Navy system: In the Navy the promotion panel decides which officers are promotable, and all of them stay on the promotion list and are promoted as soon as funds are made available, which may take more than a year, i.e. they no longer have to compete for that next promotion.

In the Foreign Service, however, if you are not promoted on one promotion list, you have to compete again to make the promotion list the next year, and so on until you do get promoted.

On the third day the lecturers explained the different levels of security classification, such as classified, confidential, secret, top secret, and eyes only, and the rules for proper handling and storing of classified documents and information. We were given basic guidelines for sound security (e.g., store everything classified in a secure file or safe—and lock it—when you leave your office; don't leaving classified material where it can be seen by persons who are not cleared for security; don't discuss classified material or information on the telephone or even refer to it with persons who are not cleared; and don't keep a diary of what you are doing, etc.

In the afternoon we had lectures on Communism, emerging countries and the role of USIA (United States Information Agency).

The fourth day was devoted completely to foreign affairs, and a description of the respective roles and relationships between the State Department and the Foreign Service, and other executive agencies of the Government

The final day of that week focused on the role and duties of a Foreign Service family in an Embassy setting, commenting on social usages and public relations.

Rita also stayed with me for the second week, because we studied the culture of the Far East and Thailand and some of the unique aspects of the languages of the area. Special briefings were arranged for the wives.

Rita gave Honey a full account of what she was doing.

Dear Honey:

Here, and finally relaxed - sure hated to leave you all. I can't help feeling guilty that I had to leave the boys there with you, but it's proved worth the effort (at least MY effort!). The classes are all concerned with the Foreign Service organization(today), duties, do's and don'ts, benefits, purpose of families abroad; associations of which we are a member.... then

Tuesday: Health, travel, purchases, mail, ship-ping effects, leaves, finances, allotments, supervision, performance and evaluation and the manual.

Wednesday: Security practices, Communism, emerging countries, USIA.

Thursday: Conduct of Foreign Affairs.

Friday: Duties and Social Usage and Public Relations.

Then next Monday, we start study of the culture of the area and language all afternoon! And some wife-briefings!

The third week - I may not stay. I'll see how it goes - is language, America, area briefings....

The apartment is a nice little one, with all the essentials. Eric had some snacks in the refrigerator, and we're very comfortable. He's going to do all the cooking and dishes. Bless his heart!

We're meeting a fellow just back from Bangkok this afternoon and I'll add more then. Now to class...

I really can hardly believe that I'm HERE. It's so like a dream, really! I feel as though this is another person! I hope the boys are being good and helpful, and your nights aren't too bad.

January 13, 1955

We were in Secretary Dulles's offices yesterday - with a very intelligent, pleasant, personable young man briefing us on foreign policy and what they have to consider when they make decisions. It was VERY impressive and luxurious I might add!

Dulles and big wheels will be going to Bangkok for a conference just after we arrive. That should be interesting.

That evening, we boarded a bus and went north to Ithaca, arriving early the next morning. We began sorting through the things we had stored at Dean of Ithaca. Bo drove out to work with us, and took some things back to Downers.

As soon as Rita returned to Downers on January 23 to get ready for our travel to Bangkok, she plunged into all the preparations that were required, choosing clothing and necessary things for living, getting shots, packing, trying to get my views on what to do with our things from Ithaca, etc. You can the sense the involvement and urgency her letters convey.

January 24, 1955
> Dear Sweeeetheart,
>
> The boys are having a tea-party with pretzels, punctuated with outbursts when one takes the other's ice cubes! I've just read *Health Hints for the Tropics* and they sent me three, so I'm sending two to you. You might pass on the others to Magill or Rassias . . . And tonight I plan to read Benedict, so will send it on, too. . .
>
> Honey and I are going to spend the day in Chicago tomorrow. . . . I'll get a pattern for your sport-shirts, and one for the boys. And I'll get the sun glasses. . . .
>
> I made cookies for Travelers Aid, and sorted my sewing, and now to bed. Tor's obsession the instant he hits the bed is "go downstairs awhile." He sure is hard to convince that it's time to go to bed! Vikar came in and cut up paper for a while, and then went to bed quietly (except for <u>three</u> glasses of water!)

January 27, late
> My darling,
>
> I'm sorry I haven't been able to take time today to sit down and write you when I was fresh. Your letters (2) came this morning, and I've been so <u>filled</u> with our love all day. It was so good to read that you miss me almost as much as I miss you. I've always wondered whether you <u>really would</u> get along better if independent of the boys and me, and I'm so happy to think that we really <u>are a part of you!</u>
>
> Somehow the days are so full here that I have no time to sit and moon over how much I miss you. I'm busy and reasonably happy, but life is just not complete. I always <u>waiting</u>, but you just don't come! That sounds funny, but it's as though someone snatched the four hours of the evening away from me!

We had another shot a few evenings ago—and now just two to go. I explained to Vikar that we <u>have</u> to have them if we want to go with Daddy (and that you had them) and he is much more understanding now. He's waiting for you to come home "<u>right now</u>" I got them each a cowboy hat and guns and tried on the hat—and said it is for their birthday when Daddy gets home—and they've asked several times <u>when</u> it will be!

Vikar entertains Tor when he gets to bed—tells him stories like *The Little Engine that Could*—and tells him <u>he</u> can go to church when he is a big boy, and so on. They have a high old time and make jokes, too. Their imagination is a little <u>too</u> good, however. Vikar calls pottying *showering* and thinks up jokes about it <u>too</u> easily.

They play <u>together</u> all day long. The chairs get pushed, and books get read and cars get pushed, and guns get shot off, and TV gets watched and Mama gets harassed. . . .

I've been sewing with Honey for the past two days. Also I weighed all our stuff from here. Please call Ithaca before you leave and find out the weight of our air cargo from there [Dean of Ithaca, where we stored our things]. I really need to know! We will have about 300 pounds of baggage, and at least 120 pounds of air cargo from here. So please find out how much is there at Dean of Ithaca. Or write. But we need to know before we leave!

The sewing has mostly been moving buttons on the boy's clothes and mending some of mine and hemming my new dresses. We're almost finished. We sit and talk and enjoy it—but it leaves no time to write!

I have a headache now. I read very late last night and was up early. The Benedict pamphlet is on its way to you (as I promised) with the health hints. I kept one here. Some cookies should arrive soon. Sorry I had no box to put them in. . . .

[The last line is written in a heart-shaped circle with a long xxxxxxxxx for kisses crossing it]

I'll close for now, dear, with a big circle for my arms around you and a cross for my kisses by the 1,000.
    Rita

Friday, January 28, 1955 late
    Sweetheart,
    I'm just out from my last trip to Chicago . . .I got a garment bag to carry my dresses and stuff, and I got a book called *McKay's Guide to the Far East and the Middle East*. EXCELLENT. I hope you didn't find it before me. I haven't had a chance to read it yet, but I can hardly keep my hands off of it! . . . .
    Everyone's just gone to bed, so I'll stop typing.
    Bo told Honey that he encouraged me to come home early Saturday morning, and she was hopping mad! She said I should have stayed in Washington 'till Sunday night! Well, you never know. . . .
    I'll go through your letters and see if I'm to answer anything. About money—I need very little here. Bo will give me $30 eventually. He gave me $5 today – and I haven't much to get. But I'll have him get your suit with some of it. . . .

    The more I think of our debts, the more certain I am that we had better plan for the nursery school. I think we had better "make do" with things there for the school, though, and spend as little money on it until the first month's tuition is in. If you could find an inexpensive (under $1.00) book on nursery schools and curriculum and activities, I'd love it. I will have no opportunity here, but will see what the library offers. . . .

    I was very interested in the lecture on materialism. It was almost as good to get it from you as from the instructor. Gee whiz, I wish you weren't going to be gone so long! I'm afraid you'll become self-sufficient again by next week. It seems so far away –

I wish you could get home sooner. I miss you so much, and I'm afraid this having you miss me is too good to last. Oh, you've got some busy nights ahead of you!

Tonight, two of Honey's friends called to say that there was a film on Siam on TV, and we all rushed down and sat on the sofa to watch it – a travelogue. Did you know that watercress is a national staple? It (the film) was interesting and Honey and Bo were goggle-eyed. I noticed afterwards that Honey had on the wrong glasses!

Ah, well—another day gone, and now the last weekend alone. We miss you so much—this great big old bed is lonesome! I hate to think of you spending time, passing time there so far away. Go to movies, darling—"button up your overcoat, you belong to us", eat good nourishing food, and watch out for the traffic. We love you so <u>very</u> much – hurry home safely.

Thousand morexxxxxxxxxxxxxx Rita and the boys

P.S. Be sure to read that thing by Benedict (45 pages). It really was excellent for understanding the people better. Just reading the book on the Far East. Says things disappear at customs, and whole pieces of luggage will disappear—does our insurance cover <u>that</u>?

Rita ran out of paper at this point and just continued, writing other things that she thought of, and using the narrow space around the edges of the letter:

Hong Kong reservations, too! Be sure whatever you get is CENTRAL. We must get our Tokyo reservations. Rate for our double at the Imperial would be $9.00, and all the other hotels are more expensive. Also, we wouldn't have to pay transportation if we stayed at the Imperial. It's not worth being far from the center of town, 'cause we'll need to bring the boys back to the hotel so often, so maybe the Imperial is our best bet.

Saturday, January 30, 1955

Darling,

The boys are rebelling—they just <u>don't</u> think it's bed time! Tor and Vikar and I all had a tetanus shot tonight. Tor never catches on to the fact that it is a shot until he is pricked! But Vikar knows the word *Rosemae* [the nurse] or *shot* even when spelled out or implied! The first thing he says every day is that he doesn't want a shot today! And he doesn't want to go downtown unless he's <u>sure</u> there'll be no shot!

Yet tonight, Vikar knew her voice when Rosemae came to the house, and said immediately that he didn't want a shot, but came out walking to her <u>pushing up his sleeve</u>, and saying he'll just have one more and then he can go with Daddy on the plane—almost crying. He's a brave little darling. Then Rosemae said, "I'll see you again before you go" and he said, "Just once more, just once more." He has an <u>awfully</u> good memory, and a <u>keen</u> ear!

I got the most darling trike for Tor today. It is small from the seat to the pedals, but has a wide wheel base and handle-bars—and I'm really delighted. Now I just have to find one for Vikar.

Sewing again today, and cookies, and organizing. My garment bag came—like yours, but black plaid—for my dresses.

When the airline offers you those little bags, be sure to get one for <u>Me, Tor & Vikar!</u>

What plane will you be on?

Do you think it's <u>safe</u> to fly we're going now, with this Formosa business?

Could you decipher my writing about hotel reservations? Be sure to get a hotel that is CENTRAL. Will we be two nights in Tokyo? I hope not! Maybe the Imperial was the cheapest in this one book because it is <u>very</u> old and moth-eaten by now! Limestone, you know. I don't care at all, just so we can "center" with the boys for a nap for them and eat, etc.

Tor is going to be baptized here at home next Sunday—nothing formal and no reception or any such—but I <u>do</u> want him baptized before we go, and your family will be here then. So is that all right with you?

When you know the definite schedule—how long each place and the airlines and all, please let me know—I know I could find out from here, but it would mean a call. Do we go Northwest the entire way? How many changes of plane? And luggage?

The boys finally gave up and went to sleep. How comforting it would be to have you come in now and talk to me, and I could lean up against you and be relaxed and happy—you could massage my back and this big old room wouldn't be lonely any more. . . .

Ah well, this was the last Saturday you'll be gone! Only six more days—really 5 1/2!

Love. . .all my love,
Rita

Below are excerpts from other letters I wrote to Rita after she had returned to Princeholm. I have not dated them, because it is not clear to me when they were sent:

This evening I was over at the International Club, and talked to a man from Thailand. He is going to stay here for a year and study agricultural education in Tennessee and Florida. . .We talked for almost three hours. . . .As I spoke of servants, he did not give me the impression that we would lose face if, say, I did some things around the house such as fix screens. Heaven knows I didn't find time to do much to help you in Ithaca—whether or not I will in Bangkok is anybody's guess. But you know that I'll try.

. . . . Say, I have a compliment for you at this end. Two people have tried to guess your age and have been wrong on the right side by six and four years. They were not trying to give you the benefit of any doubt, either; they just thought you looked too fresh and radiant to be "pushing thirty.". . .

I find it <u>hard</u> to get used to being alone, to not knowing that you're close by, to not having you say, "How's it going?" I say *hard*; I should say *impossible*, because I'm not used to being alone yet and don't know that I ever could be fully used to it. So, when I'm not reading or studying Thai I feel an inner compulsion to tramp around the city or be in some sort of company, like at a concert or a movie.

That feeling is new to me; it could only have come because of our being together. When you're not here it's as if a part of me were gone, and as if I have to go looking for it in a crowd somewhere or try to forget about it by reading. So although I haven't progressed much in the way of being non-critical, I still am radically different from what I was that June in 1950. Therefore, I've lost (and I'm not complaining about it at all—in fact wouldn't have it any other way) a lot of my self-sufficiency, because I have no control over the emptiness caused by being away from you. . . .

I'm sorry that Honey had the task of taking the children to get their haircut, and of consoling them after their shots. I hope that taking care of them was not too much of a task for her for the two weeks. She was really a saviour for us, though. What we would have done if she hadn't taken the children, I can't imagine. In fact, what we would have done if she hadn't been helping us all along this last half-year is impossible to say. We certainly would have had one dickens of a time; that much is clear.

To say thanks for help of that kind and that magnitude seems forced somehow—how can thanks be enough? Ever? If somehow you could make it clear to Honey how truly grateful I really am, and how I would say thanks myself, and often, if those thanks could convey my gratitude—if you could tell her that and convince her of it, you'd take a load off my back.

It's not that I haven't tried to do it myself; I have. But I have yet to be able to show gratitude to Honey in a way which I thought got across. With Bo it's different; somehow with him I'm able to speak out and feel that my gratitude is expressed and fully understood. I know that you have said that I should say thanks at a time when the occasion doesn't seem to demand it, i.e., when the thanks do not seem obligatory. Sometimes I've puzzled over ways of doing just that, and after minutes of trying to approach it in various ways, I have given up because to me it would have seemed entirely too premeditated—too much as if I had made up a nice little speech. . . .

. . . .Just $2^{1/2}$ more days or so, and we'll be together again. It seems like years since we were at 1475 Euclid, and ages since I left Downers. I feel like a kite in a slow wind; I just keep drifting and don't move until I get reeled in—reel me in quick!! I feel more and more that we have at last become a real family <u>unit</u>! I know that I don't think of myself as whole except as somehow what passes for my SELF includes both you and the boys. That last sentence would never have passed on one of my Freshman English papers, but I think the meaning is clear. Ah's lonely, gal! And a big handprint for you. I love you soooo much, and will be waiting impatiently until Friday.

100000000000000000000000000000000000000 more,   Stinky

Below is the travel schedule I prepared and sent to Rita:
  ETD DC – 5:30 p.m. Feb. 4   American 261
  ETA Chicago – 6:45 p.m.
  ETD Chicago – 3:00 p.m. Feb. 8   Northwest 107
  ETA Seattle – 10:00 p.m.
  ETD Seattle – 10:15 p.m. Feb. 8   Northwest 1
  ETA Tokyo – 9:00 p.m. Feb. 10
  ETD Tokyo – 1:30 a.m. Feb. 12   PanAm 5
  ETA Hong Kong 8:45 a.m.
  ETD Hong Kong 8:00 a.m. Feb. 14   PanAm 7
  ETA Bangkok 2:00 p.m.